SEX, THERAPY, AND KIDS

A Norton Professional Book

SEX, THERAPY, AND KIDS

Addressing Their Concerns
Through Talk and Play

SHARON LAMB

W · W · NORTON

NEW YORK · LONDON

For information about permission to reproduce
selections from this book, write to
Permissions, W. W. Norton & Company, Inc.
500 Fifth Avenue, New York, NY 10110

Composition and book design by Viewtistic, Inc.
Manufacturing by RR Donnelley-Harrisonburg
Production Manager: Leeann Graham

Library of Congress Cataloging-in-Publication Data
Lamb, Sharon.
Sex, therapy, and kids : addressing their concerns through talk and play /
Sharon Lamb.
    p.   cm.
"A Norton professional book."
Includes bibliographical references and index.
ISBN-13: 978-0-393-70479-2
ISBN-10: 0-393-70479-3
1. Children and sex. 2. Children—Sexual behavior. 3. Psychosexual
disorders in children. 4. Sex therapy. I. Title.
RJ506.P72L36 2006
618.92'8583—dc22   2006045317

W. W. Norton & Company, Inc., 500 Fifth Avenue, New York, NY 10110
www.wwnorton.com
W. W. Norton & Company, Ltd., Castle House, 75/76 Wells Street, London
W1T 3QT

1 2 3 4 5 6 7 8 9 0

Contents

CONTENTS

CHAPTER 5

Preface

The idea for this book percolated for two years after Deborah
Malmud approached me to write it. Initially I thought that I
hadn't seen enough children who brought sexual material into
therapy and that because of this lack I wouldn't have enough case
material for a book. But as the idea of the book stayed with me, I
began to remember all the little incidents that arose in therapy
sessions over the years, incidents that took me by surprise in my
early years in Child Psychiatry at Massachusetts General Hospital,
incidents that students brought to me in supervision, and more
recent talks and events that have occurred in my small practice in
Vermont.

The second hurdle to overcome was whether I had anything
cohesive to say about such material. I have strong feelings about
the importance of sex education in the lives of young people, and
equally strong feelings about play and its role in therapy with children. I don't think therapy should be education, but in my own
work, when sexual issues emerge, I hope that playing and talking
communicate information about sex that is more particular to the
child or teen and also more clarifying than a simple course.

While I always have something to say, I'm never quite sure I have the right or the expertise to say it, so along with the reassurance of those memories from my clinical practice, I consulted friends and therapists whom I respect. Some have coauthored chapters with me; others gave me in-depth interviews and permission to write about some of their clients if I combined features with those of some of my clients.

The case material presented here is either (1) a combination of two cases, (2) a combination of two cases with some extra material made up, or (3) an invented case. It pains me to present anything but case material from the lives of clients I know. I feel dishonest making things up. I also worry that my former clients won't know how much I appreciated them for who they were and that the changes or embellishments mean something they're not meant to mean. I worry that parents will read bits and be certain I'm describing their own child when I'm not. And I worry for students who get training using these made-up cases, cases that always seem to turn out fine. I struggled with this last issue the most. In writing some of these cases, I found that the narratives demanded endings when often there were none. People dropped out of therapy, parents refused to bring children back, a child was removed from the foster home never to be seen again, or I only heard about this child once in a supervision session. Yet the narrative seemed to demand that no problem be left unresolved. In a narrative it is rare that an issue is brought up in therapy, only touched upon, and then dropped without follow-up, while in real-life therapy this happens all the time. We often don't follow up on important points, and certain issues are never resolved or even talked about again after a particular session. In my teaching, I am confronted with students who believe they must enter a session knowing exactly what to do, their own self-consciousness interfering with the very basic listening skills I try to teach. I hate to contribute to their unrealistic expectations by presenting fully formed cases of interesting children and teens for whom I delivered perfect therapy, from which these clients emerged psychologically whole. In the cases presented here, I've tried to present some failures, some topics raised just once and dropped, and some kids who drifted out of my room and life before more could happen. If the demands of storytelling won over accuracy, I apologize in advance and encourage my students and other therapists to continue to share their experiences so we all may learn from failures as well as successes.

Acknowledgments

I am indebted to those people with whom I frequently discuss therapy in supervision: John and Teresa Meyer, and David Van Buskirk, a counseling psychologist, a clinical psychologist, and a psychiatrist/psychoanalyst. I also sometimes depend on my father-in-law, psychoanalyst Shelley Orgel, for discussions about "sex and agression" as they arise in therapy, feeling that the psychoanalytic perspective he offers brings much more depth to my understanding of the place of sex and sexuality in my patients' lives as well as within the psychotherapy session. Actually, all of the members of the Orgel family—including Shelley, my mother-in-law, Doris, a children's books author, my psychoanalyst brother-in-law Jeremy Orgel, psychologist sister-in-laws Laura Orgel and Ling Chen-Orgel, and my husband, Paul, a pianist who puts up with these conversations—make family get-togethers fertile ground for gaining support, stories, and valuable information about the art of psychotherapy.

There are other psychotherapists I've learned from. Some I spoke directly with for this book, and others I've learned from through their treatment of people I know. I wish to thank Diane Anstadt, Judy Christensen, Bob Emmons, Ed Epstein, Gale

Golden, Trevor Hanbridge, Rachel Hare-Mustin, Jeanne Kellner, Susan Lillich, Brenda Phillips, Thomas Reilley, Charles Rossi, Polly Young-Eisendrath, Andrea Waldo, and Beth Wermuth Nichols for their contributions to this book. My students who began their work as therapeutic presences at Woodside Juvenile Correctional Facility, Baird Center for Children, Rock Point School, the Department of Children and Families in Vermont, the Howard Center, and Northeastern Family Institute share with me in supervision their insecurities, fears, and moving stories of connections with children and teens at these places. I am grateful for their openness.

Four women, two of whom I never met, influenced my play therapy work. Virginia Potter, the social worker I saw at Evanston Township High School when I was 15, gave me Virginia Axline's *In Search of Dibs,* which remains a classic to this day, and encouraged me to play with the little toys at the front of her desk while I talked. I also had the great fortune to read in my early graduate school years Jesse Taft's, *Time-Limited Psychotherapy.* This book spoke to me in a way no other book on psychotherapy has or probably will in its treatment of the therapy hour as a time alive with the significance of what it means to live and die, to be a human being. I continue to think about my clients in ways influenced by Taft—what is their problem in living? How can I help them to be able to take what is offered from the world around them while still living with the limits of what can be had? The fourth influential woman is Rachel Hare-Mustin, who, with a sparkle in her eye, encouraged me and all her students to think outside the box and approach psychotherapy like a puzzle, a game.

Peter Chubinsky trained me to do play therapy and remains the rare psychiatrist who knows how to play with kids. For three years at Massachusetts General Hospital's child psychiatry clinic, he supervised my work. Rather than asking me to conform to a narrow child psychiatry model, he appreciated my developmental psychology background, supported me, and challenged me to think about all the meanings of the play. He and his wife, social worker Edie Raskin, dear friends, supply me with the best beach conversations about therapy I've ever had. Peter also reviewed several chapters.

I admire the work of Jeanne Marecek, Deb Tolman, Lyn Mikel Brown, Janice Haaken, Judith Levine, Michelle Fine, Lyn Ponton, Toni Cavanaugh Johnson, David Finkelhor, Iliana Gil, Lynn Phillips, Richard Bromfield, and Morton Chethik. Their writings and views have been highly influential in this work. I also admire and love talking to my colleagues on APA's Sexualization of Girls Task Force, as well as Leslie Cameron and Gwen Keita. Their ideas surely influenced Chapter 5 in its final stages.

I feel very fortunate to have the services of Erin Cole, Denise Brault, and the Saint Michael's College library staff, particularly Kristin Hindes, Mike Arena, and Kathy Godlewski, who work quickly and tirelessly to get me materials I need. Erin Cole was incredibly helpful to this project in every way and I am amazed and truly pleased to have found an undergraduate research assistant of such caliber.

I am indebted to Glenda Russell, (Clinical and Research Consultant at New Leaf Services for Our Community in San Francisco, and now in independent practice in Boulder, CO), Janis Bohan (Professor Emerita, Metropolitan State College of Denver, CO), and Stan Baker (Clinical Director, Howard Community Services, Burlington, VT) for agreeing to coauthor two chapters. I learned so much from these three people, and their presence in this book elevates the thinking. I also thank Dave van Buskirk for his close reading of many chapters.

I'm very grateful to have such an intelligent agent as Carol Mann, who knows psychology, thinks about ideas, and keeps a pulse on changing times in publishing and the field. Deborah Malmud at Norton had the original idea for the book and has remained an interested, intelligent, and extremely helpful editor

—a real pleasure to work with. Michael McGandy, whose virtual and trustworthy e-presence was always helpful and friendly, moved the book along toward publication and improved my writing.

Final thanks to my sons. I apologize for all the times I don't practice what I preach, not providing the fascinating conversations about sex that I urge therapists and parents to engage in. Perhaps it's better that it remains unacknowledged that when Mommy goes into her office, she's writing about sex. In spite of that, both my boys seem to have gleaned some of my values from bits of conversations here and there and seem to be vibrantly wonderful beings poised for full lives ahead. I dedicate this book to them.

SEX, THERAPY, AND KIDS

Knowing What's Normative

Amy has brought a mini–boom box to her therapy session. She's a chubby, rosy little 9-year-old whom you find adorable even though she's oppositional, rude, and impulsive at school, home, and quite frequently in your weekly therapy hour. Today she wants to dance for you to her favorite music. You smile and welcome her, expecting to mirror back to her that she's a lovely and creative child.

As she sets up the boom box on your dollhouse table and starts the music, a different look comes into her eye. It's not the look of anticipation you saw earlier, or the look that shows she's getting quite attached to you, nor is it the look of seriousness some dancers get as they pause and focus before dancing; it's a rather seductive look, one that used to be called bedroom eyes. She presses PLAY on the boom box, and as Beyonce starts to sing, Amy quickly rolls up her shirt to make her belly show and pulls her stretchy sleeves down to expose her shoulders. She dances and it's a very sexy dance. She bumps, she grinds, she strokes her body as she moves to the music, she gives looks over her shoulder, arches her back and sticks out her chest, then flips her long hair over her head in front of her, emerging from the mane like a tigress. She's part Disney, part Britney, and she's making you very uncomfortable.

Should you smile as she proceeds, hoping she doesn't actually do a striptease? Should you simply acknowledge with a nod that she is dancing for you? How can you step in and ask her to talk about her dance and her feelings without dashing her hopes that you will admire her and reflect back to her your acceptance? How might you acknowledge that she wants to be sexy and adored without also encouraging a sexuality that is blatantly too old for her, as well as too objectified? Should you have stopped her from rolling up her shirt? Suddenly your response to all this seems very important and way too complicated.

It's different when a teen comes in and you already have established an implicit or explicit agreement with her that she can talk about all sorts of issues in confidence. Or is it? Jennifer comes in with a tale to tell that begins with her performing oral sex on two different boys at a party last Saturday night. Before you can ask her how she felt at the time and how she feels now about that—our old standby questions—she whizzes past what may be minor incidents to her in order to tell you a story of betrayal by her best girlfriend, who told another girl at the party a secret Jennifer had told only her. The tale of friendship and betrayal is long and involved and you sit there with an uncomfortable feeling that maybe you should get back to the oral sex at some point. Frantically you search your memory for facts about sexually transmitted diseases (STDs) and oral sex. There are issues of danger, of self-esteem, and of performing for boys, issues also about sexual pleasure, and yet, will you seem like a voyeuristic adult if you try to bring Jennifer back to that topic? After all, issues of friendship and betrayal are at the core of an adolescent's life as well.

Margaret calls and is crying on the phone when she leaves her message. You return the call and discover she has just been told by her son that he is gay—not that he *thinks* he is gay but that he *is* gay. And yet, she says, how can he know? He doesn't have any experience and he's never had a girlfriend. He's just 14. Is he just saying this because he wants to fit in with his gay friend (this is Vermont!)? Is it because he has asthma and can't do sports? Margaret is scared to death that the younger children in the family might find out. Could they be influenced by him to be gay too? Even if that's not possible, won't they be teased at school about their big brother? She would like you to assess him to see if he's "really" gay, to tell him that this could be just a phase, and also to get him to stop announcing this to everybody. You would like to help her, but what you have to say right now might not be what she wants to hear. And you want to meet her son and hear what he has to say. You feel a mix of empathy, because she feels that this is quite possibly the worst thing that could have happened to her and her family, and distance as you wonder how in this day and age people can still feel that "being gay" can be caught like a cold.

Sexual issues and talk about sex and sexuality do not come up in every session, nor do sexual issues emerge with every client or family we see in therapy. But they can appear quite by surprise, often throwing even a psychoanalytically trained therapist for a loop. Over the years, in my classes as well as supervisory sessions, students and colleagues have brought in examples of sexual play and talk that have surprised them. Of course I ask, "What did you say?" Most of these well-meaning, intelligent, and rather sophisticated students and colleagues say, "Nothing: I didn't know what to say."

Why say nothing in response to a child's humping of two dollhouse figures or a teen's reference to a hookup last weekend? To be fair, the practice of psychotherapy demands a lot of silence, letting a client's words hover in the air so that clients can ponder them, reflect on them, pursue them, or drop them according to their own inclinations. We therapists hope that our silence expresses nonjudgment and neutrality. But I've been wondering if this silence around sex comes out of a wish to play it safe. Is it such a good strategy when it comes to sexual concerns of children brought up in play and the experiences that teens talk about with us? When we are silent in response to sexual material introduced in the therapy hour, we mimic and reproduce a world that excites and confuses our clients and yet provides them with little guidance or space for processing. In fact, our clients may indeed be reproducing the world around them when sexual material suddenly pops up in their play, just like the commercials on TV or pop-up ads on their computers that intrude on them to sell things using sex.

This is just to say that some of the sexual material brought up in therapy sessions doesn't speak to the deepest, darkest issues of instinctual desire but merely expresses the way children and teens are incorporating the sexual world around them (and the sexual world as represented by marketers) into their play and their identities. This incorporation generally happens without benefit of reflection and without time to integrate feelings and new knowledge with other aspects of who they are. It is then a therapist's responsibility to slow down children or adolescents, to help them reflect on what they are taking in about the sexual world, and how these perceptions may influence the people they are and the adults they will become.

Sex is hard to talk about in a therapy session and brings up mixed feelings in clients and therapists alike. To pursue these conversations or moments of play in therapy, we worry as therapists that we are contributing to the overstimulation of the child. We worry that the child will see us pursuing the play or topic because *we* are stimulated by it, that we might convey that it's especially delightful play, more interesting than mommies and daddies taking care of the babies in the dollhouse or the ins and outs of arguments with a boyfriend that a teenage girl may share. These are important worries I will address.

We also worry that we do not have permission from parents to talk about these things with their child and that if word got back to the parents, they might fire us, sue us, or simply be angry that we provided their child with some information they did not want their child to have. Rest assured that there are ways to discuss these kinds of issues with parents up front, at the beginning of therapy, so that a therapist can feel safer talking with a child.

Therapists also sometimes feel ill equipped to talk to teens about sex, knowing that sometimes the teens know more than we do about newer practices and the context in which sex takes place. When we need to ask questions to understand what exactly "hooking up" means to a teen in her particular world, we worry that such talk is voyeuristic and that, like the rest of society, we have too much interest in the sex lives of adolescents.

But when we are silent, we also worry that our silence lets children stew in their own concerns, providing no assistance in making sense of the world they see or the fantasies in their heads. And we worry with teens that they won't get the adult help they need to acquire accurate information or see the long-term consequences of their behaviors.

These concerns are addressed in Chapter 1, specifically when I discuss guidelines for therapists, and also throughout the book in my discussion of various cases. First, though, it is important to lay out what exactly is going on in the sexual world of children and teens.

SEX IN THE LIVES OF CHILDREN: THE WORLD AROUND THEM

Many children live in a world that we expect to be contained and protective. But even the most protected children are exposed to sexual material that can be confusing, exciting, and overstimulating.

Porn Sex, Overexposure

In children's worlds, unfortunately, all too often they confront not only overstimulating material on TV, but also the porn produced by the porn industry that might come across on the computer screen or be found in the video store, their parents' bedroom, or in school passed around by other kids. God forbid your daughter wants to be a cheerleader and looks up cheerleading on the Web. She'll have to wade through 10 porn sites before she reaches a "cheer club."

Brandy's mother called to ask for an appointment because while in a video store, Brandy had wandered to the adult corner and saw a picture of a woman giving a man oral sex on the cover of a video box. Brandy brought up this photo to her mother in conversation constantly in the weeks that followed, and her mother thought that this viewing had done permanent damage. In therapy, it became clear that Brandy was temperamentally the kind of kid who got overstimulated by almost everything. Different children will react differently to exposure to inappropriate material. The sad thing is that pornographic images are too much a part of our culture to be able to spare children from this confusing material.

In addition to the porn produced by the porn industry, there are all sorts of references to porn in their lives, like cartoon characters who do stripteases, lap dances, or erotic dances on a chair, pulling cartoon showers to drench them with water (see *Shrek 2*). These references are so common nowadays and we may be becoming so immune that we forget that these images derive from the world of porn. A child pretending to do a lap dance in her imaginary play in your therapy office might indeed be imitating a sexy rabbit from a cartoon she saw on Saturday morning.

And then there's the in-between stuff that they may see on MTV, one of the places where "raunch culture," as Ariel Levy describes it in her book, *Female Chauvinist Pigs*, has crossed over.

Sure the girls are clothed, but they're wearing the stuff of pornography—hot pants, G-strings, lingerie—and bumping and grinding like strippers of old. TV sitcoms as well produce comic characters that are sex-starved sex objects as well as girl-on-girl kissing for male delight.

It's been my experience that parents do not and cannot monitor this stuff closely enough. Sure there are parents who give up on the small stuff and bring young kids to PG-13 movies, even letting them watch R-rated movies at home. And there are parents who give in to their children's appeals to be more grown-up like their older siblings. But most parents I know care, yet they find that there simply is too much of this stuff out there to be able to monitor it closely enough. Kids today will be exposed to porn and we need to help them understand it and process it. It is confusing and it will come out in therapy.

Victimization

Another exposure to sex and sexual material is through a child's own victimization. Whenever a child brings up sexual material in therapy, we therapists have been trained to look for indications that the child has been sexually abused, and it's a realistic concern. Children who have been sexually abused do bring sexual material into the play hour. It is important for a therapist to ask about abuse when a child does. But in my experience, abuse is more likely to be revealed in a child's narration of events in her life rather than through questioning. For example, "Like the time my dad tied me up with his tie. . . ." The therapist catches on and repeats as a question, "Your dad tied you up?" This discussion leads to a disclosure of abuse. Play about the abuse seems to come after the disclosure and can go on for years, as it did with Nick, whom I write about in Chapter 3, who was abused by his father and in a game he called "mad scientist" made me sit on the chair with the slippery snakes.

Sex talk or play in therapy may be an indication of abuse. But children and teens have healthy and positive sexual lives also. We clinicians tend to dwell on the dangers and negative possibilities when we could also be supporting children and teens to understand their sexual selves in ways appropriate to their developmental age. Even when a child has been sexually abused, the goal is not to process the experience so that sex is never again worked on in the therapy session; the goal is to process the experience in such a way that it no longer controls the child and he or she can go on to talk about sexual experiences and thoughts that are normative for his or her age. Thus, knowing what's normative is even more important when working with sexually abused children.

SEXUAL DEVELOPMENT IN CHILDREN AND TEENS

How do we know what's normative in children's sexual development? Don't go to the library, because you won't find it in any books. In fact, most of the research done on children's sexuality is about what parents and social workers have observed rather than about what children have experienced, what they think about, or how they feel. Toni Cavanaugh Johnson and Eliana Gil are pioneers in this field, and Johnson has laid out tables and charts depicting the range of normative to abusive behaviors discovered in children. These charts are helpful and can be ordered from her Web site (http://www.tcavjohn.com). But these two clinicians come from an abuse perspective, delineating disordered and problematic behavior for professionals and courts.

I come from a health and resiliency perspective, primarily working with children who come to outpatient therapy for issues other than coercive, troubling sexualized behavior. I believe this book adds to the pioneering work of Johnson and Gil, and William Friedrich, too, by including information about and strategies for working with most children, not just sexually acting-out children. I also focus on what we know about children and adolescents through studying normal development. For child therapists, that's a wonderful place to start.

SO WHAT IS NORMATIVE?

Young children (age 3 or 4) rarely engage in deeply complicated games of imagination with other children, but from age 5 onward, children's imaginative play with others can become intense and full of conflictual material. In my own research asking adult women and men to reflect back on the sexual games they played as children, they played few games before age seven. When children are very young, their interests seem to be in "I'll show you mine if you show me yours" games. They also may sit on their bathroom floors looking at, touching, and even trying to taste their private areas. Curiosity, pleasure, interest—all of these are motivating factors in young children's play with their own genitals and the genitals of other children. We know that young children as well as older children masturbate or touch themselves. Of course it is easier to observe in the 3-year-old than in the 8-year-old, but it is common.

As children get older, their play includes more games of imagination. They also enter a wider social realm. In grade school, children play games about sex with each other, and their games can reproduce what they see in the world around them. They report playing house and, for example, at the end of the day, when the man comes home (often these scripts are sexist too), the husband and wife lie in bed together. This sometimes thrilling part of the game involved kissing or humping, and is played in same-sex or mixed-sex pairs. There are other games of imagination that kids play involving scenarios they may have seen in the movies or on TV, pretending to be captors and captives, making one child strip for another, even pretending to be dead bodies because those bodies are often so voluptuous when presented on TV shows like *CSI*, which many children watch. One woman I interviewed for my book *The Secret Lives of Girls* (Lamb, 2002) reported to me she played "beauty pageant" and would sit on the imaginary judges' laps trying to seduce them to vote for her. One child I interviewed told me about playing prostitute with her friends. These scenarios could involve actual touching and sexual feelings.

While those imaginary games tend to occur in paired play and sometimes threesomes, grade school children also become involved in some group games of sexual daring. One of the boys in an earlier study I conducted with Mary Coakley wrote about a game played in his neighborhood of doctors' children, where the children would take turns being the patient and all the children would get a turn to poke. Another group game he described took place in the woods near his house, where someone would have to get naked in front of the rest of the group. These games of vulnerability and daring, rather than mutual sharing, seem to be about the excitement of getting caught as much as they're about exposing private parts and the differences between girls and boys.

These group games and sometimes the one-on-one games of children can involve exploitation and what social service agencies now call abuse. I hesitate to call it abuse even though it is, because calling it abuse usually kicks in agency responses to sex offenses that are more appropriate to adult offenders. A bunch of older boys ask a girl and her friend into the woods, surround them, and make them pull down their pants. They run away afterward and the girls, crying, scared, and ashamed, return home. A 13-year-old girl puts the hand of a 7-year-old boy she is babysitting on her newly formed breast. The boy tells his parents and they send him to therapy to see if this confusing incident has hurt him in some permanent way. As in all children's play, there is mutual fun and there is bullying, there is friendship and there is exploitation, there is sharing and there is coercion. Children act out their interests as well as their worries in play and this more troublesome stuff does occur. In Chapter 4, I talk about that shady area between play and abuse and how to talk to children, victims, initiators, and participants about it.

Such games are coercive. But coercion and bullying are a part of children's play naturally, all over the world. While they are wrong, just as we don't send a child into long-term treatment for a single incident of bullying in the school, or girlfighting as it is called when it's between girls, we don't need to send children into long-term treatment if they at one time make other children play a sexual game or show someone their private parts. It's bad behavior. It's troubling. But it doesn't a sex offender make; and it is normative. Normative does not equal right or even desirable behavior. It simply indicates what kind of behavior you can expect to see at certain ages in certain societies by some children.

So, in general, what is normative in childhood, aside from some bullying? Sexual play is intermittent and not part of children's play activities constantly. When children play at sexual games, they play with children of similar age and the games are mostly mutual. The affect might be silly and excited, but there also may be guilt and anxiety—let's remember, this is a forbidden activity, often done in secret. The play is done for various reasons: curiosity, experimentation, exploration—and don't forget fun. Even more important, children are trying to assimilate the sexual material they hear about and see in their worlds, as well as responding to sexual feelings this material produces in them. Play is a wonderful way for a child to try to understand all of the above.

What's Normative in Teens

It would seem that normative sexual behavior for teens and preteens is much more known than ever before. Indeed, every year *Time, Newsweek,* or *U.S. News & World Report* trots out a tired old story about teens and sex. In addition to these recycled articles, there are surveys, books, and magazines. It seems as if the media can't get enough of teen sex—everybody seems to be concerned with how much they are doing and when. While there may be new and increasing attention to teen sex, underlying the drama it's the same old worry—keeping girls virgin. Sure, there are certain risks to early pregnancy and other risks involved with early sex. Still, discussion of preventing early sex is almost always aimed at girls' health and reputation. So few public discussions ever bring up what might be problematic for boys about early sex. A therapist can't buy into the notion that teen sex can only be problematic for girls.

Of late, it seems that the media have taken a particular interest in oral sex, although the specific worry about this act is never clearly articulated. Are we as a nation to be worried about oral sex because middle schoolers may be taking the act lightly and not with the seriousness they take other kinds of sex? Are we to be worried because they don't know about the STD dangers involved with oral sex and think it's free of danger? Are we to worry about the sexism—girls are performing oral sex on boys more than boys on girls? Or are we simply to worry that kids are just doing way too much way too early? Think of the level of excitement, fear, and anxiety that "rainbow party" and "football team" stories have pro-duced—and then ask yourself, about what exactly?

Therapists tend to focus on what early sex might mean to the individual teen, and this is a good place to begin. But it is also important to have some data about risks and about what is nor-mative.

Boys that mature early tend to be seen as more popular by their peers than boys who mature later. But girls who are early maturers are at greater risk than girls who mature later. Normative data generally tell us when certain kids of certain races, genders, religions, and socioeconomic classes are more likely to have sex. There is indeed a wealth of data on this subject and it's good to know. But there is more to sex in adolescence than intercourse, and this we know less about. We do know that about two thirds of teen boys masturbate and about a third of girls do (though this may be an underestimation, given the nature of surveys). Knowing that can help a therapist normalize a teen's practices as well as worries about it. What do we know about the other sexual practices of adolescence? Most of it is, to use a legal term, hearsay.

Hooking up could be simply extended kissing; it could be having sex; it could mean that two people are getting together in a kind of boyfriend-and-girlfriend relationship; or it could mean the two got together for a night. Much like *making out,* hooking up means various things at various ages and to various groups in various parts of the country.

Oral sex? There is talk of and joking about it in every middle school and high school across the country. But what are the real data? It's probably more rare than you would think, according to a recent survey (Jayson, 2005). What is interesting about the presentation of this survey by the media is that by combining age groups, they can give us the impression that oral sex is rampant among teens. But if you study the statistics more carefully, it's really in late high school and early college when teens experience their first oral sex, boosting the statistic up to 55% by age 17. In these reports, we are never told what exactly is problematic about teens having oral sex.

"Friends with benefits"? Again, the phrase could mean just that. In Chapter 5, I describe a girl who made a deal with a male friend that they would have sex with each other whenever one felt horny, and that neither could ever refuse the other. There are others who use the phrase *friends with benefits* to describe the beginning of a relationship when the two partners haven't yet made a commitment to be labeled a couple. Still others use this phrase to describe the weaning phase of a breakup.

Sexual confusion? Yes, plenty of teens wonder about same-sex attractions. It's a very difficult topic to research given the variation in the acceptance of lesbian or gay male sexuality in high schools in different geographic areas. The data show us that 8–14% have had some same-sex experience and 27% of girls and 18% of boys in grades 7–12 report sexual fantasies of both genders.

Teen pregnancy and risk? It's good to know about the rates of contraceptive use and how ignorant most teens are with regard to usage. One study by Crosby and Yarber shows that ⅓ to ½ of adolescents have serious misconceptions about condom use (Crosby & Yarber, 2001). In another study only 30% of adolescents could correctly define ovulation (Hockenberry-Eaton, Richman, Dilorio, Rivero, & Maibach, 1996). Research focusing on early sex (because early sex is correlated with pregnancy) shows us that teens from single-parent families tend to become sexually active earlier, even when other factors are controlled like the financial situation of the family, religion, and race. Father absence puts girls at risk for early sex and not just because of the loss of income or the stress of divorce (loss and lack of contact). There are also psychological issues that arise in terms of feeling wanted and loved by a man. When an adolescent participates in other adultlike or so-called deviant behaviors (e.g., drug use, alcohol use, smoking), she or he is more likely to have early intercourse. Alcohol has a particularly strong relationship with early sex. Depression, too, is a predictor for girls. Academic achievement and involvement in extracurricular activities have the reverse effect. Time spent in homework and school-related activities delay first sex longer for girls than for boys. The earlier a teen moves into a monogamous, love-oriented relationship, particularly girls, the earlier she will have sex.

Family dynamics play a role. When a child has warm, supportive, and communicative parents, the child is less likely to engage in early sex, maybe because parents will have an influence on what peers their child hangs out with. When a parent is harsh, a teen engages in other minor deviant behaviors that over time can be associated with early sex. Parental influence, not surprisingly, diminishes over time.

Therapists need to know this normative data. But they also need to be able to ask how things are in a particular teen's life, in her social group, in his school, in her family. Statistics are about teens in general; they're group norms. It may not matter that in general parents have less influence over high school kids when you have a teen crying in your office because she feels she has let her mother down. But it may be very useful to know some statistics about HIV when a teen is sitting there panic stricken that she might have AIDS because she had sex with her boyfriend and then found out that he had two-timed her the week before with another girl, or when your teen client goes to an adult gay bar, passing for a much older person, and has sex with some unknown college student in his car in the parking lot.

It's good to have some data, but providing information is not our primary purpose. So, if a teen asks whether she's not a virgin if a boy has used his finger, you as a therapist wouldn't really have an answer. You could provide an answer by referencing what you think to be general public opinion. But instead, you might want to explore her own meaning of *virgin* and her feelings about masturbation. If another girl asks how to get her boyfriend to stop pawing her all the time in public, statistics will get you nowhere. If she doesn't like it, she has a right to stop it and needs help to find a way to communicate that to him. Your work will probably be to help her find her voice or explore her continued relationship with a boy who isn't responding to her requests to stop. If another girl asks you if the gynecologist can tell her mother she's having sex without the girl giving the gynecologist permission to do so, you should be able to give her an answer to that question, even if you want to explore her relationship with her mother and why this is a frightening idea.

* * * *

Finally, when considering what's normal for teens, it's good to remember that some teens have little sexual curiosity in adolescence, or few sexual feelings. There is a lot more variation in sexual desire and interest than one would believe, given the media depiction of adolescence as a time of raging hormones.

While we're trained to see and understand pathology, to do so we also need to understand sexual health. Few of us have a good sense of what that is, although we should make that a goal. If we as therapists develop our sense of what sexual health looks like in the 8-year-old as well as the 14-year-old, we know what we are working toward and we can help children to be able to integrate their sexual feelings and sexuality into their whole selves. In so doing, therapists can provide a service, not only to the clients they see, but to the communities around them in advancing a more positive and integrative view of sexual development. It's my hope that this book will help therapists have the courage to address sexual issues in their sessions with even the youngest of clients, if such issues should arise.

CHAPTER ONE

General Principles and Guidelines

Psychotherapy is an art involving nuanced responding and empathic listening, and so it is difficult to describe what an individual therapist ought to do for very specific and individual issues. But I can more generally describe my own approach and present some general principles from my own practice that others might use as guidelines. I want to clarify from the start, however, that I won't be writing very much on adolescents who commit crimes or whose sexual behavior is so disturbed that they are considered by many to be "juvenile sex offenders" and sent to specialized treatment groups and placements. An extensive literature exists already on their treatment. I'm sympathetic to the plights of these boys who often come from abusive experiences and chaotic households, but my style of treatment would probably not work as well as the more cognitive-behavioral programs that are in the literature. While extensive literature also exists on the treatment of sexually abused children, I think that my more normative approach adds something to this literature; thus I do discuss this kind of therapy in Chapter 3.

My guidelines are meant to help primarily those psychotherapists in outpatient practice and caseworkers who work with children in residential treatment who present with some sexual issues or concerns. The issues I deal with are the kinds of sexual issues that arise in most therapeutic practices when therapists encounter children and teens. My decision to include some material and exclude others is based on my own work in private practice in Pennsylvania and Vermont and at a major teaching hospital in Boston, the work of my students interning in residential placements, and the work of my peers and colleagues in Vermont, Oregon, Illinois, and Massachusetts.

GENERAL APPROACH

Because I've been trained in humanistic, existential, psychoanalytic, family systems, and cognitive-behavioral strategies, my work represents a combination of these modalities. But an underlying focus of mine when working with children and adolescents is attending to the affect and affective sense surrounding a topic or play activity. This is particularly useful when working with sexual material in that sexual material in therapy can be overstimulating. I will use the word *overstimulation* quite a bit in describing children, teens, or even the world around them; it describes an underlying affective sense. Human beings need optimal levels of stimulation to remain engaged in the world. When I moved to Vermont, after living in cities all my life, I felt chronically understimulated. I found myself loving my visits to New York, where a million textual and visual messages, sights, sounds, and smells hit you at once. Over the 10 years I've lived here, my body has accustomed itself to the peacefulness and pace of the natural surroundings. Now when I visit New York, after a day or two of walking about, I am exhausted. Another example of overstimulation is the idea that parents can give TMI (too much information). Kids use that slang expression to tell parents that they just don't want that much information about a topic or their parents' lives.

Why? Because they physiologically and psychologically can't take it or don't want to deal with it.

I used the example of sensory overstimulation to describe my reactions to Vermont and New York. But we can get over stimulated by knowledge or even by a simple act. We as a species like habit. We like routine. But we also like excitement and surprises. We're attracted to information, people, and events that are exciting, some of us more than others. But there's only so much of that that a person can take.

The feeling of overstimulation is like being overwhelmed, maybe even excited, but not in a good way. Perhaps for some children or adolescents who seek out the state of overstimulation it feels good at first, but both the bodily and mental excitement are overwhelming, too much to manage, beyond one's resources, a stress. When people are overstimulated they might just shut out the overstimulating material or shut down in response to it. This is one theory of why sexually abused children dissociate when they are being abused. They also might become anxious and confused, unable to contain the affect they feel, needing to act it out or talk about it or play. They might become too preoccupied with the material that is confusing or anxiety provoking.

Whenever a child or teen is anxious about the material she is talking about or playing out, a therapist ought to be able to see signs that the client is feeling stressed, whether because she seems overly invested and a little out of control, unaware of herself, or because she seems distracted and driven in the play. This is of particular concern for children who have been sexually abused, because we see this overstimulation or even self-stimulation as a reliving or reexperiencing of the abuse, and because of that want to stop it. Such reliving of the abusive experience in the therapy hour can make children feel unsafe and out of control. They may even seem dissociated, and it's important for therapists not to encourage dissociation in the therapy hour.

It's good to train oneself to observe this affective sense under-lying talk or play, because if such overstimulating play is hap-pening in the therapy session, you can bet it's happening outside of the room. Therapy is the place in which these emotions, even bodily feelings, can be experienced in the safe presence of another who will protect and allow the time and space to process them and get some reflective distance.

But how do therapists make stimulating material unstimu-lating to the child without simply pushing the child to leave the material alone and move on to pleasanter things, more manage-able topics and emotions? This is crucial to my approach. Therapists can model a neutral, distanced reflective process with their clients that allows them to stay with the material. And thera-pists can help clients to distance themselves from it in order to talk about it or continue playing in a way that's productive. For a child, that might mean transferring the play from the dollhouse to the drawing table. For more competent older children, it might mean stopping and reflecting on the feelings they have while playing that game, thus interrupting the game with process and talk. For teens, it might mean asking them to reflect on how they feel in narrating a story or asking them questions about their feelings and thoughts at the time of the incident they are narrating. Of course, therapists ask these kinds of questions all the time, but over time it's good to develop a sense of what question will bring teens or children to a place where they can recover a therapeutic attitude toward these events and acts. I've called this approach displacement, but it means very literally displacing the feelings from one's mind and body into the play, into the more distanced talk, and not taking one's feelings toward one thing or person and directing them toward another (the older psychoanalytic meaning of the defense, displacement). This is the essence of my first guideline for treating children and adolescents when sexual issues emerge. It's a general guideline for child psychotherapy. The rest of the guidelines in this chapter are more specific to sex talk, play, and therapy.

1. Think of playing and talking as acts that modulate affect and address overstimulation.
2. Recognize society's influence on the lives of children and teens and try to assess and understand the child's individual capacity to contain this stimulation from outside.
3. Make therapy a safe place for a child or adolescent while at the same time welcoming talk about uncomfortable topics.
4. Discuss confidentiality.
5. Control your reactions and understand yourself as a sexual person.
6. Get permission from parents to talk about sex when it arises.
7. Therapy isn't education, but sometimes a little sex education is necessary.
8. Give permission to children and teens to express and experience pleasure.
9. Keep in mind that sex does not equal danger.
10. When necessary, seek supervision; when impossible, refer out.

THINK OF PLAYING AND TALKING AS ACTS THAT MODULATE AFFECT

Invite play that gives room for exploration and that allows a child to enact or represent very personal thoughts and feelings outside of the self, through art, puppets, dolls, or storytelling. By doing so, you give a child the opportunity to reflect on unacceptable and confusing thoughts and feelings without having to own them and describe them. This distance from the issues at hand helps children become more reflective about what they may be experiencing, try out solutions to problems, express secret motives and hidden desires, and indirectly gain a kind of therapeutic support that they might not be able to ask for or admit they need. Talk with teens can have the same goals; thus, talk about "friends" and hypothetical others allows a teen to project, displace, think about, propose solutions to, and work out issues at some distance rather than through direct venting and addressing of the problems. Talk with teens can take on a playlike quality of exploration even when the topics are very real. And the therapist's attitude toward this talk, that it is an exploration, a subtype of intensive play rather than a consultation (in which the therapist gives advice), can help teens build within themselves the resources to successfully modulate overwhelming feelings and thoughts when they arise.

RECOGNIZE SOCIETY'S INFLUENCE
ON THE LIVES OF CHILDREN

To assess and understand a child's individual capacity to contain stimulation from outside, therapists will need to educate themselves on what actual children and teens are watching, playing, listening to, and reading. This will prevent a therapist from making the assumption that if a child has certain sexual knowledge, that child has been abused. Society places enormous demands on children to integrate all sorts of conflicting and exciting sexual material, and it's good when they bring this material into the therapy session. Asking, "Where did you hear about that?" or "Did you see that on TV?" is, however, not the way to approach this material, only because that conveys to children or teens that they are mere reproducers of culture and doesn't get at the question of why this particular cartoon or that particular sitcom scene was repeated in play or narrated in talk. The culture provides the raw material and the individual's own issues and concerns wrap around it and use the raw material to work out some problem in talk or play. So why is it still important to know where that raw material comes from? To see the individual child's variations on the theme and to understand what aspects of the game or the TV show or movie the child may not have noticed or which might have been forgotten in favor of another aspect. For example, a teen might bring up a scene from a movie where there was a big fight between a mother and a son, and the therapist, who also saw that movie might ask, "Did you think the fight had anything to do with her discomfort with her son's sexuality?" The teen may not have even informed the therapist that the boy in the movie was gay. And when a kid is talking nonstop about a video game, a therapist might want to ask about the aspect of the game that has gotten a lot of media attention, that a player gets points for running over certain people in the game.

It's sometimes difficult to assess how much a child can take in from this outside world of stimulation. Parents learn the hard way when little children wake up in the night with nightmares from watching even *The Wizard of Oz* at too young an age. (It's quite a scary movie to them!) Nightmares, preoccupation, discussion of material that seems too old for them, compulsive play, constant questions, the answers to which are never enough—these are all signs that a child has had too much and is trying to get some understanding or handle on material that is difficult for him or her to process. It's difficult for parents to protect their kids from this kind of overstimulation, but they can do their best to reassure after the fact. Therapists need to make their therapy space safe from this kind of confusing excitement and, when a child brings in such material, help the child to modulate his or her feelings around these overwhelming topics.

MAKE THERAPY A SAFE PLACE AND WELCOME DISCUSSION OF SEXUAL ISSUES

Children and teens need to feel that they can ask about sex and introduce sexual material into their play without fear of an over-reaction from a therapist. Creating therapy as a place for exploration is one way many of us open up this space to our clients. Setting up boundaries around confidentiality from the beginning is another. Modulating one's reactions to this kind of material is a third.

When first meeting with a child or adolescent, a therapist needs to describe the process of therapy. Many simply sit and let the child or teen take the lead by inviting a child to explore the room or asking a teen what she or he has been told about therapy. This is fine. But I also advocate describing what therapy can be. A therapist can speak directly with children about how feeling free to talk when they want or just play when they want might help them to think or feel differently about things in their lives that might make them worried, sad, or angry. Sometimes even just playing can help kids understand themselves better, make good decisions, find people to help when they need help, or come up with a solution themselves about the things that might be bothering them.

How does a therapist give signals to a teen that therapy is a safe space to talk about sex? Some of us do not give signals at all but directly state that sort of thing at the beginning of therapy. For example, a therapist might say outright, "Therapy is a place where you can explore feelings that concern you, work out ways in which you want to respond to or interact with other people in your life, make plans or set goals, and just get support around things that trouble you. Some of the things you may want to talk about could involve your family relationships, school and its pressures, your sexual feelings or the sexual experiences you may be having, or your friendships." In this introduction, sexual feelings are thrown into the mix as a part of teenage life and an area in which teens may have feelings or concerns.

Sometimes in the middle of a session, a therapist may have to ask explicitly about sex to understand the issue being discussed. Nina discussed, for example, the burden her boyfriend had become to her but how she loved him and couldn't break up with him. I asked her, "Is sex an issue, too?" I could have put out a more tentative question along with information by saying, "I don't know if you and Angus have had sex or how far you've gone, but it's sometimes the case that if a girl has had sex for the first time with her boyfriend that she feels it reflects poorly on her if she and he break up, or that this first sex isn't or wasn't important, and possibly was a mistake. Is something like that also playing into your decision to stay together with him?" The last question, of course, is based on a hunch, and yet it provides information for Nina that allows her to explore that issue in relation to breaking up.

At other times when a teen is talking about a relationship and talking about everything but sex, a therapist may feel she or he has to explicitly give permission to bring that up. "I notice that you've never talked about any sexual relationship that's developed between you and your boyfriend/girlfriend and I don't know if that's important to what we're talking about, but I want you to know that therapy is a good place to process some of those feelings, and those feelings may be a part of what you're working on in your relationship. Is there anything I can do to help you feel comfortable talking about any concerns or feelings you might have?" This may also break the ice with a teen girl who is romantically involved with another girl or a teen boy involved with another boy, both of whom may feel that with a heterosexual therapist, they can only talk about the relationship itself. A therapist might want to add, "I don't know if that's important to you to talk about right now, but I hope I can make you feel safe enough in here to explore those feelings if they're part of the relationship you're concerned about." Again, that sort of question doesn't come out of the blue. When I spoke like that to a girl I was seeing in therapy, it seemed clear that she wanted to tell me about her desires for another girl but didn't know how. When I ventured the topic, with relief she poured out her mixed feelings and even discussed a sexual fantasy she had about her new friend.

Creating a safe space in which to discuss sex seriously may be more difficult than a therapist thinks with a heterosexual boy who identifies with mainstream masculine culture. He's up for jokes and innuendoes. But with regard to his worries and vulnerabilities, there are several reasons why a boy may feel unsafe. He may feel different from other boys. He may also feel that sharing any vulnerability makes him less masculine. In his world, being a knower and having done sexual things is equivalent to having power; not knowing and not having done much makes him feel small.

Creating a safe space for a boy to speak about sex and sexual concerns may involve respecting him as a person with a lot of sexual knowledge already. The teen feels powerful simply to know what Justin did to Dori and to know what the word he's using means. He feels cool and doesn't want to be told that Justin may have been lying, or that this particular sex act sounds unlikely, or even that he got it wrong. On the other hand, competitive with his peers to be in the know, he's eager to get information that will enable him to call someone's bluff and to be able to provide juicy bits of information about sex to his peers. This may mean that creating a safe space is allowing some locker room talk and not being too quick to correct distortions.

Therapists may also need to make it safe for teens to talk about issues around masturbation directly so that therapists can help teens with any concerns or fears about it. A therapist might include the topic in a general conversation about sex, saying how it's true that boys masturbate and masturbate a lot. Sometimes it helps to use the strategy of talking about "another boy" or generic "boys" so that it's not so intense or direct when a conversation about sex begins. "I once saw a boy who was worried about . . ." or "I've seen a lot of boys who worry if they masturbate too much." This sneaky strategy has its problems. It makes it seem as if all these other boys were much more open when talking about sex than the boy who's now in the office. Also, it may raise questions about whether you're going to reveal stuff about this boy's sexual life to the next boy in the office. But sometimes it's really effective to bring in a sort of virtual group therapy. It's in your knowledge of other boys, not your book reading, that you will gain a boy's trust when you reassure him about what's normal or normative for his age group and what may be harmful to him or others. A therapist can also simply say, "I wonder what other guys your age do," as in, "I wonder what other guys your age do when a girl says no to sex" and "I wonder what guys do next when their girlfriend does say yes to sex."

DISCUSS CONFIDENTIALITY

Every therapist should know that discussing confidentiality at the beginning of therapy with a child or a teen is a way to ensure safety in the therapeutic process. But privilege and confidentiality are two different things. The law in some states says that there is no client-therapist privilege between child patient and therapist. These kinds of laws are in direct conflict with the ethical guidelines of the American Psychological Association and all the therapeutic professions. Therapists need to promise confidentiality for therapy to become a place where children and teens can feel free to discuss their most troubling issues. That's why a therapist needs to get agreement from a parent at the beginning of the therapy process. Therapists need to explain to parents that to do therapy with their child, the therapist will need to promise confidentiality. The therapist should explain the limits of that confidentiality to the parents and assure them that she or he will be available for meetings to update the parents and provide some advice, but that the child or teen will have some say with regard to what the therapist can share. Most parents understand the need for confidentiality and I don't ask them to sign an agreement of understanding, although legally that might be a smart thing to do.

A therapist needs to explain confidentiality and the boundaries of confidentiality with a child. One way, with younger children, is to say that the therapist can keep a secret and that according to the job, must keep everything they talk about a secret if a child doesn't want his or her parents to know something. I tell a child directly that I won't talk to the child's parents about things the child says or does or has done in sessions, unless the child gives permission or if the child is planning to do something that would really hurt himself or someone else. Then, of course, I describe the circumstances in which I will need to talk to the parents. I explain to kids that I need to talk to their parents occasionally to keep them informed, but when I do I will first check out with the child what I am going to say and whether there are certain things the child prefers I keep secret. This has worked well for me. Before a meeting with parents, I have discussed with my young clients why I wanted to meet with their parents and what I wanted to say. In all but one case, the child has given me permission to say what I wanted to say. Most of them add things that they'd like me to tell their parents, such as, "Can you ask them if I can stay up on Sundays to watch a TV show?" I respond that I'll tell their parents about their request, then ask why this is so important.

It's different with teens. I find that therapists should be very explicit with regard to what we need to report, which is a teen's intention to do harm to himself or herself, or to another person (or to someone's property, in some states). With drug use, sexual activity, eating disorders, cutting behaviors, or sneaking out of the house at night, I specifically tell teens that although all of these are harmful to themselves, I would not discuss them with parents unless the teen gave permission. I tell them there may be good reasons to share this with parents or good reasons not to. Confidentiality is especially important to adolescents because generally, teens don't believe that people can keep secrets, mostly because hardly anybody in their lives does keep a secret and many of them have been hurt by this. It helps to emphasize that it's not just a promise but a professional ethic, and that we as therapists know that for therapy to really work we all have to be totally strict about confidentiality. One way to emphasize this is to say explicitly that you will not say anything to the teen's parents without first getting permission from him or her and that if ever you felt the parents could benefit from having some information, you would discuss this with the teen first and yield to his or her decision (excluding the usual exceptions to the confidentiality rule). Before parent meetings, I also ask teens if they would like to be present and what they would like me to say if their parents ask about drug use or sex. I tell them I can't lie, but give examples of possible ways I might handle the question, such as, "Samantha and I discussed whether what she does with her friends is something you and I can talk about and she would like to be asked these questions directly and not have me discuss any of this with you." I would then add that I support their daughter's willingness to talk to her parents and know that these conversations are hard to have, but that they should try to have them.

Most of the time, we who work individually with adolescents don't meet too frequently with the parents, just occasionally to let them know that therapy is progressing, to let them air any concerns, and to give them a chance to see what might be going on and who their daughter is spending so much time talking to. I think it's important to meet with the parents when working with teens. Not meeting with the parents can give teens a false impression that they are on their own when they're not and many times don't have to be; parents can be valuable resources at one time or another in a teen's life. Even when there is a lot of hostility between parents and teen, a therapist wants to convey the possibility that the parents can be used as a resource.

Discussing confidentiality can potentially have other wonderful repercussions. It's good for both girls and boys to actively think about what they want to share and what they don't. For teen girls particularly, the idea that they have active, not passive, control over this is important. This is really a core adolescent issue for girls in particular and is not unrelated to sexuality in general. It means that a girl is developing an identity that is separate from others and that the choices she makes are her own. Emphasizing that what this ethic of confidentiality gives her is the space to work out her decisions before or after she makes them without fear of disapproval is important. The therapy room becomes then a model for the space in the teen's head, her mind, that reflective room that she can call her own in which the question "What do I want?" can be deliberated.

CONTROL YOUR REACTIONS

Beyond keeping therapy a private and reflective space, a therapist needs to control his or her reactions to sexual material. Teen girls in particular have become accustomed to the culture's strong and constant interest in the sex lives of teen girls. A therapist should be able to give a teen girl the impression that sexual material can be discussed seriously and in a nonstimulating, nonexploitative way. If a girl feels you're getting way too interested in her sexual exploits, it's just not going to be therapeutic. And many have a keen ear for this. They know and feel the culture's interest in their sexual lives. Teen boys may feel there are cultural expectations about their own sexuality that the therapist holds and hopes to hear about. Without showing too much interest, therapists need to simply make the point somewhere, sometime that therapy is a good place to discuss sex. And they need to make clear that they're open to hearing about all kinds of sexuality and sexual experiences since this is a time in the lives of teens when they are developing as sexual people with interests, fantasies, and new experiences.

Sexual material in therapy can be overstimulating to the therapist. What were we told in graduate school? Hopefully, we were all told to do our own work. But how many of us are willing to look at our sexuality and feelings about sex? Family therapists are aware of the way parents in midlife crisis can become overinterested in their teenagers' exploits for vicarious pleasure and how having a sexually active teenager in the house can awaken dormant desires in parents who feel they are losing youth and the sexual energy that supposedly goes along with that. All this is true of the child psychotherapist too. The young therapist just out of graduate school may overidentify with the joys and pleasures of the beginning sexual life of a teen, not picking up on the anxiety and defensive bravado. The midlife therapist may get a charge out of sexual stories with a prurient interest in all the "new" things kids do today. The older therapist, whose training rarely has included anything about sexuality except as it relates to Freudian instincts, may become overstimulated when a teen shares too much.

Knowing oneself as a sexual person is the most important way a therapist can address these feelings. What is unsatisfying in one's own life may stay unsatisfying, but doing work to address it after one becomes aware of the lack of satisfaction, can prevent a therapist from acting out by making unpredictable or self-interested comments to a client.

But it's not only a therapist's sex life that rears its head when working with teenagers and children on sexual material; it's also a therapist's whole attitude towards sexual material. I think of some of my friends who are therapists, and I see a wide variation in their willingness to talk about sexual material, whether it's sex in the news, their own sexual experiences, or what they know of the lives of their children. To some people, sex is simply far too private a matter; and I wonder if they convey this attitude to their clients. My hunch is that these same therapists might never ask the question, "And did that excite you?" or "Did you feel any sexual pleasure?" but instead guess at the answers to these questions. This strategy may work, but it also implicitly suggests to a client what a therapist may not be able or willing to talk about.

This brings up the issue of self-presentation. Therapists need to choose how much they will share with their clients. As discussed at the end of Chapter 8, it may be a big decision for a therapist to tell a teen that the therapist is gay if the teen asks, or it may be something the therapist says to a teen in the first session when introducing herself or himself. It will be important for the therapist to discuss with a teen what that means to the teen and to provide some reassurance that the therapist has training and experience with teens who are straight, gay, confused, or just wondering.

Adolescents are all too willing and able to project their own difficult feelings onto a therapist. If a teen feels ambivalently about her own sexual experience, it's hard to contain and hold onto all feelings at the same time—she wanted it, she enjoys it, she hates herself for it, she's dirty. It's then easier to defend against the ambivalence by accepting only the positive and projecting the negative judgments onto someone else, often a parent, leading the teen to believe that the parent is making her feel dirty and bad about that experience. Therapists can be used in that way by teens and need to be aware when such projections come their way.

Therapists also need to be aware of what vibes they may give off in terms of their interest or disapproval about teenagers and sex or that aspects of their person might suggest to an adolescent certain ways of being, judging, and feeling. The gray-haired woman? "Surely," a teen will think, "I can't talk about sex with her. She'll be shocked by tales of oral sex." The youngish female therapist who wears short skirts to sessions? Surely she'll be cool and understand. The middle-aged maternal therapist who has teens of her own? Surely she'd disapprove, and surely her own kids don't do things like that! The young, handsome male therapist? Boy, will he ever be interested in these stories! My point is that there are some cultural stereotypes that will make it easier for a teenager to project onto you ideas about sexuality and your reaction to the teen according to his or her own fears and concerns. Giving the impression that you're open to anything, even that you've heard it all and will not be shocked, may help to project back an image of acceptance. Looks of concern may need to be explicitly interpreted for the teen as your look of concern rather than being left open to interpretation as a look of disapproval. One teen said to a friend of mine after revealing some sexual activity she had kept secret for months, "I didn't tell you that because I thought you'd disapprove." The therapist replied, "I wonder if you yourself disapproved in some way and didn't want to deal with that yet." I might alternately have said, depending on the particular girl, "I wonder why my concern for you is felt as disapproval—a judgment, rather than as concern for your well-being."

GET PERMISSION FROM PARENTS

With younger children, it is really difficult to anticipate that one will need permission from parents to talk about sex, because often questions come up spontaneously in a session. A therapist may not know if she or he has permission to discuss facts with a child. "What is fuck?" asks one child. Without his parents' permission, perhaps a therapist shouldn't be explaining what is meant by it. It seems safer to say, "What do you think it means?" or "Where have you heard that word?" or even, more coyly, "That's an interesting word you've found." Sending a child back to his or her parents to ask the same question can feel like an important therapeutic moment has been lost from the session. Yet a therapist can acknowledge that the child feels he or she can ask the therapist important questions about life and people.

Therapist: You want to know what *fuck* means. [*Here the therapist suggests to the child that it is ok to use this "bad" word in the session by repeating it.*]
Child: Jermaine told me that it meant two people doing sex.
T: What did you think about that answer?
C: I think it's right. That's something that grown-ups and teenagers like my brother do. [*Here the child seems to be asking for reassurance that he doesn't have to*

worry about such matters because he is a child, and yet he also shows some interest in his brother's sex life, which may be confusing or stimulating to him. A therapist might pursue both.]

T: Yes, it is something that concerns grown-ups and teenagers, but little kids are sometimes interested in what it is and what it means, especially when they have older brothers at home. [*And so on.*]

This is a conversation that could take place in any therapy room without consultation with parents. But often a therapist will be able to discuss in a session with parents their own provision of sex education in the home. At a parent meeting, a therapist can ask if they've talked to their child about sex and what they've told the child, what they think their child has seen, and how would they like the therapist to handle such questions when they come up in therapy. This can open the way to an honest discussion about how much a child needs to know, and how much this particular child needs to know.

In some ways, talk about sex in child therapy is similar to questions about Santa Claus. If a child were to ask a therapist, "Is Santa real?" no therapist would come right out and say, "No, dear. It's just your daddy and mommy putting out the presents on Christmas morning." Instead, the therapist would ask, "What do you think?" And if the child were to push and push for an answer, a therapist would reflect on how important it was for the child to know and maybe even how frustrating it was that his parents and therapist would not answer. A discussion could then ensue regarding why this was such an important question right now and whether or not the child had a sense about this that he was maybe afraid to voice.

Same with sex. When a child asked me if I had sex with my husband, I didn't think it was important to answer the child truthfully. It was fairly obvious that he thought it was true or he wouldn't be asking. Instead, I asked why it was important to him to know that. He replied that he was pretty certain that his parents had sex, but they wouldn't admit it to him. They just said, "What do you think?"

Therapist: And what if it were true that your parents have sex?
Boy: Eeeewwwwww!
Th: That would be pretty disturbing to you. And pretty interesting too, I might guess. [*I thought it was important to acknowledge the interest as well as the yuckiness.*]

With teenagers it's slightly different. Presumably a therapist has told parents that what happens in the room needs to be kept confidential and that the therapist is available for updates or help in a crisis but will keep the therapy pretty much exclusively between teen and therapist. I usually explain that this helps them in their transition to adulthood, that even though parents want to know everything that's going on in their kids' lives, it's more important that kids have somewhere to bring things they are struggling with before they feel comfortable discussing them with their parents. I reassure parents that if their child is in danger I will tell them and that I often encourage teens to share parts of their lives with their parents when I think parents would want to know and could be helpful to the teen. Then I mention that sex and drugs are two areas that teens need utter confidentiality about in order to be able to talk to a therapist about them, and that parents should know that not only will I talk to teens about their feelings and motives in these two areas, I will give them the message that they should be protecting themselves. I tell parents that sometimes a teen might say something like, "My therapist said . . ." and it may sound as if I'm neutral or supportive of activities a parent disapproves of. I tell them that often that's not the case, but if parents feel uncomfortable, they should talk to me. My goal isn't to prohibit, discipline, or monitor (as parents do), but to help teens process what they're doing so they can lead healthier lives and make good choices.

THERAPY ISN'T SEX EDUCATION: BUT SOMETIMES IT'S NECESSARY

Should therapists provide sex education for clients? Most do, and for several good reasons, but it's important to realize that there are changes and perhaps even costs to the therapeutic relationship when therapists move to an educator's role. Some therapists I know jump at the chance to provide real information to teenagers who have collected more myths and distortions than the *National Enquirer*. I think that sometimes therapists jump in simply because it's tiring to reflect, sit back, process, and explore, and it feels good to be direct and provide "really useful" information that is difficult for a teen to get elsewhere. I also think that therapists of teens from difficult families have a desire to assume the good parent role, so much so that they might leap to do so around sexual issues before thinking through whether education from the therapist is therapeutic.

In general, I think it's a good idea for therapists to provide this information to their teenage clients. However, therapists can become sex educators too soon and leave too little space for discussion of the feelings involved and the concerns that the adolescent is trying to express that may underlie the sexual question. Often a return to the educational resources at the end of the session works well, a sort of "aside" that makes the information important but not central to the work you are doing: "By the way, I wanted to let you know that I discovered that people *can* get STDs from oral sex. I was surprised by that myself. Would you like to know about the Web site I found helpful for this kind of information?"

Some therapists give out books. I'm a little more selfish than that. I've found that teenagers rarely return anything I loan to them. But sometimes an adolescent has so little correct information that a whole book is necessary. None of the therapists I've spoken with ask permission from parents to provide this kind of information to a teenage girl or boy. And most leave it up to the teen whether or not to share the book with the parent who picks up the teen from therapy. But in cases where the parents are against sex education, for example, if the girl or boy comes from a fundamentalist religious background, or in cases where the parents have no idea that their teen may be sexually active, it may be good to give teens some time to read parts of the book in your office or to ask you questions, the answers to which may be in the book. One can't make up for a whole missed curriculum through a single session, but giving a girl the feeling that there is important and accurate information out there and ways to get it, that there are places she can go and library books to peruse, and that it might feel empowering to go after that education, is important.

Also, therapists ought not to jump too quickly to assume a girl's lack of sex education is a reflection of the culture. Girls in particular have been socialized in our culture to be passive about their sexuality and their sex education. It may be important to explore why she hasn't been interested in obtaining this information for herself and why she hasn't asked before now. Not to blame the girl—these kinds of questions can lead to a discussion of feelings of guilt or shame about sexuality, feelings that girls often have that they're not supposed to be interested in sex, and that they should wait for a boy or man to teach them.

Those teens who seem to have a lot of information may have gotten that information from TV and the movies but may be embarrassed to say so. Therapists of teens ought to be watching a lot of TV and going to teen movies. Shows like *Friends* and *Sex*

37

and the City give a lot of information, for example, that cool girls get Brazilian waxes and talk sex nonstop with their friends. This kind of teenage life is reflected in the magazines they read like *CosmoGIRL!* and *Cosmo* itself as well as serial books like *Gossip Girls*. Research shows that teenagers who read and watch this stuff get a higher sense of self-efficacy about sex; that is, they feel and think they can do it, do it better, and do it with more competence. Perhaps they can, but they've learned a particular Hollywood way of doing it, a way that seems sophisticated but that separates sex from the heart and soul of adolescent development and interpersonal relationships. Can a therapist address the distortions in this form of media? Yes, by talking about media representations of sex versus how a girl might feel inside, by moving the discussion from how she might look and what image she might be projecting as a sexual person to what her own feelings, concerns, and sexual goals are.

As noted earlier, boys too are in desperate need of sex education and also may feel too vulnerable to show their peers that they don't know what a word means or an act is. We also know that the majority of teen boys have visited a porn Web site. So, with teen boys, sex education in therapy might be necessary to correct distortions. Therapists can help a boy himself be the judge of whether what he sees or hears is accurate, and doing so may help him to distrust other messages he's getting and seek out accurate information.

Kids and teens who have been sexually abused are in desperate need of accurate and real sex education, and therapists who work with them might make special efforts to understand what they have learned about sex from being exploited. Those who work with sexually abused kids and teens who experienced sexual pleasure or orgasm in their abuse often tell children that their bodies respond naturally to stimulation and that this response isn't an indication that they were complicit in the act. It's true that some children who have been sexually abused have more sexualized feelings and reactions to their environment. Rather than dismissing these feelings as products of the abuse, though, a therapist might talk about how pleasure is good but coercion is bad, and that it's a child's responsibility, after being abused, to make sure that he or she learn to seek pleasure in appropriate ways so that he or she can grow up to have healthy relationships with others.

GIVE PERMISSION TO EXPRESS
AND EXPERIENCE PLEASURE

Therapists need to give permission to express and experience pleasure to all children and teens, not just those whose ideas about sex have been corrupted by abusers. All too often, parents and sex education programs focus on the dangers of sex for teens and rarely on sexual feelings. When sexual feelings are discussed, they're treated as a biological phenomenon, not tied to relationships, exciting events, or fantasies.

There is one simple way to introduce this concept in therapy, and that is to name it: "Did that feel pleasurable?", "Did you enjoy doing that?", "I'm wondering if that felt good and how you handled that?", "Were those powerful pleasurable feelings?" And when one suspects that pleasure wasn't involved, as in so many teen girls' experiences, a therapist might ask, "And was there sexual pleasure in that for you too? Or were you going along because you felt close to him?" In some cases, a therapist ought to label this as a problem: "I'm wondering why sexual pleasure is not so much of interest to you in your sexual relationship with Joe."

Again, when working with kids who have been exploited, a therapist might want to hold out the idea that there will someday be a kind of pleasure in sex for them. When Tina first started seeing boys, having previously been abused by her stepfather over a six year period, I asked her, "And so do you and these guys, after the dance, kiss and do stuff?" She said yes, sometimes.

Therapist: And does it feel nice? And feel good to be doing that?
Tina: Yes.
Th: (probing) Does it remind you in any way of your stepfather and does that inter-fere at all with the pleasure of beginning your teen years?
T: Oh God, *no*! He was so old and these boys are my age!
Th: Just checking. Because I would want for you to have the joys of first kisses and the rest, without having to think about Bob.

In Chapter 3, I write in more depth about how important it is to not relabel all sexual feelings in abused children as reactions to the abuse, all attempts to have normal sexual play as acting out. Sometimes these children become oversexualized, but the response should not be to tell them to shut out all sexual feelings and urges. Instead, therapists need to help them to understand their feelings and find appropriate means of expression.

SEX DOES NOT EQUAL DANGER

Teen tales of sexual exploits may often contain a hidden mes-sage—that sex is danger and that a teen is playing with fire. Sex can be dangerous, no doubt. And most sex education programs will give incredibly detailed information about STDs and the dan-gers of early sex. In the best of the sex education programs you will see, as Kirby (1997) wrote, curricula that address AIDS pre-vention, information about the risks of unprotected intercourse, exercises that address social pressures on sexual behavior, and practice for communication, negotiation, and refusal. Still, you won't find much about pleasure. You won't find much about finding one's sexual self or understanding one's own sexual iden-tity. And you'll rarely find something about the gender roles and the way gender plays a part in negotiations around sex, sexual feelings, and societal attitudes about sex.

Therapists should keep in mind that there is more to sex than danger, and that teens are aware of this and have few people with whom they can talk about it. As I traveled around giving book talks on *The Secret Lives of Girls*, I was struck with how many young women wished they could talk about sex with their mothers. While I don't know if young men wish the same, I presume that they also would like to get an adult man's serious perspective of what sex means to him. How do sexual feelings develop, what's normal about the various kinds of ways we can get sexual pleasure, and how does one understand one's body and oneself as a sexual person? These are questions research cannot provide great answers for, but they are integral to becoming a psychologically healthy teen.

If a teen is in therapy, he or she has some problems, symptoms, or issues, whether they stem from a fragile biological makeup, cognitive distortions that have developed and taken hold over time, poor object relations, or life circumstances that are overwhelming. If our job is to help teens feel whole, to develop a strong sense of self, to check themselves when they have impulses do things they know are harmful to themselves or others, and to be able to put themselves forward into the world of work and relationships in a positive way, then we can't ignore their developing sexuality.

With sex education the way it is, and parents fearful that talk equals action or when they are absent in emotional or other very real ways to their teens, therapists may be the ones who need to address these questions while also keeping in mind the risks. To identify too closely with the perspective that says a teen is too young, too immature, too poorly informed, and too at risk will be to turn off a teen from talking about sex in therapy. As in most things in life, knowledge is power, and when we encourage teens to seek knowledge about themselves and about sex in general, we give them more power to make healthy decisions about their sexual lives.

WHEN NECESSARY, SEEK SUPERVISION OR REFER OUT

In writing this book, my hope is that therapists will understand what is typical for children and teens at different ages and that, knowing this, they will not be afraid to follow through with discussion or play that addresses these topics. For some therapists, talking about sex or addressing sexual issues in play will still be uncomfortable, and I hope that these therapists will seek supervision or start their own peer supervision groups to process such material. I also hope that many therapists who work with education or judicial systems will start to see sexual acting out a little differently and, rather than referring out to specialized sex offense groups, will begin to work with these children individually. Therapists who feel comfortable treating victims of sexual abuse will learn that the sex talk and acts of these children can't always be categorized as overstimulation and sometimes are simply the talk and acts of children who desperately need to learn about sex and how to deal with their sexual feelings from caring adults. If therapists can approach teen sexuality from a perspective that allows teens the right to explore, to learn about themselves and their bodies, and to experience pleasure, then therapists can better help teens to protect themselves, make reasonable choices, and enjoy their future sexual relationships. But for all of us who have been given too much information from the media and too little real discussion, we need to seek out support and discussion to arrive at a place that makes us more confident that we are good resources for teens to turn to.

While I urge therapists to seek knowledge, self-knowledge, and supervision on these topics as they do this work, I recognize that some may need to refer out. When kids scare us, we can't work with them, and when supervision does not quell our fears, we need to refer out. When we have strong religious or moral judgments that may be in conflict with providing healthy support and advice to kids, we need to check this out in supervision first, and then refer out. There's no shame in recognizing our limitations in working with children and adolescents. And if we always put the client's needs first, then at times we may have to recognize that the client needs another therapist.

CHAPTER TWO

Sexual Issues in Play
With Nonabused Children

One of the most important goals of this book is to give therapists guidelines with regard to how to handle, talk about, and pursue issues of a sexual nature with *nonabused* children and teens in therapy. Sex is a part of life. It's part of children's lives to a certain extent, too. Children are learning about their own sexual feelings as well as how sex is represented in the world around them, so it doesn't make sense for therapists to train themselves only or primarily in the work of sexual victimization or sexual offense.

SEXUAL ABUSE EVERYWHERE

Admittedly, I used to be one of those therapists who knew far too much about the responses of sexually abused children and far too little about normative sexuality. That's partly because child therapists working in clinics and hospital settings see a lot of children who've been sexually abused. At Massachusetts General Hospital, in the 1980s, where I began seeing children, it seemed as if every new case I was given was a child who had been sexually abused. I thought that there was an epidemic. So did others, and because of that we may have been overly vigilant at the time, suspecting abuse where there was none.

When I moved on to a private practice while still training graduate students, by and large, my practice included children with a range of other difficulties. One 7-year-old had anger problems. Another 6-year-old said he wanted to kill himself. A few were coping with their parents' divorce and having frequent meltdowns from the stress. Some had difficulties making friends in grade school. Others were simply too much to handle. One 5-year-old girl was still seriously mourning a dog who had died a year before; a 4-year-old was sleeping on the floor with her ear to the door to hear her parents leave for work before she woke (the nanny brought her to therapy). Others presented with anxieties and phobias, such as fear of dogs preventing a preteen girl from going to the summer camp she loved, or fear of bus rides after a school bus accident.

Even with the variety of problems and issues these children brought to the therapy session, occasionally some sexual topic, innuendo, or act emerged. In my early years as a therapist, when this occurred, my first assumption was that these children had been sexually abused, that sex talk or sexual play equaled overstimulation, and that overstimulation came from abuse.

I wasn't influenced to think this way only because of the kinds of cases I had seen at Massachusetts General. I was also a product of the times. I learned how to practice therapy in an era of increasing attention to sexual abuse, an era when we truly believed that children never lied about something so serious. (How could they get that kind of explicit information, we asked?) It was an era in which therapists blamed themselves and their profession for not noticing signs of abuse and not validating the claims of children who had been abused. I also trained at a time when parents were bombarded with messages about the sexual abuse of children, from the *Oprah* show to made-for-TV movies to the good touch/bad touch programs in the schools. Because of this increased awareness, parents were bringing in their children for evaluation in record numbers.

That made it difficult to work with sexual talk or play in a therapy session as indicative of anything other than abuse, for, as soon as it arose, our antennae went up. Had this child been sexually abused? I even kept a family of anatomically correct dolls close at hand for this reason. Occasionally, an inquisitive child would find them (they weren't in a locked cabinet), do a little exploration, and drop them. To my mind, that was a sign of a healthy, nonabused child's lack of interest in the dolls. Now I think differently. If a child were to be interested in anatomically correct dolls, I would not assume that this was a sign of abuse. I would begin by simply noting that this child has questions, interest, and possibly concerns about private parts or, to put it even more mildly, dolls with private parts.

WHAT'S APPROPRIATE WHEN?

Most of us who have researched child sexuality believe that in the elementary school years, sexual interest takes a backseat to interest in academics, skills, sports, activities, and other developmental growth opportunities. Likewise, most of us believe that sexual interests return or emerge in the preteen child in the middle school years, and that because of cultural changes, hormones, or whatnot (some of us are more interested in biology driving this change; others, like myself, are more interested in the culture), these feelings come on strong and in a confusing way.

In general, sexual interests do take a backseat during these years. But we exaggerate the difference. The last decade's biologizing of everything psychological with the concomitant rise of the pharmaceutical industry makes us overemphasize the relationship between hormones and sexual interest and de-emphasize the relationship between culture and experience. The culture lays out a developmental framework of when it's appropriate for kids to have certain interests, and kids get plenty of messages teaching them this cultural agenda. From Saturday morning cartoons to commercials for fruit twisters, kids are shown that in the middle school years, other-sex attraction is more important than or different from their same-sex friendships. It's no wonder that a quarter of 10–12-year-old-girls believe the appropriate time for a romantic relationship is 12–13 (Girls Scouts of America, 2000). Another study shows 20% of urban girls have had a boyfriend by 6th grade and 47% of urban 6th grade boys have had a girlfriend (O'Donnell, Stueve, & Wilson-Simmons, 2006). It's also no wonder that middle school girls are set up against other girls in competition for boys and then blamed as "mean girls."

There certainly are developmental differences in children's capacity to think about sexual experience and feel sexual. But these differences interact with a culture that, at times, can be too much for a child. I do not believe, as some therapists do, that anytime a child talks about sex or plays out a sexual theme in therapy this is an indication that he or she has been overstimulated. But when we are exploring the sexual issues that emerge, that's a good place to begin. In Chapter 3, I outline what I consider to be signs of overstimulation versus signs of abuse.

ADDRESSING OVERSTIMULATION, IN THE FLESH

There are two ways children who have not been sexually abused may themselves be preoccupied with sex or engaged in active processing of sexual feelings and interests. One comes from overstimulation from the culture. The other comes from an internal or intrapsychic overstimulation that was perhaps initiated by something in their surroundings. Of course, the internal and the external are in constant interaction, as the following two examples show. And therapists would do well to acknowledge the outside culture as well as the internal motivations for sex talk and sex play, while staying at a remove. To join in the play would be to drop one's reflective stance, to possibly cross some boundaries and, in the end, make a child feel unsafe.

Amy bounced into the therapy session exuding preteen excitement bubbling over. You may recall her as the girl with the boom box described in the introduction. She came into the session having planned to perform a dance for me, rolled up her shirt, and struck a sexy pose. What would have created this urge in Amy? Did she want my attention? Was she trying to seduce me in some way? Did she want my motherly approval of her sexual being? These were the internal sources I considered. Or had she seen these dancers on TV, felt she needed to learn that sexy way of dancing, and thought therapy was a good place to show her progress in the imitation of the dance? As such, the source would be from the outside world, and her bringing the action into therapy an event in service of her need for confirmation and approval.

When she rolled up her shirt to show her midriff and pulled down her sleeves so that her shoulders showed, I didn't stop her. Had I been a male therapist, perhaps I should have stopped her, but how? I picture the best male therapists I know and think they probably would say in gentle voices, "Wait a minute before you start, Amy." But then what? "That's inappropriate in here. . . ." That would sound like a real put-down, a scolding. We ought to be mindful of the fact that the word *inappropriate* is overused in the schools as a scold to redirect a whole host of behaviors. Might he say, "Amy, it seems as if you want to look sexy for me?" I don't think so; that would sound like an invitation. He could set a limit, a gentle limit: "We don't undress, even a little bit, in the therapy room," calling it undressing rather than dressing sexy. I would add to that gentle limit by saying, "We can make believe that you're dressed in some fancy dance costume instead of acting it out. How do you imagine yourself looking as a dancer?" and, in that way, inviting her not to act out her fantasy so directly but to talk about it. This fits with my approach of helping a child distance herself from her desires in therapy so that she might be able to reflect on them.

I was less uncomfortable than a man might have been in that situation and simply let it go. So Amy turned on the boom box and began her dance. First she leaned far forward, and let her hair fall over her face and touch the ground. She then flipped it back and brushed it away from her face. She turned around at one point, stuck her butt out, and jiggled it. She also smoothed her hands up and down the sides of her body. At one point in the dance she put both hands on her crotch. At another point she placed both hands across her chest, shook her head "no" with a pouty look, then turned around on her heels, looked over her shoulder, and beckoned with a finger that the audience follow her swinging butt. My conclusion? This girl had definitely been watching MTV.

I let her finish her dance. I smiled gently as I watched, laughing a little at her over-the-top sexy acts, but not in a way that I thought might be humiliating to her. She didn't seem to be dancing for me per se but for some imaginary male audience. I was simply there to admire and permit without disapproval. I could do that easily, but didn't I also need to address the downside of being a sexual object? Sure there's lots of attention for a girl who gets up and dances sexy on the bar, but there are repercussions.

"You looked a lot like the girls I've seen dancing on music videos," I said. "Yeah. I can show you what Ciara does in the song 'Oh,'" Amy replied, at which point she dropped to her knees, spread her legs, and started moving her body up and down as if sitting on someone and having sex that way.

Therapist: Where is she when she's doing that?
Amy: On the roof of a car.
Th: Is the car moving?
A: No, I don't think so.
Th: Hmmmmm.

Amy was sweating and flushed and wanted to turn on the boom box again and do another dance for me. I wanted to process more.

Th: Let's talk a little bit more before you do another dance. [*introducing a pause for reflection*] You do all the sexy moves that the grown-up women on the videos do, don't you? (nonchalantly)
A: Yes! I watch them every day after school.
Th: And it's fun for you to dance sexy.
A: Yes. (emphatically)

I thought about Amy and her issues, knowing that at school she felt like a dirty rejected kid, longing to be pretty, even if it were pretty in an MTV sexy-girl way. She was learning about sex as a way to get attention.

Th: I wonder if you've noticed or think that girls who dance sexy get a lot of attention from boys.
A: (nonchalantly) Yeah, boys like to watch girls' butts and boobs.
Th: It feels good to be noticed, even if it's just for shaking your butt, and not for your beautiful eyes or the smart things you say. [*Here I injected a bit of my feminism, hoping to introduce to Amy that there were other things to admire about her.*]

While I could go on and talk about the downside of being admired for one's sexiness, that would have been a hard sell. Still, it's important to go there at some point. Amy needed to know that she was picking up on something most girls learn about early, that sexiness is an easy way to get the attention they might long for. It was thus important for me to give her attention for what she was doing, to acknowledge her potential to be sexy, woman to girl, but also to point out what other talents she might have. She was good at imitating some of those dance steps. And look at how she knew all the lyrics.

But the funny thing was, after I briefly admired Amy for her many talents, she seemed to be quite ready to move on, as if admiration wasn't what she really wanted, but closeness. Admiration is a brief and quick fix, a self-esteem booster, but Amy, a rejected child in so many ways, wanted a deeper kind of acceptance, the closeness a child feels when she's accepted and connected, if only for 50 minutes, to someone. We settled down, side by side, next to the dollhouse, and Amy relaxed into a safe and exploratory dollhouse play.

SOMETIMES IT'S DIFFICULT TO MOVE
TO THAT REFLECTIVE SPACE

When a child brings a therapist's attention to her own body, it feels safer to help her displace it onto dolls or drawings or talk, where there's more distance and the therapist's reactions are less personal. This strategy is part of all the play therapy I do. But a therapist still needs to be aware of just how much distance a child needs in order to process the material. One would think that drawing might provide that distance, and exploratory play seems to be productive for children. But for some children even drawings can stimulate.

A colleague, Gordon, was seeing a boy in therapy, Jake, who said to him, "Let's draw a picture of a butt." Gordon, a laid-back kind of therapist, was comfortable waiting to see what would happen next. His client then drew a picture of a butt and put lots of marks on it. "What are those?" Gordon asked. His client replied, "Pimples." Jake then scribbled all over the picture of the butt and afterward tore it up. This kind of reaction to his own drawing indicates it was stressful for him to draw it. He couldn't sit with what he had drawn and talk about it, or even reflect quietly. Wanting to draw a picture of a butt could indicate some worries about private parts or about defecation. Add the pimples and this kind of drawing could indicate shame or even disgust with his body. Often anxious children put little dots all over the dresses when drawing a person or lots of little things flying around in the sky in their drawings of houses, inserting what looks like a lot of nervous energy. Butts were obviously making this boy nervous. I would address this affect directly: "You tore up that picture of a butt. Did something about it make you angry or nervous?" "It was disgusting," Jake might say. I would respond to this by helping Jake distance from that feeling of disgust, to reflect on it: "Butts are private parts and so some people think it's disgusting to think about or be interested in them." Jake might go on to say, "And they can be covered with poop!" The therapist has an obligation to respond but also to tamp down the excitement about butts by speaking in a matter-of-fact tone—"Yup, they can be clean or covered with poop or even pimples. Lots of different kinds of butts I guess. But, you know, it's really babies' butts that get covered with poop. Most everyone wipes their butts clean after pooping when they're older." Talking like that can overstimulate a kid, but it can also normalize it, make it less exotic. The therapist here responds, "Yes. It's a butt. No big deal. Yes, we can talk about poop, but like grown-up kids and not little babies." He conveys something relaxing and nonthreatening about it. In so doing, we haven't really gotten to why the butt is so exciting to him. But this kind of measured response can lead the way to more focused talk on sex and the body or more general talk about feelings about the self.

A calm, measured response can open the way for a more distanced discussion later about anxieties, or it can simply reassure in the moment. For example, another little boy playing in therapy lifted the skirt of a dollhouse doll and tried to peer underneath. His therapist, a young man in his 30s, asked, "What do you see?"

Boy: Nothing.
Therapist: What do you *want* to see?
B: Nothing.

Th: So, everything's okay! [*The therapist sensed curiosity, possible anxiety, and responded to it.*]

B: Yes.

SEXUAL PLAY OR TALK FROM CHILDREN
WITH MILD DEVELOPMENTAL DELAYS

Some of the times that sexual talk or play most commonly shock us in therapy is when we are working with children with mild nonverbal developmental delays or compulsions. These are usually children or teens who don't have a diagnosis but may be more literal thinking or impulsive than other kids. We see them in therapy through parent or school referrals, but many of them don't get help or services from any agencies. Whatever disability they have is too mild. But if they do get services, it's usually in school around their reading or math skills. The kind of kid I'm describing is socially awkward and so does not have the same restraint that most children have. His thoughts, shared in a session, can be rather shocking. Take, for example, Jeremy, an 11-year-old boy who tended to perseverate. In one session I allowed him to use up my roll of tape taping things together, and after that he would bring tape to the sessions and politely ask me which piece of furniture in the office it would be okay for him to tape up that day, not to enhance the beauty of the furniture but to aid in holding all the pieces together! He checked out all the furniture and would get particularly excited if some table leg seemed loose and in need of taping to the table top. I understood this act to be symbolic to an extent, as his parents' divorce had affected him deeply, but also perhaps a random choice that fit with his tendency to get stuck on and compulsive about certain interests. During session, while taping the small table in the room, he openly said to me that he couldn't stop himself from thinking about a scene in his head in which he held a gun to his teacher, made her undress, and then tied her up naked. It was interesting, of course, that he didn't tape her up, as expected, but I was quite shocked when this boy, not yet even a preteen, shared this fantasy with me. Was it a fantasy? Or was it a "brain hiccup," as some psychiatrists who treat obsessive-compulsive disorder like to call an obsessive thought? He seemed quite worried about this thought and earnest in his request that I help him to stop thinking about that. I wondered whether his cognitive issues (literal thinking, to be more exact) prevented him from seeing this as a fantasy and what worried him was whether he might sometime do such a thing. As a feminist, didn't I have a responsibility to steer young people away from these kinds of fantasies, or at least to help them see them as degrading to women? But I stayed with him and his feelings. I reflected back to him: "This image is really upsetting you." "Yeah," he replied. "It keeps coming back into my head and I can't get rid of it." With a kid like Jeremy, it wouldn't be good to engage him in play to work out some of these issues. Rather, play was difficult for him and instantly became obsessive.

And he was complaining of an obsession. In the past, through play, I have helped children who were obsessing about a trauma. Mariah, a little girl who seemed to be compelled to act out "The Three Little Pigs" with me, always played the wolf, whereas I was assigned the part of the three little pigs, trembling and helpless in my house when the wolf came to the door. She was reenacting a sexual abuse experience. Dustin, a little boy who had been terrified when held down by doctors and nurses to be given a spinal tap, seemed to need to play over and over with me a scene in which I was to be an innocent little boy, walking down the road, licking a lollipop, when confronted by an "army guy" (played by Dustin) who stuck a gun in my back. Working through these traumas in play helped these two children find moments of power and ways to change the scenario, eventually even to let the compulsion go.

But this seemed quite different. I explored with Jeremy if he knew what it was like to be tied up. I didn't think he had been abused, but I wanted to check for abusive experiences. It seemed to me also that he might have quite easily and regularly seen any number of women held at gunpoint and forced to get undressed on TV. So I then asked, "Is that something you've seen in a book or on TV?" He said no but then talked about a show that had some very similar scene. He was a very literal person and so did not at once see the similarity between his scene and the TV scene. I gently explained, "Sometimes, when we get angry at a person, other scenes of angry people come into our head and get mixed into our thoughts and feelings." I also pointed out that sometimes teachers can make a kid feel dumb and a kid might want to make a teacher feel dumb and embarrassed too (*humiliated* was not a word I thought he would understand).

Did we play out this scene with the dolls? Within the therapy session? No way. He needed help getting that image out of his head and replacing it with another. Literal as he was, play therapy was unlikely to provide much relief to him. I gave him two ideas to work with. One came from an old form of cognitive-behavioral therapy that has been shown to work for some, although in general it has limited effectiveness. That's Meichenbaum's therapy involving, first, simply shouting "Stop" to oneself (silently) when a problematic thought or self-statement comes into one's head (Meichenbaum & Deffenbacher, 1988). I also gave Jeremy ideas for a kind of image to replace that troublesome one. "What would you think," I asked him, "if you changed the channel of the TV in your mind to something that's more appropriate to say to a teacher if you feel mad?" Together we created a picture of a kid sitting across the desk from a teacher saying, "You made me mad today." I then asked him to say the sentence with me, and then to picture it in his head: "How do you picture your teacher responding? What do you think happens next? Let's fill in the scene. Where is she sitting? What's on her desk? How does the conversation go? What's the look on her face? Are you so angry you slam your fist down on the desk?" By adding some emotion to this new image, I was hoping to have it catch on as a replacement to the old one. Together we created an image, granted one that may not have been so compelling, but one he found he could successfully switch to.

The next week, he reported that he didn't have that problem with that image anymore. I didn't press him and ask if my technique had worked, although I was curious. That would have been for my benefit, and he was off taping my couch!

EXTERNAL STIMULATION:
OUR SEXUAL WORLD AND WELCOME TO IT

Like Jeremy, most kids see and experience any number of sexual images that are difficult to process. But some children come with fewer defenses, less of an ability to shut out stimulation, with fewer boundaries between them and the outside world. Given that there are kids like that, consider what they're seeing.

Watch Saturday morning cartoons or children's movies from a grown-up perspective and you'll see cartoon animals doing mini stripteases, batting their eyelashes, and wiggling their butts. You'll see male animals' eyes popping out at cartoon females with big busts. You'll see voyeurs looking at sexy cartoon shadows against a closed backlit shade. You'll see out-and-out sexual harassment if you watch that French skunk, Pepé Le Pew. You'll see females getting chased around desks, and girls chasing boys to kiss them on the playground at recess. A lot of these cartoons are written by young guys in California, inserting their own brand of humor, however sexist and inappropriate, into these cartoons in order to create adult asides and amusing double entendres for themselves, their friends, and the parents who may watch alongside their kids.

But you don't have to look at the innuendoes in cartoons for sexual stimulation of young kids, because many kids watch all sorts of things on TV and at the movies. It seems that parents use PG-13 as the cutoff for movies their kids of all ages can see. This is problematic because PG-13 means everything is basically okay except the word *fuck* and explicit footage of sex. People having sex in bed is fine. As long as you don't see the naked bodies, what's a little humping? And there are plenty of references to having sex, references to girl-on-girl kissing, to cute butts, to oral sex, as long as the language is clever enough for most kids to miss it and nothing explicit is shown. I hear about these movies in therapy sessions and I see young kids at the theater when I go to watch PG-13 movies. Even supposedly sweet movies impress kids with a teenage life that's ahead by including sexy partying scenes with hot tubbing. For example, in *Ella Enchanted,* when Ella enters the land of the giants she encounters swimsuit model, Heidi Klum in her halter top and miniskirt, among other sexy giants, drinking martini-like drinks and partying all night. The little girl in the audience doesn't know it's Heidi Klum the swimsuit model, but the director sure does, and shots of her sexy dancing light up the 20-foot screen. Kids also hear quite a few sex scenes when they're not shown on the screen. Quite a few young kids can understand and actually make the sounds of a woman wild with ecstasy before they even know what sex is.

Many kids bring these images and sounds into therapy. They act them out in the dollhouse. They play dress-up and dance sexy. They show you that these images stick in their minds. And these images develop into other images. A therapist can and should open up the talk around the play to likely sources, because if this play is repeating something watched or heard, it was most likely troubling to the child. But therapists needn't worry about finding the specific source. Addressing the concern is much more important.

EXTERNAL AND INTERNAL STIMULATION AND THE DEFENSELESS CHILD

Some children have fewer defenses than others when it comes to processing and understanding stimulating material from the world around them. Some may express confusion quite openly and inappropriately; others are very sensitive, alert sponges. With these kids we need to dig a little deeper to discover just what they saw or heard that aroused worries, and with more expressive kids we need to be very clear about what's appropriate or not to spew back into the world. Helping these children desensitize themselves to the world, to be able to play out an issue in the dollhouse without becoming disorganized, upset, or more worried, is like helping them to set up some boundaries in the world at large.

Eddy was 8-years-old, a child from an upper-middle-class family in the suburbs of Philadelphia, and had enjoyed months of play making puppets fart and having me respond in total shock. As a child working hard on self-control, these moments of puppet lack of control, actually a hostile and directed "lack of control," gave him a lot of pleasure. I saw it as a safety valve and saw therapy as a place to act out some of his angry feelings about what he perceived to be overcontrol by the adults in his life, pressuring him to mature before he was ready. It was so difficult for him to behave at school and at home that therapy was a kind of respite room from the world where he was asked to hold everything in. It was great that he could displace this onto puppets rather than truly acting it out as some kids do. Therapists vary in their tolerance of flatulence in a session. While I tend to ask children if I can take them to the bathroom downstairs, other therapists have been known to angrily request kids to control their farting.

One day in play, Eddy discovered the Barbie dolls. They were in a plastic box on the floor along with all the other dolls, including some cheap Kewpie baby dolls with little ruffled outfits and bows in their hair. The Barbies were instantly stimulating to him. I used to have a rule for anyone sharing the toys in the group office in Philadelphia where we trained students. I wanted our students to learn to respect the toys and keep the office the same, session after session, in order to provide a safe and consistent environment for the kids who came back week after week. I taught my students always to leave the Barbies clothed. Sometimes it's shocking for a child to open a big box of dolls and be confronted with a nude Barbie. It should be the child's choice whether or not to take Barbie's clothes off. And generally the therapy room should be a nonstimulating environment, someplace safe and peaceful in which the child can present his or her own worries, not the ones the room evokes. That way you know, when a child sees your painting of a grassy field and wonders if there are poisonous snakes in the grass, that you didn't introduce that fear by putting up scary pictures in the office; it's the child's projection onto the painting.

When Eddy found the Barbies, they were dressed. But he began running his fingers over the breasts of the Barbies, and then his demeanor changed to a certain kind of urgency to undress the Barbies. Anyone who's played with Barbies dressing and undressing them knows this is not an easy task. Once Barbie was disrobed, Eddy sat back and sighed with relief, looking at Barbie naked. I offered a remark that guessed at his curiosity. "You really wanted to see Barbie naked," I said, with no trace of judgment. "Yes," he exclaimed and went through the other Barbie dolls. As he was undressing his second Barbie, he noticed a bald Kewpie doll and brought her out. Calling her a "he," he announced that this was the evil guy who had spied on Barbie and then captured her. He then had the Evil Baby approach Barbie and yell at her, "Lay down!" He made the Barbie doll lie down and then Evil Baby began to feel her breasts. My comment was something like, "Evil Baby wants Barbie's breasts," remembering that Evil Baby was actually a baby. Eddy then had the baby nurse from Barbie, thus confirming that his interest in Barbie, though sexual, also had to do with some longing for that early experience with his mother. No wonder it was a baby doll who fit the bill as Barbie's attacker! Eddy then had Evil Baby begin to lick at Barbie's crotch. This was rather shocking to me. Eddy was quite involved and relishing the play, making licking and slurping noises. And I thought, "I probably should stop this. Other therapists would probably stop this."

Was Eddy getting overstimulated by the play? He was certainly intensely involved, the way kids get when they are deeply into the fantasy they're unraveling. Was the therapist getting overstimulated by the play? Yes. There was a mixture of discomfort and anxiety. It seemed odd to let him go on. A safe question might distance us both from the play.

Therapist: So what's Evil Baby doing?
Eddy: (instantly) Licking her private parts.
Th: What's Barbie doing?
E: She's trying to get away, but she's in his power.

Okay. Now, how to ask the next question—how the hell did an 8-year-old find out anything about oral sex? Did he see it on a porn channel on TV? Did he walk in on his older brother or his parents? Could he possibly have invented this on his own? I asked, "I'm wondering if you ever saw someone do that." It's good to be nonchalant and erase any tone that might suggest such an act is shocking or wrong. And I asked this when he seemed to be through with the play. He replied, "No." I then asked him about whether his 15-year-old brother ever brought his girlfriend to the house. He got rather excited by this question and said that yes, he did, and they closed their bedroom door and that sometimes he tried to sneak around them to catch them kissing, and once he did see them kissing. I asked, "So what did you see?" He described a typical scene of two kids sitting on a couch kissing, adding that his brother caught him and chased him away. When asked if he found that interesting, he denied it and said, "No, yuck." I then asked questions I would ask if I were doing a sexual abuse evaluation, still in a nonchalant voice. Nothing.

Eddie took up the trucks and cars and began to make a road scene on the floor, giving me some time to think about his play. I continued to think about it all week and wondered if he would bring up that play again. He did, three more times, and then he moved on. He moved on to typical latency-age activities in the session. No more doll play; no more dress-ups; no more puppets; no more imagination. Instead we played catch, checkers, basketball (with a spongy ball and a minihoop) and we talked about school-work and friendships. It wasn't until months later that I put it all together.

I called a parent meeting. Without revealing to his mother exactly what he was playing in the session, I asked her about Eddy's interests at home with his older brother, and whether he might have been exposed to some sexual material in movies and TV. She said that they kept a pretty close eye on what he watched on TV and that his brother did bring his girlfriends home occasionally. She added that Eddy had always had a kind of interest in her sexual life, which was pretty nonexistent since the divorce—but that she had to be careful not to get undressed around him at home, because he would get overexcited and very silly.

This play seemed to have been a turning point for Eddy, after which he put aside some of his stimulating feelings toward his mother. I concluded that Eddy was probably overstimulated not by something on TV, or his brother, but by his mother as a sexual being. She was convincing in relating her efforts to protect him from seeing, learning, hearing too much. So I understood Eddy to be enacting a psychoanalytic theme in therapy. Combining elements of babyhood and adult sex, longing for mother and knowing someday he would be a sexual adult with lascivious intent, Eddy invented a play that involved both. An immature kid, Eddy had trouble tamping down the sexual feelings that normally are aroused in childhood through living with and loving one's family. Many kids sail through the latency-age years forgetting about those earlier feelings and ignorant of the feelings to come. Eddy mixed them all together. As he grew out of the babyish years and was unable to securely find a place for himself in the latency era among his peers, he was bombarded with and unprotected from external and internal thoughts about sex and sexuality that were confusing to him. What was it exactly that adults do together? What do breasts and mothers have to do with it? Can little boys have sex? Can babies? Is it evil to think about sex or feel desire? And why must he be deprived of his mother? Why couldn't he just take what he wanted? Morality, self-control, feelings about growing up, feelings about sexuality—these were not conscious thoughts in Eddy's head. But they were part of the confusion that led him into this particular play. He needed to play it out a bit and put it away on his own. Play therapy is wonderful that way because you can see a child process and outgrow certain thoughts, putting aside certain wishes.

BARBIE, OVERSTIMULATION, AND A CHILD'S BODILY EXCITEMENT

Let's entertain the idea that Barbie herself is overstimulating. Why keep Barbie dolls in the office if they can be so stimulating to children? I believe we mustn't be afraid of these things—not Barbies, not guns. Kids confront these stimulating things as part of childhood outside the office, and inside they have the good fortune of someone there to talk with them about the feelings that arise. They also have someone who can help them regulate their bodily feelings when they can't.

Children do get physical excited when engaged in play. Play demands physical investment. A therapist can see this when children dress up or swing from the rafters. There is an emotional intensity in their bodies as they crash the cars together or sing out the fire engine's siren as it races across the room to put out the fire on the desk. Therapy creates a liminal space of real and not real, where a child can wholly invest in the play, really get into it, without fear of consequences or disapproval. The magic of this can only happen when therapy is a safe space.

But when kids get overstimulated, the space doesn't feel safe anymore. It's hard for a therapist to detect this overstimulation but it's so important. It doesn't feel like an overinvestment in the play, because productive play often is very preoccupying. What a therapist will feel is anxiety, coming from a child's awareness that he is not quite in control of his body. There's no flow in the play, but the child seems to jump from topic to topic and is antsy in his seat. He may accidentally brush up against you or say something that sounds a bit disorganized. It's at this time that you might find a way to pull the child back from the play into the world of talk or into a different form of play. A therapist could ask a question or make a suggestion: "Let's stop playing for a while and talk about . . . ." or "Do you think we can stop with the dollhouse now? I'd like you to draw me a picture of some of the things you're playing." Through these requests, the child, by focusing outside of himself, calms his body.

ALL PLAY, NO TALK

There are kids who show no emotion and barely talk in therapy, and for these kids it's very difficult to determine their level of excitement, their worries, and whether they are stressed by what they are playing. These are the ones that my students complain most about—"She won't talk to me." I constantly remind them that therapy can take place without words, that especially with children, play has the power to organize their emotions for them and present their wishes and fears in a way that makes them more easily understood and mastered.

Mike was one kid who never seemed to show much emotion or connection in therapy. He enjoyed building Lego models and was quite good at them, but at 8-years-old, he found talk a little boring. He was seeing me not for any specific reason but because at Massachusetts General we used the child guidance model to help families. This model has the psychologist seeing the child in play therapy and the mother meeting at the same time with a social worker. This mother had come for therapy after her husband had been sent to jail and her older child had gotten in trouble at school. She, the older son, and her younger son, Mike, were automatically assigned therapists. That's how we treated families back then, individually. After all, Mike's father was in jail; they lived in poverty; his mother seemed to the social worker to need a bit of help in basic parenting issues; Mike could naturally use a little one-on-one time. The mother's therapist also let us, the two children's therapists, know that the mother was a little inappropriate with her sons, asking them to scrub her back when she was in the tub, and sharing with them information that might be too stimulating for them at their age. The social worker was working with the mother to share less and create better boundaries in the home.

It wasn't until Mike moved past the Legos and on to the dollhouse that I began to wonder what exactly his father was in jail for. It turned out his father had robbed a house, and so Mike's play about burglars entering the dollhouse and disrupting the whole family sleeping was fairly obvious. When he tied up a female doll in his play, I went to his mother's therapist and asked her to get more details from Mike's mother. As it turned out, Mike's father had tied up and raped a woman during one of his burglaries. He was sent away for a long time. What was this to Mike? He had hardly known his father before, given that his dad didn't live with them and rarely had visited. In his poor Boston neighborhood, he had known his father as a guy who occasionally dropped in to say hi or whom he would run into on the street when playing hockey.

The problem was that his mother told him why his father was arrested and what his father had done. He had this information but he was unable to talk about it. That may have been because Mike was unable to talk about most things. He built with Legos and played with the dollhouse, but he didn't talk. This is where I had to have faith that my putting things into words would help.

As Mike set up the dollhouse, I asked, "Is this a family?" "Uh huh," said this nonverbal child. "And here the mother and her children are all asleep, very peaceful," I added. He went on silently. He made the burglars go around the house looking in windows. I narrated, "Here are the burglars looking for a way to get in." I was careful to try to represent what he was doing as simply as possible. I wanted him to begin to internalize an observing ego voice, as the psychoanalysts of the ego psychology school called it. An observing ego is a distancing voice, not harsh and evaluative like a scolding conscience or superego, nor overly excited, but reflective and separate from the emotion and action. And I wanted to give him words to describe what was happening, eventually emotion words that might describe his feelings.

As the burglars entered the house through the windows and woke up the family, I narrated, "The kids are trying to hide under the bed," and added, "They're frightened." Mike, a boy of few words, added about the mother in the house, "They're tying her up." A therapist's choice at that point might be to repeat what the child has said, to indicate that she's with him and has heard him; or she could take the perspective of the victim and play at her crying or trying to escape. Or she might ask the boy, "Is she trying to escape or is she just crying there?" The therapist could also take the perspective of the burglar. "He doesn't care about her feelings or how frightened she is!" or "He is angry at the woman." It's best to avoid being evaluative, as in "He's mean" or "He's bad!" First of all, even if his father is mean or bad, that's not exactly where the child is in terms of trying to understand what his father did. Second of all, if we think of play as a dream in which every role is played by the child, we want to help him feel the feeling or express the worry or idea that's in him in relation to his father's act, and not our own ideas about people who tie up women and rape them.

I recall that after a while Mike stopped the play and seemed stuck about what to do next.

Therapist: You know about why your father is in jail.
Mike: Yes, he raped a woman when he was burglaring a house.
Th: (gently) Do you know what rape is?

He said that it was tying a woman up and getting on top of her and "doing sex."

Th: (neutrally) What do you think about that?
M: (with emotion) Disgusting!
Th: It must be confusing for you to know about this. You must be wondering why your father would do such a thing.
M: (silence)

Thinking about where to go, I tried to tune into Mike's affect. Was he excited in his play? I didn't think so. Was it compulsive? No. Where was he coming from? The burglars were buddies; they helped each other open windows and climb into the house. This was about identification with other guys. This was about being a part of the experience; it was his father, whether he knew him well or not.

Th: Your father's in jail now.
M: (as he busied himself in the dollhouse) Uh huh.

Th: He did a bad thing, and the judge thought it was good for him to be in jail so he couldn't hurt someone again and so that he could think about what he did and try to be a better person.

M: (still silent)

Th: (guessing) But he's your dad and I bet that you might miss him sometimes.

Perhaps Mike was furious, but generally little boys who have bad dads sometimes still miss them, and there's so little space for that emotion to be expressed to others. I went on, "Sometimes it might have felt like he was a good dad to you or rather that he *could* have been a good dad to you." Mike offered, "He took us for ice cream once." I, of course, was thinking this was sad and pathetic, but said, "Yes, and that day you enjoyed being with your dad?" He was silent. Perhaps he didn't quite enjoy being with his dad that day but was struggling to remember something nice his dad did. I changed my line of thinking and said, "That day he took you for ice cream, you hoped he would be a really good dad to you." I think I hit on something there. Mike was silent, paused in play, and yet there was something in his demeanor that seemed to indicate that hope was the right emotion. What I did was to make my comments not about his dad's horrible sex act, but about Mike's longing for his dad to be a different kind of dad, a buddy, a friend, a guy to look up to. It would have been a mistake to talk about how wrong it was to tie women up and rape them— implying that Mike needed to know that. His dad was in jail for it and that was clear already. The sexual part of the play was just part of the scene, not a sexual investment on his part.

Therapists can get upset rather quickly when a child brings sexually violent material into the playroom, worrying about abuse or future offenses. But calm and thoughtful observation can help a therapist sort out from the beginning whether sex is really what's worrying the child. It would be wrong to lecture or comment on the evilness of rape with a young child. With Mike it wasn't the rape per se that was on his mind. His affect and his investment in the play seemed to be elsewhere. Sure, he was using a woman in his play as the basis around which camaraderie was built, but my hope was that helping him to acknowledge that longing in himself and having someone to his feelings of disappointment in his dad would help him in the future to not need to act out or form relationships with other men around the degradation of women.

SEXUAL MATERIAL COMES AND GOES

These examples indicate that butts and private parts as well as sex acts and sexual violence can be a part of kids' lives. Some kids can get involved and concerned about sexual issues much more readily than others. Some kids have had to deal with exposure to some pretty awful knowledge at a very young age. For many children, sexual material comes and goes as a small part of their lives, but spend a day in an elementary school and you'll hear plenty of jokes and references to make you wonder whether all kids are preoccupied with sexual themes. Sexual themes, yes. But this interest isn't always sexual in the way adults think about sex. Butts and private parts are part of the world around them and, like other parts of their lives, they raise concerns, and they reflect concerns having to do with the self. The important thing to remember is that the content of the sexual talk and play, these references to sex and body parts, often have much more to do with a child's concerns about herself and her place in her family, school, and world than about the actual sex act or body part itself. Treating them as such breaks through feelings of shame and worry to enable a child to be whole in a session.

PROBLEMATIC SEXUAL BEHAVIORS

While most therapists agree that sexual play between children is normal and natural, certain acts raise concerns, for two reasons.

The first is that they indicate to clinicians that a child has been exposed to material that might be too adult for him or her and that this exposure was abusive or may have been learned through abuse. The second is that a child may actually be abusing another child if he or she coerced the child to play a game and there was some power differential between the two. There has been some research and writing that has served to help professionals working with the justice system to differentiate play from abuse. Toni Cavanaugh Johnson (2004a, 2004b) created a chart of behaviors classed as "natural and healthy," "of concern," or "seek professional help." Under "of concern" for kindergarten through fourth graders, she lists: Keeps getting caught peeking at others doing bathroom functions; uses dirty words with adults after adults have consistently said no; continues to rub genitals in public after being told no; romanticizes all relationships; makes sexual sounds (sighs, moans); continuous fascination with nude pictures; wants to play games with much younger or older kids; draws genitals on some nude figures; wants to compare genitals with much older or much younger children; continuously wants to touch genitals, breasts, or buttocks of other children; French kissing; puts something in own rectum or genitals or those of another child; touches genitals of animals; frequently plays doctor and gets caught after being told no, and so on. The theme for the behaviors listed as "of concern" is that children show some obsession, compulsion, or lack of control through continuous acts or speech after time has elapsed or after a grown-up has told them no.

As a list of behaviors about which a parent ought to be concerned, these make sense. Some of these acts certainly are an indication of a preoccupation with sex at an early age. My criticism of this list, however, is that in my interviews with adult women, I spoke to quite a few who claimed that in childhood they had this very fascination. And it wasn't a fascination that eclipsed other activities. They still drew pictures of nonnude people, rode their bikes, played with other kids, and did their homework. Secret drawings of nude people, playing doctor even after being caught with that one friend, feeling strongly interested in seeing other people naked, or returning to that dirty magazine found on the playground over and over again—all of these kinds of behaviors were concerning to the kids themselves at the time. (When I did interviews with adult women about their sexual histories, those adults who identified themselves as preoccupied with sex when they were young were very concerned about their "normality.") One student who felt stimulated by and obsessed with playing naked Barbies also thought she was a "pervert" as a child. These women were concerned about their interests because they felt that they shouldn't be doing this, and yet they felt compelled to do it anyway.

The trouble is that children come prepared to feel sexual feelings when stimulated, and we live in an environment that is sexually stimulating for kids. If they find a way to express these feelings and respond to the sexual stimulation they're getting from their environment, sexual play and sexual feelings are self-reinforcing. Guilt and shame may make them stop, or other childhood activities that are fun and interesting may take precedence.

Let's take a closer look at that list. Many of those activities raise concern because they are public. Children who are so overstimulated that they don't hide what they are doing from the adults around them, or, children who are so out of touch with public mores that they don't realize what they're doing may be offensive to others. Most of the people I've interviewed or from whom I've collected survey data state that they tried to hide what they did from the adults and that this was part of the fun of it. Some informed me that once caught, their moms didn't ask them to stop but simply closed the door and talked with them later about it.

I've come up with my own easy-to-use list of five general guidelines for problematic sexual behavior in children. I repeat them in Chapter 4, where they might help clinicians distinguish play from abuse:

1. Play that is *not mutual* because one child is coerced, older, has much more power in the relationship, or tricks another child into playing a game is problematic. Just as bullying goes on in the world of nonsexual play, a one-time incident is sometimes not so problematic. But if this sexual bullying recurs, then I would call the behavior problematic. A rule to go by is to think about bullying in the schools, what passes for normal, and what deserves greater attention.

2. If not coercive, is it a *boundary violation*? Is someone else made to feel uncomfortable by the act, forced to watch, for example? Are someone's rights violated? Does someone else feel intruded upon? These boundary violations are another example of problematic behavior.

3. Is the behavior looking too *persistent, compulsive, or obsessive* in that it occurs in public places and/or the child seems not to be in control? Does the child seem unable to stop? Is the child choosing this play or behavior over other activities and interests? It's often compulsive sexual acting out that gets children noticed.

4. Is it *harmful to the child*? For example, is it harmful physically? Or, is it harmful socially? Is this behavior so persistent that it is interfering with other play, other activities, other interests? Or, is it harmful psychologically because the child is preoccupied with guilt and shame about the acts?

5. Is it *adultlike or unusual* in some other way? Of course, this is the trickiest of categories. It certainly isn't odd or unusual for little girls to dress up like adult women in Victoria's Secret bras and panties and prance around, but it is very adultlike. It wouldn't be of concern unless this was a kind of persistent play. Yet any reasonable adult would agree that sex with an animal is unusual, even if not adultlike. Is it odd, unusual, and adultlike for a 6-year-old

to want to French kiss his sister? That doesn't make him a sex offender; just a child that you want to work with a little more around overstimulation. When two 9-year-olds are performing oral sex on each other, you don't want to tell them simply to stop, but to process their discovery of this sex act, their feelings about it, their shame, and their interest. If they were caught once and haven't pursued it, it remains just that, an unusual and adult like sexual behavior, influenced by the media, exposure in real life, or chance.

When children rub their genitals so hard they hurt or when children force other children to take off their clothes or coerce them to play sexual games, when children expose themselves in public or masturbate to nude pictures, it is clear such children should see a therapist. But any of these signs of concern do not necessarily indicate that a child has been abused. Take, for example, Gwen, who was referred for an evaluation because she had been masturbating constantly at school. The preschool teachers were incredibly worried. They knew this could be a sign that she had been sexually abused because the compulsive and public quality of this rubbing looked very different from the behavior of the other preschool children, who occasionally touched themselves and then returned to other play. Moreover, the preschool teachers didn't like this girl's father. It was unclear what came first, their suspicions or their dislike, but they found him "creepy." He was a geeky computer software developer who didn't wash his hair often enough or dress very well, even though he was quite wealthy and able to afford the expensive preschool little Gwen was attending. He was socially awkward and the preschool teachers didn't like him hanging around, seemingly having difficulty separating from his daughter, when Gwen was dropped off at school. This was odd behavior for a dad who, in their minds, typically separates much more easily than a mom.

73

The therapist who evaluated Gwen was concerned about sexual abuse too, but knew that compulsive masturbation in a 4-year-old could arise from a number of other things as well. It was certainly a self-reinforcing behavior, and it could be self-soothing. An interview with Gwen's parents showed that they were concerned about it too. She hadn't done it much at home and when she had, they had asked her to stop but were afraid of making her feel bad about her body if they scolded her or were too harsh in preventing her from doing this. The therapist asked about the home, sleeping arrangements, the marriage, the presence of overstimulating material. All fine. There just didn't seem to be much to go on. The parents seemed like they knew a bit about child rearing and they cared a lot about their daughter.

Gwen came into the playroom rather cautiously but immediately went to the dollhouse. Like most children her age, she picked up the family dolls and labeled them mom, dad, and baby. In play she had the mom, dad, and baby interact well in the dollhouse and presented this therapist with a bedtime scene. When a child presents a bedtime scene, a therapist should consider whether the child is dealing with issues of attachment and separation. Of course, it's a dollhouse, there are beds and bedrooms; the house generally evokes this kind of scene. Still, the rehearsal in play of a goodnight scenario could indicate worries about goodnights, or the need to replay some very intimate attachment scene with the parents. In Gwen's play, the parents tucked their child in together, kissed the boy goodnight (Gwen distanced herself from the play by choosing a boy doll), and then went downstairs to watch TV. No fears or worries were expressed directly except that when the mom tucked the little boy into the bed, she said, "You're going to school tomorrow." Thinking this might be a clue, this therapist then said, "Let's make it be morning and time for school." Gwen obliged and soon in the dollhouse it was morning, and there was a lot of activity around what to do to get ready for school. A whole lot of activity! The amount of detail and activity relating to going to school was very different from the amount of activity that going to bed and kissing parents goodnight produced. This child was probably anxious about school, anxious about separation, which, of course, was thoroughly normal developmentally. Come to think of it, she was rather a well-put-together little girl who seemed poised and focused. Not the kind of girl who would cry and scream upon separation, demanding what she needed when she needed it. She dealt with her anxiety on her own, and rubbing herself was most likely very self-soothing.

Gwen's therapist was faced with a dilemma. Should she go on to do a smallish sexual abuse evaluation, asking Gwen questions about her private parts and whether other people touched her? She was experienced enough to know how to ask those questions as well as how to read the answers in a way that didn't influence the child very much. However, she also knew that asking any questions about this would put some ideas into Gwen's head that possibly weren't there.

So she opted simply to talk about touching private parts in public.

Therapist: Sometimes at school, your mommy and daddy told me, you rub your private parts a lot. They are worried because that's something kids do in private, not at school. And even though it feels good, your parents want you to do other things too that make you feel good, not just that, but things that help you to learn and play at school.

Gwen: (quiet, all eyes)

Th: (continuing in a reassuring way) I know lots of children who do rub their private parts. But as they get older, they learn not to do this at school, and to do it just sometimes in bed when they're alone because it feels good. [*Here the therapist tried to give a sex-positive message.*] Other times, when kids want to touch themselves, they sometimes touch other things. I bet you do this too. Is your BurryBurry [*she had been introduced to Gwen's teddy bear earlier, named BurryBurry*] something you also like to touch?

G: (nods yes)

Th: Is he nice to hold and touch?

G: (hugs BurryBurry close to her so that the therapist wouldn't even *think* of touching him)

Th: Well, I'd like you sometimes to touch BurryBurry instead of your private parts. Can I see how you touch BurryBurry in a way that makes you feel good?

G: (strokes his head)

Th: And can you rub him like you might be worried about something and rubbing him might help?

G: (rubs him)

Then the therapist told Gwen simply that she should try to sometimes rub BurryBurry instead of her private parts, especially at school because school is for learning and playing with other children, not a good place to rub her private parts. This therapist then met with the preschool teachers and the parents separately to tell them how to lovingly reward her for touching her teddy bear instead of her vagina. She gave them stickers to reward this different behavior and told the parents to do this in a loving way, ignoring the rubbing of the vagina, but rewarding the rubbing of the bear. When she checked back in a month, this behavioral intervention had worked.

I like what she did. She worked hard to make sure that the child did not feel bad. She also made the child feel that she was already on the way to growing out of this behavior by showing her that she already used her teddy bear in that way. She also made it seem more grown-up to use the stuffed animal. And she linked what she believed to be the cause, worry, to the behavior.

Part of this therapist's role was to also educate the preschool teachers that not all sexual behavior is a sign of sexual abuse. A child, especially an anxious child, can get fixated on a certain soothing behavior, and rubbing oneself does feel good and focuses one inward, shutting out the overstimulating world around a child. Of course there was a glimmer of worry that the therapist had overlooked potential abuse. There always is, but she had to trust her instincts that not all sexual behavior is a sign of abuse. And with the parents, this therapist discussed her concern that Gwen might feel that she had to rely on herself a little too much with regard to her worries. There were things that her parents could do to encourage Gwen to talk about worries in a way that released them rather than rehearsing them. Turning to her teddy bear was one solution. They could also encourage her to tell her teacher if she ever felt that she missed her mommy and daddy at school. Her teacher would give her a hug and help direct her to an activity.

There are other cases where therapists get the sense over time that abuse perhaps has occurred, but it becomes difficult to prove it and one has to simply alert social services, which can do a more thorough investigation. I supervised a case of a 4-year-old girl who had a speech impediment. She would enter the playroom and immediately attack the dollhouse, lining up all the dolls and, regardless of gender, putting them all in twos, one on top of the other, saying, "They're humping." She was able to indicate to the therapist that she should play the role of the "man watching." This man watching was first displaced onto a male doll who was poised at the window, and then frustratingly removed from the window and put in the corner of the room where all the dolls were humping. Then she was able to convey to my supervisee that she needed to be the man watching. It's always tricky when therapists are asked to involve themselves in difficult positions in play. I've always avoided being the one to shoot the child or kill someone else. I also advised my supervisee to insist on representing herself with a doll. So she took a doll and made it represent herself watching within the play. Why? The feelings of overstimulation in play may become too intense, the feelings of lack of boundaries reproduced. Therapists need to represent boundaries and safety in play. They represent safety within the session by keeping a close eye on overstimulation, and when necessary, they alert the department of social services to investigate.

* * * *

Yes, we therapists need to be aware that some play looks like an indication of abuse. But I would argue that focusing too closely on whether the play reflects abuse leads a therapist to miss other information that a child conveys through play and may also lead a therapist to ignore other influences, both intrapsychic and environmental, that might be at the heart of the behavior or play in question. Sexual abuse of a child is a horrible thing and we wouldn't want to miss detecting it because if we did, worst of all, the abuse might continue. Children who have been abused often become symptomatic. Their play is traumatic, full of alarming metaphors, some acting out, and puzzling disorganization. The next chapter gives examples of children in treatment who present with some of these behaviors and symptoms, in hopes of clarifying the difference.

CHAPTER THREE

Working With Children Who Have Been Abused

My work with sexually abused children began as an intern at Massachusetts General Hospital. At that time, it struck me that much like adult victims, children were coping primarily with issues of betrayal, loss, boundary violations, bodily fears, and most important, issues of power and control. What better place to address these concerns than in the therapy room, where safety and trust are established, where boundaries are reinforced and limit setting is clear, where a child can experience bodily excitement and be helped to understand it and then back away from it, and where children are given the power to direct a session in many directions.

I learned early on from sexual abuse therapist Esther Deblinger that it is important to address issues about sexual abuse directly. Otherwise a child is sometimes induced to follow a pattern of avoidance and even dissociation when issues, thoughts, or feelings about the abuse arise. For many children who have been sexually abused, their strategy of coping is not to deal directly with the problem. Many cannot. Their abusers are far too powerful and they may feel complicit and ashamed. They thus develop ways of coping that involve avoiding thinking about the abuse, avoiding the perpetrator, and even dissociating during the abuse, removing themselves psychologically from the scene to preserve themselves and their well-being. In the long run, though adaptive at the time, these responses are maladaptive and children shouldn't be encouraged to continue responding in this way when there are people who can lend support. Moreover, if they are no longer being abused, talking about their abuse gives them the opportunity to develop other ways of coping that are more mature and healthy and will serve them well in the future.

Thus, I recommend speaking directly with children about their abuse in a way that takes seriously the events they experienced, that doesn't allow the events to be shoved aside, and that sets as a model for them a way to talk about the abuse so that it can be integrated into the whole of who they are without it being a central defining feature of the self.

Keeping those goals in mind, play is essential. As an abused child and a therapist play, the therapist can help the child temper memories and feelings by acknowledging what in the play may be reminiscent of the abuse and what feelings may be evoked in play that need discussion. Rather than demanding conversation, a therapist, while observing play, playing along, and commenting on play, shows a child that together they are cognizant that they are working on those feelings that are a result of the abuse. Remember that the play actually is a way of talking about the abuse. No therapist should worry about how to start a conversation about the abuse, thinking that talk is more important or more therapeutic than play. It isn't. But clueing into the abuse as it arises in play and allowing the child to enact and play out these issues in productive ways is particularly essential with younger children.

It's important to realize, however, that when children become involved in play, sometimes play becomes a reenactment. The primary job of the therapist is to figure out when the play is productive and when it is compulsive repetition or overstimulating to the child. A therapist needs to read the affect and make a determination of how much in control a child feels while playing the game. When play is spontaneous and intense and also productive, a therapist will always find that a child is the director as well as the actor, that there's a person involved, the child herself, figuring out what to do next, deliberating. When a child seems compelled, driven, or out of control, it will be important for a therapist to step in and help the child to distance herself from her play. As a young therapist I was less able to recognize when a child was getting overly stimulated, focusing more frequently on myself and what I would say or do next. My students tell me the same is true for them, that when they first begin to do therapy, they have a hard time focusing on what the client is saying or doing because they're constantly worrying about what they will say in response and whether it will be the right thing, or whether they will have anything to say. Paying attention to the anxiety level of the child at play seems almost too much for them.

The play of sexually abused children doesn't often have sexual components in it; rather it has components relating to the trauma, like the child I described earlier who compulsively reenacted the wolf scene from "The Three Little Pigs." What a terrifying moment that must have been for each of the pigs as the wolf stood at his door.

Play may have sexual elements in it, but here is what's tricky. Sexually abused children will also have some interest in sex that is normative, picking up on talk or images from their environment or even their own developing attention to this area of life. Therapists will be tempted to relate these children's interest and questions back to the abuse, but that's because therapists have so little education about normative sexual development in children that they think they are seeing reenactments or overstimulation even when a child is trying to understand natural interest as it arises.

Must a child be forever a victim of abuse? One would think so, to read the literature. However, we know that many kids, the majority actually, grow up to have little symptomatology and to feel that they have moved beyond their abuse. They are no longer defined by it. Therapists need to take care not to reconfirm children's victim status over and over by interpreting all sexual material as pertaining to the abuse. And they must also truly believe that all children, but especially those who have been abused, deserve an adequate sex education, to understand their bodies, their selves, their fantasies, and their impulses.

EXCITING PLAY AND BOUNDARY VIOLATIONS

Nick was one of the first children I ever saw in therapy. He was both excited and worried to have me as a therapist. We had a nice first session in which he turned out all the lights and instructed me to sit under the table with him and tell scary stories. We shared the storytellings and I was careful to follow his lead. He seemed to like me and, as a beginning therapist, I was grateful for that. I don't think a therapist ever really gets over that need to be liked by a child, but it's particularly strong when a therapist is just starting out in practice.

I think it was because Nick liked me that he became interested in my religion. Coming from a fundamentalist Christian home, he wondered if I were Christian too. His mother had told him that she thought I was Jewish, and in a session he asked me if I was. I asked what it would mean to him if I were. He had said that if I were Jewish, that would mean that I might go to hell because only Christians would be saved when the judgment came. This was rather harsh talk from a 7-year-old; I reflected that he was worried about what might happen to me. I understood that he saw the world as a dangerous place ever since he had been sexually abused by an uncle who had lived with him in his house for two years, having full access to him and his sister when his mother was out. This uncle was now in jail for the horrible abuse he perpetrated, drugging his niece, Nick's sister, and Nick, forcing them to have a form of sex together, and also raping each one of them at knife-point, more than once, and sometimes while wearing a scary Halloween mask.

Given this horrific abuse experience, perhaps it was easier for Nick to see me as the one in danger than to remember himself in danger and risk reexperiencing that terror. He had been constantly in danger in his own home and it wasn't the abuse alone, but the threats from his uncle that he would kill Nick's mother if Nick ever told on him. To state the obvious, that is too much fear and responsibility for a young child to have. And this young child came to therapy seeing that his therapist, another woman there to protect him, was in danger and he had to save her.

He resolved this fear in the following way. Relieved and almost jubilant, he came to the next session and announced that my name was in the Bible and so I would be protected. I was the Lamb of God! (For readers who might have forgotten this, Lamb is my last name.) He had even brought his bible in to show me where the word *lamb* was in the Bible. His mother had helped him to find it. He didn't have to look out for me; God would.

After getting beyond that beginning, Nick still remained preoccupied with me and my safety in play. But over time, as he used me as a projective screen for his own experience, he also began to see me as both a sexual object and a potential victim, enacting both of these roles that he had played at home, through me and my presence. The first sign that he was seeing me in some sexualized way came when he was about eight. He stroked my leg, feeling the pantyhose material from knee to ankle as he sat on the floor and I sat next to him on a minichair. At the time, I experienced this as affectionate and not sexual. He was feeling close to me and trusting, and I just didn't know what to say so I said, "You're feeling the material on my leg," or something plainly reflective like that.

I knew I should have responded to this as a boundary violation, but I was young and waited to ask my supervisor what I should have said. My supervisor at the time, a female psychoanalyst from Hungary, immediately saw this as sexual and said I must address this gently. "That's inappropriate," though, sounded too rejecting. Perhaps a gentle, "Nick, that's one of the things we don't do in therapy together. When we feel close, we tell each other how we feel, and then we can talk about it." That would be skirting the sexual issue. To be more direct about the sexual aspect, I might have said gently, "Nick, we don't talk much about what your uncle did, but when a grown-up sexually abuses a little kid, the child can get confused about what's the right kind of affection between a grown-up and a kid. Your uncle didn't treat you like a kid. And he didn't treat you well at all. He was mean and he made you do things and think about things that kids shouldn't have to do or think about. When you're in therapy with me, we can't make what happened to you disappear, but we can talk about it. And when you touched my leg back then, I wondered if maybe you didn't know that this was something kids don't usually do with grown-ups. When we're together in therapy, when you feel close to me, you can tell me, or smile at me with your wonderful smile." It might have been good to even add, "I don't want you to feel bad for doing that. I just want you to understand that if there aren't rules about touching in here, you might begin to feel unsafe, because you knew a grown-up who didn't care about any of those rules." I like the speech for what it covers. But if a child is anxious, it is way too long and possibly could make him feel more anxious. The sentiment expressed is right. The message has to be that boundaries are good even when they feel like a rejection because they make people feel safe.

The fact that I didn't set a boundary around that incident may have opened the way for what happened a few weeks later when Nick, as soon as he walked into the office, jumped up and kissed me on the lips. As in a car accident, the seconds seemed to go by slowly as I tried to determine how to respond without hurting him. He was only 8-years-old, and yet this was not a peck. He pressed his lips on mine and held them there, hugging me around the shoulders and neck. I pushed him away as gently as possible, trying to think of what to say, but before I could say a word he burst into tears.

What was going on with him outside of therapy that he was bringing in these boundary tests with me? What was going on inside the session? Did Nick need me to show him there were boundaries here, that even though we were getting close, there would be no abuse? I thought back to the first day he came to my office and insisted we turn off all the lights, sit under the table, and tell scary stories. Could we bond together against the dark and the frightening outside world? This seemed to be his first question. Now his question was whether I could be trusted and whether he could trust himself with this closeness.

The abuse by Nick's uncle was harsh, unsympathetic, and cruel, so Nick's stroking and kissing didn't seem to me to be a straight reenactment. Yet a reenactment of a boundary violation it was. He liked me and so it all came out in a kinder, gentler way. Kids who have been sexually abused often don't have good boundaries with adults and other kids. So as Nick cried in my office, I spoke to him about boundaries and feeling safe. I also told him how I felt close to him too, but that because I was a grown-up and his therapist, we didn't express this kind of closeness with a kiss. He was embarrassed and refused to talk about it. In the continuity of the sessions that followed, the closeness expressed through play and talking, some of the damage of what must have felt like a rejection was undone. Yet I can't help but think that after the first feeling of rejection, Nick might have felt a bit safer with that boundary made.

NICK AND THE CHAIR OF THE SLIPPERY SNAKES

In the year that followed, Nick moved such reenactments into play, and although they were not explicitly sexual, he was addressing the sexual abuse. One imaginary game he repeated over many sessions was that of a "mad scientist" who forces a young girl, played by myself in his scenario, to sit on the chair with the slippery snakes. The coercion, the phallic symbols, the double entendre of the word *mad*? What else could this scenario represent? And yet it was healthy and important to play this game as long as he didn't get overstimulated.

How do I tell if a child is getting overstimulated by the play? The sheer repetition of the same game with little change is a clue. Shutting out the therapist as a person is another. If the game can be reflected on while in play, then one gets the sense that processing of the experience is happening simultaneously with this changed reenactment. And reflecting on the game while a child is in the midst of it is the very thing that helps a child to maintain a safe distance from a stimulating reenactment.

Perhaps this process is similar to what happens in eye movement desensitization therapy. My understanding of it is that in the retelling of a traumatic event, a certain part of the brain is engaged that leads a client to relive the experience in the retelling. The eye movement purportedly engages another part of the brain and allows cognitions, helpful thoughts, to become integrated into the reexperiencing. So, while people may be reexperiencing their trauma, they may also be saying to themselves things like, "This won't happen again," "I'm safe now," and "I was able to get myself out of there"—positive thoughts about the future, the present, and their control in traumatic situations.

When a child is engaged in play and he will still talk to you about where to place the chair and how the responses should go, when he can stop in the middle and talk about what he is feeling rather than brushing your questions irritably away, then there's some room for processing the event. When his eyes glaze over and you get the feeling of inevitability and lack of control over the events, then it's time to step aside and talk. Play can be healing, but it can also be overstimulating and produce anxieties. And there's no literature to support that simply reenacting an abusive experience is healing and helpful.

So, Nick was the mad scientist, and he pretended to tie me up. I was instructed to cower and cry, but not to try to escape. Then he set up a chair at the back of the room, all by itself. And in the game, I would be made to wait, anxious and scared, while he played around with his chemistry vials and such, until he was ready for me. At this point, he would walk toward me and I was meant to back up, resisting, so that I wouldn't have to reach the chair. Nick the boy instructed me to look scared and try to resist even though I couldn't. The way I played the victim was to represent the victim as a person with thoughts and plans while being forced to do something horrible. Victimization takes away the personhood of the one victimized, and it sometimes takes a long time for victims to recapture all the things they thought and did to try to help them-selves, but this is important because it reaffirms to them that they were there, present, and a person in the midst of the victimization. Edna Foa and Norah Feeny's work (e.g., Foa, Hembree, Cahill, Ranch, & Riggs, 2005) with sufferers of posttraumatic stress dis-order (PTSD) shows that after many opportunities to relive their traumas by speaking them to a therapist and into a tape recorder at home, trauma victims begin to retell their story in a way that captures themselves as subjects, as agents within the victimizing situation. Thus, playing the victim, I spoke thoughts aloud. I spoke scared thoughts: "I'm so frightened. What is he going to do?" I spoke planful thoughts, "Maybe I can fight him and run out of the room. What if I call out? Will someone hear me and come help?" (After all, I was instructed by Nick not to escape but not to stop planning an escape.) I spoke words of justice and anger: "This is unfair. This scientist is crazy and why do I have to suffer?" While Nick was feeling some mastery over the situation by identifying with the aggressor, I was trying to give him a victim he could identify with, more complex than the helpless and frightened little nothing he may believe he had become in his uncle's hands.

What's so important about this kind of play is that when it's done carefully and without much excitement, a child is given a chance to respond and react intellectually, given pause to examine the feelings of perpetrator and victim, without quite understanding how close to home all of it is. I see no need to remind the child that something similar to the game happened to him. Play is a form of indirect processing and can work on its own. Occasionally I may relate the play to an actual experience, but this is often when the play breaks down and the child seems unable to make use of it. If Nick became emotional at something the victim said, I might say, "Let's stop for a minute. It was hard to hear the little girl planning to escape, right? You have some feelings about that. Maybe they have something to do with a time when you couldn't escape." Or, "Let's stop a minute. You look kind of scared when you're being the mad scientist. Tell me what you're feeling. Is the scientist scared to be so mean? Or are you remembering how scary other people you know have been?" These kinds of promptings can happen gently and privately alongside the play. It's a way of using the feelings that the play brings up, and attending to what about those feelings interferes with the play. If we think of play as healthy childhood activity, then we are always in tune with what interferes with creativity, play, the ability to cope.

WORKING WITH THE CHRONICALLY OUT-OF-CONTROL CHILD

Some kids seem unable to play and yet feel compelled to act out their abuse in a session. Fred, 8-years-old, was in residential treatment at the time he saw my student and immediately asked if he could be her boyfriend. What a perfect question for the beginning of therapy! Please therapist, where is the boundary? Fred had watched hours and hours of porn with his stepfather, who also at times masturbated in front of Fred. He was removed from his stepfather's home and sent to live with his mother, his mother's new husband, and her two children from that marriage. But Fred was so out of control and so sexual, she couldn't tolerate having him around. Hyperactive and with no respect for boundaries, he engaged in touching and undressing with the younger children in the home. Hence his removal from the home and placement in a residential center.

But Fred couldn't play. He ran around the room, going from one toy to the other. Was it overstimulation, hyperactivity, or both? This was difficult to tell. He wanted to sit on my student's lap. He'd run by and touch her on the behind. He was a whirling dervish of sexual innuendoes and petty thieveries. Before she could process the last act, he'd cross another boundary, leaving this student exhausted and on edge. A quick "no" left him instantly depressed and ashamed, but not for long before he was bouncing off the walls.

Fred's sexualized behavior begged for help with boundaries and self-control. And my student couldn't slow him down enough to address these issues. But it was not good for Fred to get away with enacting these violations. So, in supervision, we decided she should make the sessions shorter to begin with, and we found some activity in which he could participate with a female therapist that he wouldn't have to sexualize. We thought up a phrase to stop him in his tracks and to get him to settle down before entering the sessions. And before coming to his sessions, he would choose what he wanted to play with—checkers, Clue, Sorry—by filling out a sheet in the classroom with his teacher.

When he came to the therapy room, it would be structured—the game would be set up and waiting for him, an invitation to sit and focus. When he was calm and focused on the game, sometimes my student was able to process some of the boundary problems. And when he would "accidentally" touch her or jump on the furniture, she would use the phrase, "That's not okay with me," which emphasized to him where the boundary was. But she said it in a way that tried to convey he simply wasn't following a rule, like a rule in the game, and not that he needed to feel ashamed. The rules of the game became a wonderful source of talk about boundaries with Fred. It worries me when I hear beginning therapists say, "We didn't do much. We just played board games." There's a wealth of play in a board game, play about restraint, about competition and aggression, about playing by the rules, about needing to win and sometimes needing to lose. Not surprisingly, Fred wanted to break the rules of the game, and by addressing what was okay and what was not okay with the therapist, acknowledging the conventional rules and how breaking the rules changed the game and made it unfair, they were talking about all rules, all boundaries.

SEXUALLY ABUSED CHILDREN AND SEX EDUCATION

Children who have been abused need and deserve to know other aspects of sex than abuse, so that they can master it intellectually and emotionally, and imagine that someday they might have a nonabusive sexual relationship with someone. All too often therapists and caseworkers shy away from providing this way of talking and learning about sex for fear of exciting the child or stimulating memories.

Summer, a girl who had been sexually abused by her uncle and older brother while living with her alcoholic mother, was probably not returning to her home. But her stay at a residential center for children with emotional difficulties was not only designed to keep her safe temporarily until a foster home was available, but to help her to deal with her emotionality, her "over-sexualized" behaviors, and her desire to kill herself. Because Summer once tried to strangle herself with a piece of string before she went to sleep at night, the staff kept belts, ropes, string, and other like objects away from her. The staff really liked her because she generally behaved at the house, doing her chores when asked and cooperating with routines. She also was able to speak about her feelings and in only two months could "process" with the staff, using the therapeutic language that they used. For example, she would say, "I don't feel safe now and I'm afraid I might look for some string." The only problem with Summer was that sometimes she became overly familiar with the male staff and when overexcited she would try to touch the kids on their buttocks. She also sometimes injected sexual talk into the conversation, and the staff had to tell her to stop. Generally they would say, "That's inappropriate" if she said something sexual, or, "Summer, you need to ask people if it's okay to touch them," when she got too close to a staff member or child. The center generally used cognitive-behavioral techniques, and these comments were consistent with that approach. The staff, young adults just out of college, focused on helping the children develop better self-control, ask for help when they needed it, and process their feelings.

One night at the residence, a staff member had put on a video as a treat for the five children staying there. They all settled down on the couch and floor in front of the TV with popcorn and drinks. The video the staff member chose was rated PG and there was a love scene in it, in which a high school girl was kissing a boy she liked. Everyone seemed to be enjoying the movie and paying attention, even during the "mushy" parts, when Summer asked, "Why am I feeling tingly in my vagina?" Although other children were present, Summer addressed her question to the two staff members there, who were also watching the movie, a woman and a man both in their early twenties. The two staff members, rather shocked and embarrassed, gave each other one of those looks: "Oh my God." And the woman said to Summer, "That's inappropriate." She later brought it up in our supervision. She was sad that Summer was so, in the house's terms, over sexualized from her abuse, so much so that she would feel that way during a rather mild kissing scene and just come out and say something like that. It also made her feel odd that this 11-year-old was having such grown-up sexual feelings.

My experience with supervising staff and interns at placements such as these is that they respond to such talk with a lot of sadness. Although staff members who work with children have a lot of positive feelings about the children. they feel uncomfortable when abuse enters the conversation. Although they are the ones who spend the most time with the children, they are taught to say things like, "You'll need to discuss that with your therapist" and "You're safe here now." Thus they miss important opportunities to process thinking and feelings about sex when they arise.

It was inappropriate for Summer to say what she did in a group of kids, even if it was understandable. It was possible that her announcment had something to do with showing a false sense of bravado but also likely that it had to do with her anxiety about the sexual feelings that the film evoked. It was also the staff member's sense that Summer was announcing this feeling because she herself thought it was strange and didn't quite know why it was happening to her just then nor how to label it. She may even have worried that something was wrong with her. Whatever motivated her remark, "That's inappropriate" can't be the final statement.

Let's first consider that what Summer was feeling was not all that strange. It may be that other children, perhaps a little older than Summer, would also feel sexual stimulation from a scene like that. Surely scenes like these are filmed in such a way as to draw viewers in, identifying with the teenagers in it, in a way that's supposed to be stimulating. And Summer needed to know that people do sometimes feel sexual feelings when they're reading a book or watching TV. Understanding this as a natural and private feeling can go a long way in preventing a girl from needing to act on these feelings. Those private moments stimulated by a movie or a book can give one pause for reflection about one's body, desire, and the future, without having to act.

It was clear to the staff members and to me that Summer's feelings in response to the movie, not just her speaking about them, could have been exaggerated and that the sexual feelings she felt were stronger than what another 11-year-old might feel because of her earlier abuse. But even if the origin of those feelings was a traumatic experience, that doesn't mean they needed to be erased or dismissed. This is the body she now had, and she needed to understand it and learn to live with it. Would it be helpful if a staff member were to suggest to Summer that she might be feeling those feelings more strongly because of her earlier abuse? I don't think so. Any statement like that might make her feel those feelings are wrong and she should dismiss them. Why would we want her to dismiss any feelings? Above all with sexually abused children, we want them to be in touch with their bodies rather than outside of them, to understand the body's feelings rather than dismiss them.

There's another sense in which we might see this experience as positive for Summer. She was feeling sexually excited by something that was rather normative for teenage girls, kissing a boyfriend. Sure she was young for that, but she had been sexually abused for years by an older brother and an uncle who had done brutal things to her, and now found herself sexually interested in a nonabusive situation. This has to be good. Wouldn't we worry more if the overly sexualized coercion scenes that occur in so many films were the scenes she responded to? Of course we would. So to respond to Summer's statement, sometime after the movie, away from the other children, a staff member might say, "When you get older, you may have someone you really feel close to, and if the two of you like each other a lot, like the people in the film, you may kiss and have some of those tingly feelings again." The message is that those are good feelings to have. Saying "That's inappropriate" may convey to a child that the feelings are wrong and shameful and that she is dirty for feeling them. And if she felt that way when she was being abused, sexually responsive, yet hurt and ashamed, it's likely that she will extend that feeling to other sexual situations. Here was a staff member's chance to help her understand that the feeling is a good feeling, but a private one, and one that she hopes Summer will have when she's older with someone she really cares about.

Recall that one of the staff members was male. Could he have had that conversation with Summer too? Yes. He might have said, "Summer, those are private feelings we all have sometimes, but it makes people uncomfortable to hear you talk about them. If you want to know more about those feelings, we can talk later about them." Given that she was so overstimulated by male staff at the house already, it would be good to give her that little bit of sex education at a different time, when she was calm and less excitable. Later, he could approach her and say in as neutral a way as possible that he wanted her to know that the feelings she was feeling are normal, and that it's good that she recognized them. But, he might add, he hopes that someday she will have a partner or husband with whom she can enjoy being close and that would be a good thing.

Finally, wasn't it good for Summer to be aware and self-reflective about her body? And wasn't it good that she wanted to talk about it? This made such a wonderful opportunity for sex education, and who needs sex education more than a child who's been harmed by sex? We tend to think that because sexually abused children get overstimulated and overwhelmed more quickly that we should avoid such topics. Children who have been abused need and deserve to know other aspects of sex than abuse so that they can master it intellectually and emotionally, and imagine that someday they might have a nonabusive sexual relationship with someone. So many victims of abuse numb out and pretend that their bodies are no longer theirs and have lifelong serious sexual dysfuntion. Summer's reflection on a bodily response was a wonderful first step toward owning her body and taking care of it.

Think of it from Summer's perspective. Next to her, on the couch, at the center, was a beautiful young woman, a staff member, who tucked her in at night, who walked around in her own body presumably safe in the world, and who cared for the children at the center. Also next to her was a handsome young man who liked children, wanted to care for them, and who wouldn't abuse them. Who better to take her aside and talk to her about her feelings than people she felt safe with, people whom she trusted, people who wouldn't abuse her? It's true that neither staff member actually was her parent; they were only there three, four, or five nights a week. But in the time Summer was at the center, these young people became so much more for the children there. They became representative of adults who care and who can be trusted, internalizable objects. As positive representations of parents who care, they help children hope for such caring in their future when they leave and move into an adoptive home or return to their parents.

"That's inappropriate" was only an appropriate response if we're thinking of the literal meaning of the phrase, but too little a response for Summer, who was left to make sense of these feelings on her own and probably also left feeling a little shameful about having spoken out and shared them. But I don't blame them. We as adults are uncomfortable talking about sexual feelings in many situations. And therapists are often shocked when some statement is made by a child in the therapy session, let alone while watching a movie together. When children have been sexually abused, it's not only statements they make but the play that they engage in with us that provides them with opportunities for sex education and for experiencing their feelings in the company of someone safe.

* * * *

These examples show how alarming, compulsive, and strange some of the traumatic talk and play of sexually abused children can be, but also how therapy proceeds as normal, exploring feelings and thoughts through play and metaphor. One might draw the conclusion that when play or behavior is less strange or just mildly provocative that a child is acting out normative sexual curiosity. That might be wrong though. The child with fewer symptoms might have had a less invasive or disturbing experience of sexual abuse or might have coped unusually well given other resources.

CHAPTER FOUR

Acting-Out and Sexually Abusive Children

Distinguishing Play From Abuse

Before examining the acting-out behaviors of sexually abusive children that are often called "sexualized" or "offending" behaviors, it's important to review my simple list from of what makes a sexual behavior problematic (see Chapter 2). The first three points indicate what would be considered more severe on a continuum from sexual play to sexual offense.

1. Play that is *not mutual* because one child is coerced, older, has much more power in the relationship, or tricks another child into playing a game is problematic.
2. When not coercive, sexual behavior that is a *boundary violation*, where someone else is made to feel uncomfortable when acted upon, asked to perform an act, or forced to watch an act, is problematic.
3. Does the behavior look too *persistent, compulsive, or obsessive* in that it occurs in public places and/or the child seems not to have self-control? Is the child choosing to do this play or behavior over other activities and interests?
4. Is it *harmful to the child* physically, socially, or psychologically?

5. Is it *adult like or unusual* in some other way? For example, is the child having sexual relations with an animal? Or are two young children attempting to have anal sex?

Although there are plenty of books on treating juvenile sex offenders, these treatments typically refer to children who have already been identified as having fairly major sexual acting-out offenses. They address, for example, teens who compulsively expose themselves, rape, or repeatedly sexually abuse younger children. These children deserve the best treatment possible, but I don't have the space here to review the kinds of treatments offered in milieu, group, and individual therapy that have been successful. There is another category of children who have acted out sexually, who have abused (by legal definition) other children, and for whom there isn't adequate knowledge about treatment strategies. For these children, those very confrontational programs about sex offending, reeducation, and violating the rights of others, programs that actually label these children sex offenders, do not seem appropriate. This chapter presents a few of these children. But first I discuss what makes sexually abused children act out and why we fear that a victim can turn so quickly into an offender.

THE ACTING OUT OF SEXUALLY ABUSED CHILDREN

As we saw in Chapter 3, children who have been sexually abused bring these issues into play sometimes in disguised form and sometimes directly. We also saw that children can get overstimulated by such play. When children are sexually abused, they are forced to cope with feelings, physical and emotional, that they're not ready for. There is fear, guilt, shame, worry, dread, sometimes physical excitement, often confusion; and, over time, children can get habituated to the abuse, coping in a way that gives them whatever control they can get within the experience, sometimes by absenting themselves (when able) by blanking out, shutting down, numbing, thinking of other things, or removing the spirit from the body. We know through studies of adults that trauma changes physiology, and that even those victims who don't obtain the full diagnosis of PTSD, still show symptoms and behaviors that indicate trauma. They go numb when stressed or space out when they should be paying attention. They may have flashbacks or reexperience their abuse in other ways. They may become self-injurious, acting out abuse on themselves. And they may act out parts of the abuse with other people.

When children reproduce their abuse in their interactions with other children and even adults, it can take various forms. Like Nick in Chapter 3, it can look like a game about something else (the mad scientist and the slippery snakes). They can also reproduce only the feeling of bodily excitement or overstimulation and not the particular abuse through, for example, play wrestling with other children. I tend to think of these attempts to bring the abuse into play or into their experiences with other children in two ways. First, I see these kids as trying to master their abuse in a way that gives them more power and control. They are redoing what happened to them but more often than not taking the part of the abuser, working the game in such a way that they slow it down, make choices, and feel more in control. They turn the passive into active, identifying with the aggressor. But even when they play out a game in which they are clearly taking the part of the victim, they are also trying to gain control of the situation, thinking through the experience, pausing to think about their own role as victim, and trying to get it right, saying things they had wanted to say or feeling the experience in a way they couldn't during the abuse.

Such play doesn't come only out of a desire to master the experience and gain control. Posttraumatic sexual play also can come out of overwhelming thoughts and feelings. Some children who have been made sexual objects for other people often have to live with a hyperreactivity to sexual stimuli, intrusion of memories of the trauma, and sexual feelings that may go beyond their years and which are experienced as more powerful and less controllable than the sexual feelings of other kids their age. They may act out on these feelings simply because, unable to suppress them, there is nothing else to do with them. It may be impossible to talk about the feelings in the moment, although we saw Summer bring up the subject to staff at her residential home in Chapter 3. It is also hard to make them go away. And with these feelings of stimulation, a child may seek out another child to play or interact with in a sexual way.

FROM VICTIM TO OFFENDER

When a child who is a victim of abuse initiates play with another child, in my experience, clinicians and caseworkers tend to interpret this play as sexual offending. Indeed, play and boundary violations may not be clear in the child's head, and the behaviors may look too adult, too coercive, or too unusual for any reasonable adult to categorize as just experimentation or just play. But all too automatically, the sexual behavior is seen as a precursor to, if not itself, a sexual offense. The thinking goes something like this: Isn't it true that most sex offenders were sexually abused as children? And because of that, shouldn't we worry when a child is sexually abused that he or she might turn out to be a sex offender?

We have enormous fear and disgust of sex offenders in our culture. To many adults, quite possibly it is the worst crime imaginable, second only to murder. Some think with glee that a sex offender will have trouble in jail, further punished by a big guy named Bubba in the next cell. Most of the general public I have spoken with, including many educated individuals, believe that sex offending is an incurable problem. They are unaware of the variety of sex offenders that exist, from severe pedophiles who are difficult to treat to the more amenable first-time offenders who became overstimulated, obsessed, and needy around a step daughter or stepson, wracked with guilt but still wrongly making excuses for their behavior. While the public seems to want to see sex offenders as monsters, there are also those who acted out only once and were able to make changes in themselves.

And there are a few problems with those statistics that report that most sex offenders were sexually abused in childhood. For one, when arrested, sex offenders may get a lighter sentence and more sympathy if they lie and say they were sexually abused during childhood. Quite a bit of the research on sex offender sexual abuse histories is based on self-report of sexual abuse, that is, a sex offender's own report about his childhood. He has a motivation to lie about that.

Also, these statistics are tricky. Most sex offenders were abused as children (Stirpe & Stermac, 2003, find 60%, and Aylwin, Studer, & Reddon, 2003 find 70%, while Worling, 1995, found only 30% of adult and 75% of adolescent sex offenders were sexually abused). However most children who are sexually abused do not grow up to offend (Widom & Ames, 1994). More recent research shows this to be less than 1%. So how can this be the case, that 30-70% of adults sex offenders and 75% of adolescent sex offenders were sexually abused as children and less than 1% of sexually abused children grow up to abuse? It would mean that there are a lot more sexually abused children out there than sex offenders, and this would make sense given that sex offenders often have more than one victim.

But the fear is there, and when a boy in particular has been abused, we worry that he will grow up to act out his abuse on other people. This, unfortunately, does not lead parents to make sure that this boy has a proper sex education, including information about how to understand and control sexual feelings, how to seek out satisfaction in appropriate ways, how to be patient, and how to understand overwhelming sexual feelings. Instead, it means adults will watch and wait.

The following cases all involve children or teens who acted out sexually. In each I describe the circumstances under which such acting out emerges and address why, for these particular kids, a juvenile justice system approach might not be warranted or the most healthy approach for all involved. The first case is a case that never was discovered, a perpetration of abuse by a teen on a younger boy, included to show how family life can contribute to acting out and how having done something that the culture considers to be a sex offense can haunt a child into adulthood. The second case shows how what might otherwise be seen as normative sexual play and games, when discovered in a child who was a victim of sexual abuse, can be interpreted as acting out or even sexual offending. The third case, much more complicated, shows how immaturity, loneliness, and an oversexualized younger child led a preteen into ongoing sexual play that looked like abuse to all the adults who subsequently came to know what was going on.

AM I A SEX OFFENDER?

Tom was 17 when I saw him, and he stated that he worried that he had been sexually abused when he was younger, although he had no memory of this. He had come from a very chaotic household with few boundaries. His father had left the home when he was 9 and his mother had brought a rather verbally abusive man and two daughters into their household for a couple of years. Tom, a quiet and composed boy, never got in trouble with Norman, his mother's explosive boyfriend, but his brother Rick, who was louder, more daring, and more argumentative, would antagonize Norman who would hit him and chase him around the house. Tom's mother, it seemed, felt helpless in the face of these tirades. While living in this madhouse, Tom felt like he lost his mother and gained a horrible father figure and a crazy sister. Norman's daughter Doreen, would visit on weekends and talk sex constantly with the boys. She was "obsessed with sex." But it wasn't just Doreen; the household itself seemed oversexualized, with Tom's mother discussing with both her boys her sex life with Norman, and encouraging her boys to become "full-blooded masculine men" by buying them posters of girls in bikinis to put up in their room.

Tom's mother brought him to therapy upon advice from the school during his senior year, at a time when he was spending a lot of time on his own, binge eating, and playing guitar endlessly while his mother was staying away many nights at her new boyfriend's house. I recognized that Tom was way too isolated with too little care for a boy that age and talked to his mother about this, with his permission. But even though his mother heard me and agreed, reports from Tom indicated that she still was leaving him alone in their condo way too much. The Department of Children and Familes would not intervene with a boy this age, so capable, and a mother who seemed to drop in just enough.

A recurring theme, then, in therapy was how difficult it was for Tom to have to take care of himself as well as how angry he was at his mother, but we also pursued Tom's idea that he might have been sexually abused by Doreen and forgotten it. His brother told him that Doreen had forced him to have sex with her and Tom wondered if the same had happened to him only he didn't remember. Therapy talk also focused on whether Tom was essentially a bad person.

Tom: I don't know. I just feel as if I have all these aggressive feelings inside, like I could hurt someone. I can picture myself raping and hurting a woman, although I would never do that.

Therapist: How often do you picture that?

T: Not very often. But I have and it's sort of scary.

Th: A woman has hurt you. Maybe you get revenge in your fantasies. Let's try to understand what the fantasy means to you before dismissing it as wrong. It's there for a reason.

I came to see Tom as being very overstimulated by his childhood experiences, akin to being traumatized, as well as continuing to be overstimulated and confused by his mother's sex talk. After much discussion of his family life past and present, we both came to see his worries about being sexually abused as a sign that indeed he felt abused. "You may never remember or know whether you were actually sexually abused, but what happened to you as a child was a form of sexual abuse," I said. He was all ears. I explained that the overstimulating stepsister who was brought into the house, the constant references to sex, his mother's lack of boundaries, and her current discussion of her sex life with her boyfriend was all too much for a boy to hear, overwhelming and exciting, and also even abusive, even if no one ever touched him. The trouble was, it was still happening. When his mom returned to the condo, if they didn't avoid each other, the only intimacy he got was talks with his mother at his bedside, listening to her stories of boyfriends, sex, and romance, men's penis sizes, and sexual adventures with this guy or that. He longed for the attention and seemed to be able to get it only by talking about sex with her.

Then an incident was revealed. Tom was supposed to go with his mother to visit his aunt at his aunt's house but told me he didn't want to go. When pushed to explain why, he shared that he "sort of" sexually abused his cousin when he was little and was afraid to see him. I told Tom that it was very brave of him to disclose that to me and that we would talk about it and try to figure out what had motivated him to do that, but first, could he tell me more of what happened? What had happened was that Tom, at about 11 or 12 years old, was left to play with his cousin, who was

5 or 6. He really liked this cousin and they would set up army figures in patterns all over the house. He didn't remember how he
initiated it, but over the week that he stayed at his aunt's house
with his mother, he touched this little boy's penis and had the little
boy touch his penis back. He couldn't remember how he felt at the
time, and as we explored the experience, it seemed clear that he
got no sexual excitement out of remembering that time, only
shame and guilt. He thought of himself as a sex offender and as a
horrible, horrible person.

This was clearly sexual abuse. But it seemed to me that calling
Tom a sexual offender at the age of 12 was extreme. Here was a
boy who had been trying to deal with all sorts of confusing sexual
feelings in a household where acting out and sexual discussion
were ever present and overstimulating. He liked his cousin; he felt
comfortable with him; he had been his play partner for the week
he was visiting his cousin's house; and he had sexual feelings that
he found difficult not to act on. What he did was wrong. But it was
understandable given his circumstances in childhood. And the
fact that he felt so enormously guilty and had never done anything
remotely like that again seemed to be a good sign.

Tom: I ruined his life.

Therapist: You may have hurt him, but we don't know if this act ruined his life.

T: It was unforgivable.

Th: You feel very, very terrible about what you did. And yet you were also only 11 or
12, with your own struggles to deal with about boundaries, and a family that
made light of boundaries at best

T: It can't be my mother's fault that I did this horrible thing.

Th: No, you did it. But you were a child. You weren't fully developed yet and didn't
have the capacity for restraint that you have today or that you'll have 10 years
from now. Your household made it difficult for you to restrain yourself from
doing something you knew was wrong, for using your cousin to play sexually.
Playing around sexually at that age was perfectly fine; using your cousin to do
it wasn't.

Tom went with his mother to visit his aunt and cousin and reported back that his cousin seemed fine. He said that his cousin was happy to see him and friendly. He also noticed that his cousin, now 11, had a bunch of friends in the neighborhood with whom he hung out.

Th: So, your cousin seems okay in lots of ways, not as if his life was ruined.

T: Yeah, it's really odd to see him that way.

Th: In your mind, you pictured him to be the victim that you also pictured yourself to be.

T: Yeah, but could I have still ruined his life? Like later in life might it all come back to him and he could end up in a mental hospital?

Th: It's a possibility that this experience might have made him vulnerable to other problems. But from what you describe, it sounds like he weathered it okay so far. While what you did was not healthy for him to experience, it was just a week in his life, and it wasn't the kind of sexual abuse that you hear of causing the most trauma—a father, a man he trusts, raping him, under coercive experiences, or using him repeatedly for his sexual pleasure. What you did happened in a relatively short time, and it may have hurt him, but statistics show that for boys, being sexually abused in these milder forms does not lead in the majority of cases to long-term psychological disorders like depression or anxiety.

T: Really?

Th: It seems as if you might want to continue to punish yourself about this because it was so wrong.

T: I can't just make excuses.

Th: No. But you can live with it and see yourself as a child back then who did something bad and a young adult right now who knows better and would never hurt a child like that. Is that true about yourself right now?

T: Yes, absolutely.

Th: This way you're deciding on what kind of man you want to be.

The phrase "the man you want to be" is an important one I use with late adolescents.

So, with Tom, the issue he brought up earlier, that he might have been sexually abused when younger, turned into the issue that he might be a sex offender. Both were true in a sense, that as a child living in such a chaotic and oversexualized house, he had felt like a victim, helpless to stop the onslaught of overwhelming information and activity that came his way; and having lived in that space, he brought those feelings, trying to master them, into his relationship with an innocent kid, becoming the aggressor, the one who did the overstimulating rather than remaining a victim of it. He had a conscience and knew it was wrong, and his enormous guilt prevented him from acting out again. The remaining task was how to be sexually assertive without being an aggressor, an offender, a sexist man. We continued to work on that.

DISTINGUISHING PLAY FROM ABUSE

As noted earlier, children who have been sexually abused may not be allowed sexual play or experimentation because their play alerts parents and officials that they may be acting out. It's a tricky issue because sexually abused children need to have positive sexual experiences and sometimes have more interest and energy to devote to sexual expression at earlier ages than children who have not been abused, whether it's in the form of reenactment or just exploration. Seen as tainted children, their play is worrisome. Will they introduce to an innocent child new and adultlike sexual behaviors? Will they coerce younger children as they were coerced, or can they be allowed the same normative experiences as other children?

Ashley and Carey had been living together for about 6 months. Ashley, 10-years-old, and her mother moved into the apartment where Carey, 8-years-old, and her mother had lived for quite some time. This move was not rash. Their mothers had been seeing each other off and on for some time and had decided to take the relationship to the next level, opening it up to the lives of their children when they moved in together. Ashley didn't know that her mother had been having a relationship with another woman, only that Carey's mom was her mom's best friend. She also knew that her mother didn't like her father very much anymore and that she was not permitted to go to her father's house. She was, in fact, only allowed supervised visits with her father at her grand-mother's house because she had been sexually abused in her father's home by a teenage boy living there. Her father didn't pro-tect her from the son of his girlfriend and although the son was now in treatment, the Department of Children and Families did not think it wise for Ashley to have to stay in the same home with this boy on visits to her father's house. Ashley was in therapy for the sexual abuse and both moms, one of whom had been sexually abused herself as a child, seemed sensitive to her needs.

Ashley's 11th birthday party was coming up and both girls were excited about it. Ashley was allowed to have six girls sleep over that night, and Carey was allowed to be there. But the night before, something happened and the party was canceled. Carey's mom walked in on Ashley and Carey in bed together, Ashley on top of Carey, humping her leg. She told the girls to "stop it right now" and sent them to separate rooms, although they had been sharing the same bedroom. Then Carey's mom called the police and asked what she should do about this. That was probably a mistake. But she didn't know where else to go for advice regarding her daughter and what she perceived had been done to her. She was angry at herself and her partner for allowing this sexually abused, now sexually acting-out girl to have unsupervised access to her daughter. And, having been abused herself as a child, Carey's mom immediately determined Ashley's behavior to be coercive and a sexual offense. The police came to talk to both moms and the next day members of a special sex abuse team came to interview both girls, who were kept home from school. They advised canceling the slumber party until everyone was sure that other little girls would be safe with Ashley, who was portrayed as a possible sexual predator. Carey was assigned a therapist to whom she could talk about what happened and who could address trauma symptoms if any arose; Ashley was assigned a therapy group to attend, in addition to her individual therapy, a special group for sexually acting-out kids. When I heard this story from a therapist I supervised, I was astonished, then outraged. Was this a sex offense? Was it "sexually acting-out behavior"? What would these two girls learn from this experience?

When I saw Tom in individual therapy, it was helpful to be able to discuss his abuse of his cousin apart from any action on the part of social services or the courts. There was no danger, and so I didn't need to report him. More often, when children are labeled sex offenders, there is a lot more to deal with in individual therapy than their feelings and motivations. They are part of a system that defines them a certain way and invites self-condemnation, shame, and embarrassment. What does it mean to one's growing sense of self, as a 12-year-old, already uncomfortable with sexual feelings, already feeling dirty from having experienced abuse, to be interviewed by police? To have a party canceled because nobody trusts you? I would imagine that a child would not only feel that she did something wrong, but that she was a terrible, terrible person, to say the least.

What Ashley and Carey did together is not atypical for girls their age. This was a case where curiosity might indeed be the appropriate word. Adjusting to a new conception of their mothers as partners and lovers, perhaps the two girls were stimulated by this knowledge. Family therapists who see blended families are well aware of the times when a newly sexual parent is difficult for a child to bear; especially when this parent is not acting the same way with the child's other parent. The interviewers who came the next day did not see Carey as manipulated by Ashley exactly. She, like Ashley, had participated in the game they were playing, husband and wife, that led to the humping. Once caught, both seemed to feel guilty and ashamed, but who was to know how Carey felt before then? Did she imagine herself a full and consenting play partner of this other girl? If Ashley was a leader and Carey a follower, did Ashley take advantage of Carey? Or did Carey introduce the game and Ashley follow? Did Ashley seek out a younger child over whom she could exert power? Or was Carey a convenient choice for a game that got sexual, given that the girls played together most every day?

The age difference makes this more problematic. Older children do have power over younger children. But is this similar to the power that an adult has over a child? I don't think so. If therapists come with assumptions that sexual coercion in children is sex offending, they may read too much into an older child's play with a younger child. If they work from a model of bullying, then it becomes possible to see that older children can bully younger children into playing games they don't want to play. Younger children may want to do things to impress the older child. There's also a different scenario to consider, the immature older child.

THE COMPLICIT YOUNGER CHILD
AND THE IMMATURE OLDER CHILD

When an adult or adolescent abuses a younger child, over time, the younger child may look forward in some ways to the experience and attention, and grow to have sexual interests herself. In the end, she feels complicit in the abuse and more ashamed than if she had been totally coerced. Of course pedophiles play on this phenomenon and find ways to make a child feel complicit, as if it's a game between the two of them. But sometimes, between children, there is mutual interest. In the following case, it was the younger child who had been sexually abused and who may have led the way for the older child to become involved with her sexually. Of course, the older child ought to have stepped back and refused, and yet both were lonely and their play seemed fun, exciting, and imaginative while also sexual. It led to Marissa's arrest.

Marissa, an eighth grader, was arrested for the sexual activities she engaged in with her neighbor, Kelly, who was in 3rd grade. They had only been neighbors for about a year. Marissa's military family moved a lot and she was rarely in one city or school for more than two years. Marissa had settled into her middle school for seventh grade, making friends with a group of boys and girls who hung out together in the local park after school. This was a somewhat advanced crowd that had tried smoking weed and drinking. And Marissa had been going out with a boy in this crowd, another seventh grader. Although they called it "going out," they mainly hung out together at the park and each other's houses and sexually had done little more than kiss. He wanted to have sex but she wouldn't, although some girls in her school and her crowd had already had sex with boys. So her boyfriend broke up with her and started dating her best friend. She and her best friend had stopped talking, but Marissa had heard from other friends that her best friend and ex-boyfriend were now having sex, and she felt bad about this. Even though she wasn't ready to have sex, she felt babyish and rejected for not doing it. There were many ways in which she wasn't ready. In fact, she still liked playing lots of games she played as a child, and did so with her next-door neighbor, Kelly. They played Clue and Monopoly and in the summer, hung out in Kelly's backyard pool. It was only 12 feet around, but a great way to have fun and keep cool in the summer. They also hung out in Kelly's basement with some of Kelly's other friends.

The games in that basement often were spun in a sexualized way. Alone together, Kelly and Marissa would play dress-up in a way that exposed parts of their bodies and made them look like prostitutes. They would also do sexy dances together to music. With Kelly's other friends, Marissa had organized a strip poker game. She also helped Kelly orchestrate a "marriage" of sorts, where two 8-year-olds, a boy and Kelly, got undressed and attempted intercourse via her instruction, but just touching his penis to her vaginal area. Their activities got exposed when at Marissa's birthday party, Kelly acted strangely in front of the older kids there. All the teens were dancing, and Kelly, thinking she was fitting in, started doing some sexy dancing with Marissa, touching her butt and actually fondling her breasts in front of the other seventh graders, who saw it and said, "Ew, gross." Kelly ran from the party crying. When her mother talked to her, she told her mother what she and Marissa had been playing at.

In therapy, Marissa's parents were mortified by what she had done. Marissa's parents described a rather healthy upbringing. There didn't seem to be any indication of abuse nor overexposure to porn or overly mature TV shows. But there was a boundary issue. Marissa was a "Daddy's girl," said her mother. And sometimes, her mother would call Marissa's father her "boyfriend" when she was teasing Marissa. She'd also tease her husband by calling Marissa his "girlfriend." As therapists, it's sometimes very difficult to get a feel for boundary violations in the home, but this was a big clue, and one could expect there were other indications that once Marissa became a preteen and possibly before, Mom and Dad had sexualized the relationship.

Marissa herself was very ashamed of what she did. She said, "I'm sorry" to the therapist and cried, asking, "Why did I do that?" It seemed that she felt that what she did was separate from how she thought of herself and that she felt very, very bad. What's wonderful was that she was not making excuses for what she did. Those who work with sexually acting-out boys are familiar with the defensive excuse making and victim blaming. Marissa blamed herself. She ignored the fact that Kelly was so young because Kelly was her best friend, the person she liked to play with the most. Because of this focus on Marissa's actions, it took a while to understand that this 8-year-old, Kelly, was not a stereotypical victim.

Marissa's victim, Kelly, was already a sexual abuse victim who had been in therapy for her abuse. For several years she had been groomed, initiated into sexual activity, and then abused by two teenage cousins who lived in the neighborhood and who taught her adult acts in a "friendly" although manipulative way. Kelly, though uncomfortable at first, became what she perceived as a willing partner to these boys and believed them to be her secret "boyfriends." Exposed and introduced to such feelings and acts at an early age, Kelly mastered this experience by repeating it with Marissa. She was perky and lively and a leader at school. An outgoing child, she actually was the one who brought up the subject of strip poker to Marissa. As if they were two teenagers, she and Marissa had had countless talks about sex and boys, Kelly advising Marissa as Marissa struggled with her mixed feelings about her ex-boyfriend now having sex with her former best friend. Marissa treated this 8-year-old as an equal, not out of motivation to take advantage of her, but because she seemed like an equal. It became clear, in talking with Marissa, that she didn't see Kelly as a child younger than she but instead as a best friend to share stories and experiments with. Kelly initiated many of their acts together. Marissa clearly also wanted a safer place to act on her sexual feelings, given her rejection of her boyfriend. Kelly, sexualized from her abuse, Marissa, vulnerable and sexually interested, both of them girls, felt safer with each other, until Kelly felt humiliated by Marissa's friends.

In therapy with someone like Marissa, it's important to explain that age differences may mean more than they seem to, while acknowledging that Kelly was also seemingly grown-up in many ways. It would be wrong to help Marissa create a narrative of this event that pictured Kelly as a sexual aggressor and initiator, even if she had experienced Kelly in this way. It would be better to talk with Marissa about how she was invited to play a role with Kelly and what in her life made her vulnerable and interested in playing this role.

It was also important to normalize the sexual feelings that Marissa was having. These teens and preteens need to know that confusion and issues regarding control over one's sexual feelings are simply a part of having sexual feelings. For Marissa in particular, it would be good to say, "Many kids your age feel sexy and have sexual desires that they're not quite sure what to do with." A therapist could add, "Some kids masturbate in their beds at night." A therapist could also add that a lot of same-sex sexual play and games occur during this time of life, including games of strip poker or "pretend" make-out sessions and that in these sessions or role-plays sometimes one or both of the kids get excited. The problem with this play was that Kelly had been sexually abused and she seemed to be way too open to engaging in teenager-type behaviors with older kids. A second problem was that Marissa didn't see that Kelly really was younger and fooled herself (that's sometimes a good word to use with kids) into believing that Kelly was a peer. In discussion, the therapist looked at both sides, saying, "It's not safe or healthy for Kelly, only 8-years-old, to be reliving all the things she did with that adolescent boy. We want her to stop thinking so much about sex and try to develop other interests, right? And it's not right for you, Marissa, to be trying out new things with an 8-year-old, although it may feel a whole lot safer than trying things out with a strange boy at school. We're not saying that you shouldn't try things out. But Kelly was not a healthy choice for you. And it wasn't because she's a girl. It's because she was younger and she had experienced some abuse that she needed to reflect on and work through rather than act out with you."

FROM PROBLEMATIC BEHAVIORS TO SEXUAL OFFENSES: OUR BELIEFS AND THE COST TO CHILDREN

There are pretty much just a handful of rules that a therapist can teach a child or teenager about what makes certain sexual behaviors abusive or problematic: Does it harm someone else? Does it harm yourself? Does it get in the way of other activities? Is it coercive or does it involve force or manipulation? Is there an age, size, or power difference between the kids? These simple rules cover a range of abuses and can help a therapist focus conversations in a way that emphasizes the client's health and well-being as well as hopes that the client could take the perspective of or have empathy for the person they might have taken advantage of. In fact, it's important to understand the whole child and not just the behavior. If a therapist establishes a good relationship with either the initiator or the victim, finding out about their lives, their concerns, their ways of coping, there are always moments in which the abuse situation can be woven into the narrative that is coconstructed with a client about his or her life without keeping it front and center at all times. But a therapist can't forget about it; it's important that these experiences become integrated.

Treating these sexually acting-out experiences as behaviors with meaning addresses another problem, which is that many of these children who act out, cross boundaries, show disrespect, manipulate, threaten, and abuse often come from homes that have had an incredible amount of sexualization present and few boundaries. One preteen boy who had been sent to residential treatment for abusing younger boys in his neighborhood came from a home in which his mother would lie around naked, passed out on the living room couch, while kids in the neighborhood came and went. Another 8-year-old lived in a home where he had witnessed his mother having sex with several different men at different times. Sometimes these more incredible boundary violations produce an overstimulated child; other times it just frightens them.

Of course, many children in horrific situations like this do grow up to abuse in their teen years, and residential placements have staff who understand how to work with kids like these, know when cognitive treatment is appropriate and when teens can understand and work more interpersonally using the support of a therapist to try to gain insight into themselves. But there are other children lost in a limbo of foster homes, who have experienced abuse and acted out in a way that was too mild to warrant residential placement, but have become unadoptable because of families' fears of taking in a potential sex offender. This is when our culture's fears of sex offenders can really hurt a child's chances to grow up healthy and loved.

For example, a student of mine worked with Aaron, who was only 9 when he was sent to a residential home. At age 8 he and his sisters had been taken out of their biological home where he had been sexually abused by his stepfather, and he in turn had sexually abused his two younger sisters. It was his abusive behavior rather than his father's abuse of him that led authorities to look into the family. His younger sister in kindergarten had tried to stick crayons in her vagina and told her teacher that her brother did that to her. The Department of Children and Families investigated and discovered that not only had Aaron been playing doctor with his two younger sisters, he had been tying them up and rubbing up against them. As the investigation went on, it became clear that the three children lived in a house where they had seen porn on TV, had seen their mother and her boyfriends having sex, and in which the new stepfather had taught Aaron how to give him oral sex and had Aaron watch as he sexually molested the two younger girls.

Aaron was a sweet boy whom all the staff cared about. He had been at the residential center for a year and had learned to control his emotional outbursts well. These had never been aggressive anyway. They were just signs of being overwhelmed by the rules, the sadness of his losses, and the feeling that he was bad and deserved to have been separated from his family. He looked forward to leaving the center and joining his two sisters in a preadoptive home where they had spent the last year. The couple who brought his sisters for visits and who occasionally took him home for a weekend were very nice and he had already started calling them Mom and Dad, mimicking his sisters. His sisters adored him and were eager for him to come live with them in this new home. And then the floor dropped out of his world. The adoptive parents decided that they wouldn't adopt Aaron, only his sisters. They thought he was too much of a risk. They were scared of him and what he might become. They loved those two girls now and wanted to protect them, and they interpreted the girls' love for their brother as sick and likely to lead to him once again having power over them.

How does a therapist talk to parents like these who already are doing something wonderful by adopting the two girls? How can one encourage them to take Aaron home without laying on the guilt? "Don't you realize," a therapist may want to scream, "that at 9 he is very unadoptable and that you may be his last chance? Don't you realize he also loves his sisters and he's made great gains in therapy?"

What made them change their mind? Aaron had been at their preadoptive home for visits with them and had become overstimulated by something on TV and started talking about sex to his sisters. The parents were in the room and told Aaron that was inappropriate, but this scared them. And they had begun thinking that they would be taking in a child who would need a lot more than his once-a-week therapy could provide. "We're not equipped" and "we're not therapists," they told Aaron's therapist. She offered them the chance to work together with Aaron in therapy so that she could help them know what to say when he was inappropriate or to help him control his words. But they were adamant. They didn't want to adopt him. They had made a connection with his sisters. Everything was going so well at home. Why introduce a boy with so many problems into the mix?

When I heard about this case, I felt deeply that this boy could have improved in a loving family. Here was a kid who had won the hearts of several staff members, who recognized what was wrong with what he did, and reflected on things he needed to work on.

Though likely to become overstimulated too easily, he had not acted out on any of the kids or staff during the year he was in residential placement. I also realized it would have been wrong for the therapist to pressure the parents any more than she had.

What was left to do with Aaron in therapy but to sit with him in his grief? He became a shell of a kid for months, although joining in the center's activities. His verbal explosions came back for a while, triggered by other kids' overstimulating behaviors and his need to shut them out. It was impossible to explain why the preadoptive parents didn't adopt him, although it was left to his therapist to do so: "They felt that two children were enough right now. They felt that your sisters needed their full attention so they could help them deal with what had happened to them. They didn't know you. If they had gotten to know you better, they would have grown to care about you like all the staff here do." Aaron wanted to know if he would ever have a family of his own, and he was assured that the staff was working to find him one and that he would still be able to visit his sisters.

Aaron was moved to a temporary foster home and we lost track of him. But it was incredibly sad to think that he might never be adopted, a kid who was fun and lovable and able to work on his behavior, but always tainted by others' perception that he was a sex offender and that he might again offend.

HOW IMPORTANT IS THE DISTINCTION
BETWEEN PLAY AND ABUSE?

If it were up to me, I would not permit any children to be called sex offenders. *Sex offender* is a term for a criminal; it often evokes a knee-jerk response that we should lock them up and throw away the key. It encourages district attorneys to advocate for teens to be tried in adult court, thereby contributing to the demise of a juvenile justice system that once envisioned rehabilitation and support as its mainstays.

Sexually acting-out youths is a much better way to refer to these children and makes room for a range of behaviors that should be addressed. I would also encourage all who work with children who act out sexually to explore the range of environmental influences that encourage this acting out, from inappropriate exposure to the media to their own abuse.

Also, the importance of defining normative sexual behavior in children can't be overstated. In all other areas of children's lives we take a developmental stance, looking at what sorts of behaviors are appropriate at different ages. Children don't discover their genitals at 14, nor do they experience their first sexual feelings at that point in time. And yet they are given so little information and sex education before then to help them to understand that these feelings may be normal and that sexual pleasure is a good thing.

* * * *

I would argue that children have a right to this education, education that continues through their school years and which helps them to process not only their own feelings and fantasies but the input from an overly sexualized world. Our culture's obsession with and simultaneous fear of sexuality hurts children. My predictions for the future are bleak:

- Most children will have too little sex education to be able to understand or cope well with feelings as they arise. Many will grow up ashamed of their bodies, with small nagging worries about size, shape, performance, and the normality of their desires.
- Most sexually abused children will grow up to think of themselves as damaged from the abuse. Others throughout their childhood will try to shield them from sexual material rather than talking to them about it.

Knowing only unhealthy and uncaring sex, they will be left on their own to try to find healthy and caring sex.

• Most sexually acting-out children will grow up thinking that sex is dirty and they are bad. They will be treated as potential sex offenders. Rather than being helped to establish views and behaviors that are normative for our culture, they will be kept from sexual material because it might overstimulate them to abuse or act out again.

Therapists alone can't provide the much-needed space to discuss sex and sexual feelings. But while our repressive, overstimulating society keeps us from providing a wide-reaching sex education, therapy is a good place to start.

CHAPTER FIVE

Teenage Girls in Therapy

Sexual Concerns and Issues

The sexual issues or supposed sexual issues of teenage girls get a lot of press in the media. It would seem that the culture can't get enough stories of girls gone wild, friends with benefits, girls performing oral sex in the hallways of middle schools, girls kissing other girls for boys' enjoyment, and girls' first sexual experiences (preventing them, describing them, controlling them). If we are honest with ourselves, we ought to admit that this is rarely for the purpose of protecting the vulnerable in a difficult world and more frequently for entertainment value, journalists playing on the public's more prurient interests. We as therapists have a responsibility to look past both the glamorizing and catastrophizing around girls' sex lives to see real girls and what their concerns are. And when they are concerned about their sexual activity or when their sexual activity is of concern to us, this is usually symptomatic of other problems in their lives, such as the need for attention, the need to be noticed, the need to have someone in the world think they are special, the need to look tough, the need to belong. Therapists who talk to girls about sexual issues are more often than not going to have these conversations around these other deeper concerns rather than around the more moralistic topic of "too much too soon."

And yet gives need to take heed of media images and the cultural influences regarding what it means to be a girl. Their task in adolescence is to negotiate how to be a woman in this world and stay true to their interests, connections, and developing selves. This sometimes means that a therapist needs to discuss and criticize those outside influences head-on, know what's "hot," what a girl is reading in magazines, what she's seeing on TV, and help her to identify her own feelings, desires, and goals in the midst of the media barrage.

Girls come with a variety of knowledge and stances toward sexuality. While sex education in the schools is lacking, some girls are proactive and have learned quite a bit from discussion with friends, the Internet, reading, movies, magazines, and TV. Some know very little. With a girl who knows very little, it may be important to explore why she hasn't been interested in obtaining this information and how it came to be that before now she hasn't asked.

What are our goals as therapists when it comes to helping teens deal with issues of sex and sexuality? For girls, one of our goals must be to help them to discover their own desire in this mixed-up world of images and messages telling them how to be sexy while insisting they remain pure. And it's important to remember that understanding oneself as a sexual being is related to psychological health. In terms of prevention, we therapists must help a girl to develop the kind of awareness of herself and her surroundings that will help her to not do dangerous things. This means, particularly for adolescents, not to act on their feelings of worthlessness, depression, or anxiety, but to bring these feelings into session so that through talking about them they may make better choices out in the world. With these more global concerns in mind, we can look at some of the common issues among adolescent girls: ambivalence around intercourse ("should I or shouldn't I," as well as "everyone's doing it but me"); pregnancy and HIV scares; same sex attraction; powerful boyfriends; and wild, acting-out but unsatisfying sex.

AM I READY?

"Doing it" or deciding "when it's right" is still a huge topic among teen girls, although these discussions may be happening at younger and younger ages. Having intercourse is seen among girls as a rite of passage, an act with intense meaning, and, as research suggests, pretty disappointing in the flesh. The first time is glamorized in the movies and on TV, and the romance narrative that many girls buy into indicates that relationships lead up to this particular moment. It proves love and suggests a lasting relationship for some. For others sexual intercourse is an entry into an exciting teenage life of partying. It's accorded such meaning that for some girls it's easier to just get drunk and have it happen.

Therapists will want to de-emphasize an excessive focus on making the decision to do it or not so that "it" doesn't have to represent that a girl is an adult, that she's made a lifelong commitment, that she's a woman now, that she's popular, or that she's wanted. I recommend treating the act, not casually, but as part of a repertoire of adultlike sexual behaviors. The emphasis for the teen girl ought to be on what she feels comfortable with, what she wants to learn about herself or her relationship, and, most important, not just what having intercourse might mean to her, but what having a sexual relationship means.

In therapy I try not to support the cultural messages girls get that the first time ought to be special nor that girls should have sex with someone they love or plan to marry. Those feminine notions that wrap love and sex together into a pretty, Disneylike package have been shown to be harmful to girls. In the short run, girls who buy into the whole notion of romance are less likely to use contraception. In the long run, girls and women may stay with men who are harmful to them because they love them, putting their boyfriend's needs and preserving the relationship before their own well-being. When a girl buys into these fairy tales, it's easier to make the decision to have intercourse, and it happens soon after the word *love* is mentioned. Where else does the phrase "If you loved me you would . . ." come from?

But if a therapist has ruled out the "wait until you're married" or "wait until you're really in love" messages, then what message is coming across? When I think about exploration, play, and development as the focus of sex in childhood and adolescence, the message is clearer. Who better to play, explore, and develop with than someone whom girls trust, whom they like to "play with," whom they spend time with doing other things, whom they talk to, whom they care about, and who seems to care about them—in short, a friend. That's why it doesn't seem very problematic if a teenage girl decides to have her first intercourse experience with her best friend or a good friend, someone she knows, feels comfortable with, cares about, and can talk to, rather than with a boyfriend.

The "friends with benefits" phenomenon was described by teens interviewed by Benoit Denizet-Lewis (2004) for the *New York Times*. Most readers eager to jump on a new alarming-teen-sexual-trend bandwagon understood Denizet-Lewis to be writing about random hookups. But he was describing a range of behaviors from drunken hookups to very carefully planned sexual experiences between friends. In fact, most of the teens he spoke to did not see having sex with friends as a replacement for dating (most hoped to have a girlfriend or boyfriend some day), but something that teens did when they didn't have time for or didn't want to have a relationship with all those "relationship issues." Or so they thought. As Denizet-Lewis's teens discovered, having a friend with benefits did not prevent messy relationship issues from emerging. Denizet-Lewis also found that a lot of planning had gone on. These teens talked over the Internet about what they might do when together, even asking each other for boundaries—"What are you comfortable with?" One teen caller in an NPR show (Conan, 2004) said that among her friends, even though there was quite a bit of friends-with-benefits sexual activity, there was a lot of mutual planning beforehand—"What are we going to do?" and "What is it going to mean?"

If a girl wanted to have sex with a friend, I would warn her that such an intense experience might raise other expectations, and that the friendship might be at risk. But I would also emphasize that it's often a wise choice to have sex with someone you feel comfortable talking about sex with and someone you know cares for you and you trust.

There's also the issue of protection. Does a therapist bring it up? All the therapists I spoke with who work with adolescents ask them about protection as soon as they reveal anything about sex activity. I suppose we all feel responsible at that moment to make sure the particular adolescent has gotten a strong enough message about safe sex. And one can argue that it would be untherapeutic for a therapist to ignore this issue even if the client were ignoring it. So I do advocate asking about it, but I also advocate treating the ability to talk about contraception, knowledge about it, where to get it, and how to use it, as one indication that the girl is taking care of herself with regard to her sexual activity.

Deirdre and I moved into a conversation about sex during a conversation about drugs. A friend of hers had mixed drugs and alcohol at a sleepover where a number of girls had been drinking and had passed out. Deirdre didn't know whether to call 911, get her mother downstairs to check out her friend, or just stay up all night monitoring her friend's breathing. We talked about her feeling responsible in this situation and how important it was to recognize when things were getting difficult and beyond her control. We also talked about how frightened and responsible she felt and about the patterns in her life that led to her assuming more responsibility than she was ready for. This was an important discussion because she would often argue in therapy that she was just as capable as any adult, given the responsibilities she had already taken on. But toward the end of the discussion I asked if she had been doing drugs. She replied she had smoked some weed because everyone was doing it but that she didn't really like it and she didn't like that she did it because everyone else was doing it, instead of making her own decisions.

This revelation made it easy for me to also ask about sex.

Therapist: I'm wondering if you might get involved (or might have gotten involved) with sex that way, just going along with what's happening, going with the flow, and only thinking about it afterward and maybe asking, "Did I really want to do that?"

Deirdre: (excitedly) Yes, that almost happened.

Th: How?

D: We were talking and Jack asked, "Do you want to?" and I said, "Yeah, like whatever." So we made a plan to do it on Saturday night but then I thought I didn't want to, I wasn't ready, so I told him we should wait.

Th: Yeah, like whatever? [*reflected as a question*]

D: Yeah. I was just like, sure, everyone does it, why not now, whatever.

While I wanted Deirdre to make thoughtful decisions in her life, I wanted to make sure in our conversation that she didn't see me as an advocate of waiting just for the sake of waiting. As I stated earlier, I don't think it's wise for adolescents to think of the first time as a huge experience they have to orchestrate as if it were their first prom; on the other hand, I'd rather that she went into any kind of sex with more reflection than "yeah whatever."

Th: So what were your concerns that led you to not do it on Saturday?

D: I guess I was concerned that I might regret it. And I knew that our relationship was kind of shaky. I mean, I don't know if we're going to break up over the summer. And I know that a lot of people, once they start doing it, that's all they ever do together. I just wasn't ready.

Deirdre was smart and brought up an important point. I stored it away for future reference and asked, "That's all they ever do because they want to do it all the time? Or that's all they ever do because they're bored and what else is there to do?" "Bored," she said authoritatively. I praised her for thinking it through, but was careful not to praise her for making the "right decision."

Deirdre's decision to not do it on one occasion probably meant that she might be doing it soon. So I brought up the topic of contraception.

Th: Would you use protection? Where would you get it?

D: Well, my sister's on the Pill and she just leaves it around the house.

Th: (quicky with shock and surpise) You know you can't just take your sister's pills. There has to be a special prescription for you and you have to take it every day for it to work.

Because Deirdre was such a competent young person and had an idea of herself as being quite aware, the one who gave her friends information, I regretted jumping in so quickly to talk information. I added more gently, a question she could answer in the affirmative, "Did you know that a doctor would give you a prescription for the Pill or some other contraception without telling your mother?" But she didn't know this. "Really?" she asked. "Yes," I replied. "For teenagers, pretty much everything you talk about with your doctor is confidential. Your doctor should have told you that."

It seemed as if it was time for a little sex education without implying that she was ready to go out there next Saturday night and do it. I wanted to convey that there is a lot of information to know that goes into making the decision and maybe it isn't just a matter of how ready a girl is. "Do you know about the different kinds of contraceptives there are?" I asked. "Yeah, they talked about it in school," she replied. "That's excellent," I said. And then I went on in some detail because it was a way of talking about a tricky issue. The tricky issue is this—most teenage girls in my experience are unwilling to explore their own bodies, even masturbate, but are willing to let a boy do whatever he wants to them. Some are disgusted with their bodies and some just feel their body doesn't belong to them. Self-objectification theory (Fredrickson & Roberts, 1997) argues that the culture teaches girls to be good sex objects in a way that alienates them from their bodies and the feelings their bodies can have.

That's why I went ahead and asked Deirdre, "I'm wondering if they showed you the diaphragm. Girls your age don't generally like to use that because it takes a real knowledge about your body to use it and presence of mind to step aside and say to a guy, 'Wait a minute while I go put this in, and now, where's that cream?' In saying it that way, I gave her information she might not know—that the diaphragm is ineffective without the cream or jelly. I also brought up an image of a girl so aware of her body and her desires that she could use the diaphragm and think ahead. "Condoms are awkward for the same reason, right?" I continued. "I mean, even though girls like to leave it to a boy, the condoms aren't as effective if you don't use them with a cream or a jelly." Recent research on girls watching an episode of *Friends* in which a condom was not effective showed only two thirds of them actually getting the message intended by the scene, that condoms aren't completely effective (Collins, Elliot, Berry, Kanouse, & Hunter, 2003; Collins, Elliot, Berry, Kanouse, Kunkel, Hunter, & Miu, 2004). With all the talk kids get about safe sex, one would think condoms are the be-all and end-all—but it's important for them to get a picture of how ineffective they sometimes can be.

Thinking about contraception or reflecting on one's readiness to have sex is sometimes antithetical to a girl's desire to make the whole thing happen spontaneously. I've had girls say to me, "I sort of knew I was going to" and I've said back, "What got in the way of your actually making a decision about this instead of just sort of knowing you were going to?" Girls want to be "swept away," in the words of Carol Cassell (1984), who wrote about this phenomenon in adult women. And yet they want to think ahead, too.

Allowing oneself to be swept away usually comes with "knowing he's the right one." A therapist can try to lend perspective to a girl who believes she's met her life partner at age 15, but it's not easy. Shandra had had sex at 13 with her boyfriend, Carlos, who was 16. They were in love and she told me that she thought this was a way to prove her love to him. It sounded to me like a real relationship that went the way of most real relationships at age 13 except that they also had had sex. When I saw Shandra, she and Carlos had already broken up. She reported that she regretted her decision now because she knew that he wasn't the right guy, and the right one would be coming into her life in the future. And now she wouldn't have a first time with him. I suggested that maybe it's difficult to know in your teens if someone really is the right one, given there's a lot more growing up to do, a lot more experiencing of life ahead. Rather than challenging the notion that the first time ought to be special, I suggested we talk about all the things that she learned from that experience that she could use in the future.

It's wonderful to be able to talk about contraception when the matter isn't urgent. So I asked whether Shandra left the contraception decisions up to Carlos? She said yes, and I asked if she thought that was a good idea now. She generally thought it was a good idea because her boyfriend had been responsible and didn't want her to get pregnant, but she talked about a couple of pregnancy scares. I told her that not all boys would take on that responsibility and that it was good that she saw that as an important feature in a guy. But even so, I added, when one partner in the couple slacks off, the other person has to be on top of that contraception issue. We then explored how it would be possible for her to take charge of that. How would she get information? How would she get to know her body well enough to understand contraception? How could she actually get condoms or the Pill and have them in the house without her mother freaking out?

And we also talked about her goal to have sex with someone in a lasting relationship, not someone like Carlos whom she had only seen for seven months. "What is a lasting relationship?" I asked. "How long will it last? If you mean years, then at what point do you know that this is going to last instead of just feeling that you want it to last because you like him so much?" I tried to introduce to her the issue of self-deception as well as the idea that there's a period in a relationship when you have a total crush on a guy and may not be so clear-headed. Feeling that this guy's the one and knowing it are totally different things.

Discussing heart versus head versus body is an interesting way for teens to talk about their sexual decision making. I don't really believe these things are separate, but the teens do, and they often talk that way. In sexual decision making, it may clarify what's going on to have a teen girl talk about what her body is saying to her (tuning in to her body), what she knows intellectually to be true, and where her heart (her emotions) is leading her. Talking in this way may help her to clarify ambivalence and where it arises within her, rather than having her project all the no's on her parents, society, and even you.

ANXIETY AROUND SEX

One of the primary ways I've experienced girls bringing up sex in therapy is through a panic about either being pregnant or getting AIDS. In every situation where this has happened, the girl was not pregnant and did not have AIDS, but the important thing was that she was bringing her anxiety in for me to hold. When this happens, therapists need to contain the anxiety so that the teen herself can run through options for action. And sometimes it may be wise to view the dramatic and heart-wrenching fear and self-loathing as a form of self-punishment. Therapists need to listen for self-punitive talk, talk that indicates that a girl thinks of herself as bad or a "slut" or dirty and deserving of punishment. And when that happens, reflecting on how harsh she is on herself can help to alleviate the anxiety as well as making room for her to think more rationally about actions she might take to discover if she is pregnant or has contracted AIDS.

Libby and Monique, two teen girls I saw separately, both had AIDS scares, and each presented with overwhelming anxiety I needed to contain. Libby was attending an alternative high school in her town and would party on the weekends with kids she didn't know from other schools and areas nearby. Monique was attending a boarding school for teens with learning disabilities and went home for Christmas break to spend time presumably with her family but mostly, day in and day out, with her boyfriend, Randall, whom she had left behind. What's similar about these two teens was the session they had after sex, when they were in a complete panic about having contracted HIV/AIDS.

Willingly and drunkenly, Libby had had sex at a party with a cute guy whom she didn't know. Monique, home for break, had had sex with her boyfriend several times before he confessed to her that while she was away at school, he had two-timed her with another girl. Monique considered this girl to be a "ho" (someone who had sex with a lot of different guys in her neighborhood); "Everyone knows that about her." I didn't know whether the other girl was as sexually active as Monique thought she was or whether this was some way to put down the other girl to her boyfriend and claim herself superior, given that his two-timing had made her feel inferior and unimportant. It's sometimes so difficult for girls to blame their boyfriends in these circumstances because they don't want to lose them. So they'll shift the blame to the "other woman" and buy into an age-old idea that women are temptresses and men hapless victims to their seductions. But Monique was totally upset that Randall could have put her at risk for a sexual disease by doing it with some "ho," and not simply totally upset that he had two-timed her.

Both of these girls had worked themselves into such a frenzy before coming into my office that each was absolutely certain that they had contracted HIV/AIDS. It's extremely difficult to address underlying concerns when a kid is that anxious, because any straying from what they see as the focus, "What will I do if I have AIDS?," is felt as unsympathetic. For Libby, I saw her underlying concern as being about her going out and having sex with people she didn't know. Libby generally thought of herself as bad, immoral, and a slut. I knew this because of our weekly conversations about her bulimia and the harsh language she used about herself with me quite frequently. She had so little self-sympathy, so little self-love or understanding. To herself, she was just bad, bad, bad, a horrible person with "absolutely no self-control," "ugly," "unlovable," "too much" for her family, and even "evil."

Monique was different. A super-tough girl from the neighborhood, with no girlfriends and only her boyfriend to hold onto, she was in pain about her boyfriend's infidelity and unable to express her vulnerability and hurt in any way but fear and blame. Of course, she must have been questioning herself about having made the wrong decision in trusting a guy like this, but he was all she had, and a back-home anchor for her that her parents weren't while she was away at this boarding school.

Monique's hurt was huge, and yet in some way she conveyed that merely being hurt about being two-timed wasn't enough, and that elevating her hurt to something more gave her room to express fear, anger, and her sense of betrayal. He had not just two-timed her like other guys two-time their girlfriends (so predictable, so banal), but he had put her life at stake. Although she was overdramatizing, her dependency on him was so strong that she felt as if her life was at stake because of this betrayal.

It was unlikely that either of these girls had contracted HIV/AIDS from one encounter with a person who was not known to be infected. And yet there was some chance. Would it be helpful to assess the chance? The accuracy of their fears? When fears are flamed from a variety of directions, addressing one direction isn't enough. I told Monique that it didn't seem very likely to me but that it was always a good idea to check it out at a clinic, have a blood test to put her mind at ease, and get some more information about how to protect herself with her boyfriend.

The real challenge for me was to sit with the anxiety in the room. Therapists are often receptacles for anxiety, and if we can contain it without becoming too anxious, our patients can leave the session a little lighter. Neither of these girls could focus for more than a brief reply when I asked about other issues, and each returned to anxiously asking me, "What are the chances that I could have HIV/AIDS?" and "What will I do if I do have AIDS?" even though I was fairly clear at the beginning that I didn't know but I didn't think the chances were very high and it sounded like they needed to check it out.

For Libby, I first did a lot of sympathetic reflection: "You're feeling very down on yourself"; "You sound like you really regret this"; "I've never seen you so scared." All of this made me feel more helpless as her anxiety increased. I went on to address the issue that she seemed to feel bad about herself because she acted in a way that felt impulsive, unthoughtful, coming from a need to be wanted and seen, maybe even held, or just to be acknowledged as sexy or sexual. I suggested that maybe that night she had acted in a way that wanted to confirm that she was bad or slutty. I went so far as to say that I thought that quite a few teenage and college-aged girls had slept with people they didn't know, and while most regretted it and didn't have as much fun as they expected nor got out of the experience what they wanted, it didn't seem to me to deserve as harsh a judgment as she was giving herself. What were her expectations before going off into a room with this guy at the party? Was she attracted to him? Did she want to have sex or just get some sexual attention? How did she feel about herself while with this guy? At the end of the session, Libby asked me to look up a clinic she could go to in the phone book.

Requests from a client for action on the part of the therapist should always be discussed and reflected upon, but coming at the end of a session where I felt so helpless to help her and she felt so anxious, her giving me something to do, really felt too good to turn down. So I opened the phone book and said, "Let's look together." What else could this request have meant? Maybe it was a way of saying she didn't trust "all the talking" to help; she needed me to do something. Or perhaps it was a request that I be a mother to her and help her through this when she couldn't possibly talk to her own mother. Maybe she just didn't want to feel alone in all this. Looking back, I wonder if I might have addressed with her earlier how hard it was to go through this alone, and how sometimes she felt she deserved to be alone in this world, and because of that pushed me away. But here she was inviting me to address those feelings through action in the moment, and I couldn't resist. We looked up the names of clinics in the phone book. She wrote a couple of phone numbers down and went off to make the calls. Had she asked me to make the call for her, would I have? Probably. And it would have been a mistake, but I probably would have done it.

I say probably because I did just that, years later, at the end of Monique's session. I gave her directions to the clinic, the phone number, and called her school to say she'd be returning there late because I had given her a therapeutic task to do downtown. Why do I know this was a mistake? Because I was taking action that she needed to decide to take, even looking up a clinic in the phone book. I was acting out of my own feelings of helplessness, because I was focusing on her neediness rather than her perception of reality. Later, I learned she didn't even go. Maybe she didn't go because she knew she probably didn't have HIV/AIDS, or maybe she felt embarrassed to walk into that clinic. Maybe my action resolved some anxiety. Or maybe therapy worked that day and she found some relief, less urgency to be checked out. I saw Monique two weeks later and she told me she and her boyfriend worked things out over the phone (she still hadn't forgiven him) and she spoke about her fights with the school about some kind of punishment she got for mouthing off, but she didn't mention going to the clinic or fear of HIV/AIDS. It wasn't until the end of the session that I asked if she had gone, and she brushed it off. "No, I wanted to get back to school right away that day. I had a lot of homework."

Lesson learned? Perhaps. But I knew the lesson before I acted, that these fears often represent other feelings that need to be addressed. These are like pregnancy scares, that come fast and furious when a girl feels uncomfortable with her new sexual experiences, when she feels young and not ready for all the responsibility of having sex. Pregnancy scares have not been so difficult and anxiety provoking for me, perhaps because the outcome, whether it was abortion or full-term pregnancy, is not the same as the imagined death from HIV/AIDS, but the girls' anxiety has been just as real for them. Unlike HIV/AIDS scares, I've often heard about pregnancy scares after the fact, when the issue has already been resolved.

Therapists need to be very careful to be open to all possible resolutions when a girl they are seeing in therapy actually is pregnant. Depending on the family situation, it may be a good idea to help her tell her parents and it may not. Research shows that only 61% of girls who seek abortions tell their mother they are pregnant and 57% of informed mothers do not tell their spouses (Henshaw & Kost, 1992). And a call to our local Planned Parenthood in my rather liberal state of Vermont informed me that the majority of girls who come in for abortions are accompanied by their boyfriends, not their mothers. The woman on the phone estimated that only about 20% of them are brought in by mothers.

Having proper support around a pregnancy decision is incredibly important, and helping a girl find other people to talk to about it is crucial. But sometimes there is no one she trusts enough not to tell others—not her best friend, not her aunt. If I have a sense that her parents will be helpful in the end, I will encourage a girl to discuss her pregnancy with her parents. I always want to support parental authority in a healthy way and when there is something a parent can offer. Most parents do have something to offer. I may ask to bring parents in and hold a joint meeting, to help the girl talk to them about what happened and what her decision is or how she would like them to help her with the decision. In anticipation of that, I might ask the teen, "What's the worst thing she would say?" or "What's the worst thing that could happen?" And then, "How likely is that?"

DOES THIS MEAN I'M A LESBIAN?

Sexual confusion is probably more common than people think. Same-sex attraction may come and go in adolescence as teens form new relationships and experiment with different forms of intimacy. Some teens may have same-sex sexual experiences and not label themselves as gay because of the stigma attached to it or because they are questioning themselves. Some may have sexual feelings for people of the same sex and not act on these feelings or speak about them with anyone, again, because of the stigma attached. The younger people are when they first acknowledge same-sex attraction, the more likely it is that they have fewer resources to help them with their confusion or with their understanding of their sexual identity. Thus, if a teen discusses sexual identity or same-sex sexual feelings with a therapist, the therapist may, at that time, be the teen's only resource. This might mean that the therapist needs to provide not only a space in which to explore these feelings but information about where teens might get good information on their own. If the teen does not want to come out to his or her parents, it will be a therapist's goal to help that teen stay connected to his or her family and the rest of the world, keeping up with schoolwork and social activities.

Therapists of adolescents see teens who are interested in getting support to come out, and I talk about these teens in Chapter 8. We also see teens who have had experiences and feelings that leave them confused. In working with these teens, it's important to emphasize that therapy may not provide them with an answer to their question, "Am I gay?" But it's good to also let them know that therapy is a place to explore those feelings and thoughts for their own sake and not simply to come up with an answer.

Diane came to my office because she had been fighting with her mother too much and demanded to see a therapist. Her parents, old-fashioned, thought that seeing a therapist was something someone only did in extreme cases, but agreed to let her come for a few sessions. As I came to understand, her acting up at home was an expression of the anxiety she was having. By bringing more attention to herself in this negative way, she got her parents to allow her to see a therapist. Entering my office, she asked me myriad questions: How many kids do I see? Where did I get those posters on the wall? Where did I get my beanbag chair? Where did I go to school? (I was still a graduate student at the time.)

I asked her why she wanted to come to therapy and told her what her mother had said over the phone. Haltingly, embarrassed, with head down and fingers entwined on her lap, Diane said that when she was younger, she had played some games with other girls and was wondering if now she might be a lesbian. I asked her what that would mean if she were a lesbian. She said that she felt as if she'd be alone all her life. I commented that many lesbians have very full lives with lots of people in them, partners, even children. She said she knew this, but the picture she couldn't get out of her mind was that she would be living alone in an attic room. What I heard was the fear that she was different and deserved ostracism.

I reassured Diane that many children play sexual games (this was before I wrote a book on the topic) and that many of these games are same-sex games. It's different with children. It doesn't necessarily mean that this is your sexual identity for life. But, I added, maybe there are feelings or attractions you have now that you're an adolescent that make you wonder.

We then talked about her other relationships in high school. I asked if she were attracted to another girl in high school and she said no, that she had a boyfriend. I asked if she and her boyfriend had a sexual relationship. Diane said yes but they hadn't gone all the way. I asked if she enjoyed being with her boyfriend and "messing around" or "hooking up" in other ways, and she said yes. Then she added, she felt that she enjoyed cuddling with her best friend just as much though and looked forward to that.

I asked about this cuddling. And she explained that while watching TV at her house or just goofing around, she and her best friend would lie against each other. They were quite affectionate and recently, just once, her friend kissed her. This is what had brought back the flood of memories about her childhood sexual play.

I asked if Diane thought this kiss was a romantic kiss. And she haltingly explained that she couldn't tell because they were always affectionate anyway, hugging and lying around next to each other, but she thinks so because her friend acted weird after the kiss, even though it was a short one. I suggested that maybe her friend had an attraction to her and was this something the two of them could talk about? She said no, that that would be "way too difficult." I asked her to imagine what might happen in that kind of talk if she could bring it up, and she pictured her friend feeling awkward and then not being her friend anymore.

Therapist: (hesitantly) Maybe you're afraid that the intensity of your own feelings might drive her away.

Diane: It's stupid but I keep thinking about that kiss. If I keep thinking about that kiss, does that mean that I want it to happen again?

Th: It could, or it could mean other things, for example, that it made you anxious. It seems that time may tell if this is something you want to pursue, and you can decide through a variety of ways, through talking about it with her, with me, or through kissing her back, or through just letting it lie and seeing what lies ahead.

We then talked about her same-sex childhood experiences. My goal was to disconnect them from her current feelings so that she might be free to experience these on their own. I talked about the surprising intensity of childhood sexual feelings, and I wanted her to know that for many children sexual feelings can be very intense. I said, "Children can have very sexual experiences that sometimes are difficult for them to cope with or understand. Some children can have orgasms in play. These can be powerful and confusing." For teens exploring childhood play, bringing up the word *orgasm* might be important. They might not realize that they experienced an orgasm or be deeply ashamed that as children their play could have created such an intense experience.

For Diane, acknowledging the confusion and possible sexual feelings the night her best friend kissed her seemed to be enough, temporarily. She didn't talk about it with her best friend and things between them seemed the same, she reported. I didn't push her to pursue it, and I only saw her a few more times. For other teens, such a kiss could open up continued discussion about fantasies, feelings, and interests. It's important to keep the conversation open to those feelings, and had Diane continued in therapy, I might have later checked in with her. "How are you feeling about your best friend? Do you ever wonder anymore about that kiss or think about her in a more romantic way?" And I would say this to let her know that the topic of her sexuality and her interests was still open. For some teens, that first kiss could be an awakening; for others, just one of many various sexual adolescent experiences that are thrown into the mix of sexual identity. If a therapist attaches a label too soon (or at all) to a teen, then the therapist may miss cues about a whole range of interests that teens develop or experiences they have.

GIRLS AND POWERFUL BOYFRIENDS

One issue that therapists have to work with when seeing teenage girls is their lack of agency in sexual situations with boyfriends. Girls have been socialized to be passive in sexual relationships, to be the one who waits to be encouraged by boys, rather than to be the one with desires and needs, the one who acts. And it's often the case that a girl will be so passive with a boyfriend that you are unsure that she wants to do what she does. Some teen girls believe that with sex, if their boyfriend asks or demands, they should just do it. These girls never give a moment's thought to pleasure. It seems as if it didn't occur to them that this might be what sex was about or that they had a say in what happens.

Lydia came from a very religious family, but she was in the public school system and met a proverbial "bad boy." They didn't talk much when they hung out together, but Lydia felt cool and admired and impressed that she was chosen by him and made part of the gang. Her parents didn't want them to be together and argued with her constantly. This was a problem because it made it harder for her to use them as a resource. She had also separated from her friends as she hung out with Ryan every day after school. So her parents sent her to therapy where in the initial session it became clear that she and Ryan had already had sex. She confessed they did it almost every day after school in his bedroom. When asked if she wanted to do it this much or if she liked to do it, she replied, "I don't know."

While a therapist may not want to ask for a lot of details in the first session, once a relationship has been established, it's good to try to get a feel for how sex goes and whether or not the girl has some agency in it. It's hard to find out details about this in therapy, but I asked, "So how does it get started when you two have sex? Can you picture it for me?" I think I asked because she seemed like such a meek person, not a kid rebelling, but a kid just wanting a relationship. She started by describing them lying on the couch together, kissing, and our conversation went somewhat like this:

Therapist: Okay, you're making out. Do you like that?
Lydia: Sort of.
Th: Sort of?
L: I guess.
Th: And then you do it?
L: Yes.
Th: Does he ask?
L: No.
Th: Do you respond to him by showing that you're enjoying yourself?
L: No.
Th: Because that's embarrassing?
L: No. I don't think I really enjoy it.
Th: So does it happen that he just pulls down your pants on his own and sticks it in?
L: Yes.
Th: Does he try to make sure that you are interested or willing, by, like, touching you?
L: No.
Th: Do you ever protest it?
L: No. Well, sometimes I pretend to want to take a nap.
Th: I'm getting the picture that you're not that willing or interested in having sex most of the time but that you're also not sure how to or that you want to say no.
L: I don't know.
Th: Sometimes it's difficult for girls to develop a voice in matters like this. Is this something we might work on?

In other conversations, Lydia revealed that her boyfriend was not very nice to her, calling her names in immature and just plain mean ways. He teased her about being fat (and she didn't seem to have an ounce of fat on her body, although that didn't stop her from worrying about his mean teasing). She later described a situation in which he demanded sex from her and she simply complied—no kissing, gentle urging, even requesting. He would say, "I've gotta have it today," and she would just sit there and let him lead the way. It all seemed to happen because he decided he wanted it, and it felt very much to me like he was using her. The task was to help her to know she had a choice about whether she would have sex or not and that there was a possibility for a different kind of relationship for her with someone else in the future.

Therapist: What would happen if you said you didn't feel like doing it?
Lydia: He would do it anyway.
Th: And what would happen if you got up and left?
L: I don't know.
Th: Might he break up with you?
L: I guess.
Th: And you want to stay with him?
L: Sort of.
Th: You want to stay with him, but you'd like him to treat you better, to be a different sort of a guy, I expect.
L: Yes.

Little by little we worked on her finding a voice in this relationship. It was my belief that if we worked on her as a person, with feelings and thoughts, and magnified them in therapy, it would be harder to ignore them and turn herself into an object for her boyfriend. This was obviously a terrible relationship, but she had to be ready to leave him, and she had to find a way to say no when she wanted to say no or to bring herself to the sexual part of the relationship as a player, someone with desires and wishes.

Another client of mine, Francesca, was under the spell of a friend, Andrew, not a boyfriend, with whom she had an arrangement to provide sex whenever he asked and vice versa. She and he had grown up together, their parents friends, he a couple years older. When she was 14, desperate to be popular, he took her under his wing. He was the older guy, leading the kind of life she wanted to lead, doing everything she wanted to do, going out to parties every weekend, hanging out with a crowd that seemed sophisticated, wearing nice clothes, driving an expensive car that his parents provided for him, and he looked hot. He gave her lessons on how to be popular, as in those Pygmalion movies. He took her out shopping for clothes, told her where to get a Brazilian wax, did makeup with her at a department store counter, making suggestions to the sales clerk, and told her how to wear her hair. He also told her how to "play" guys. Together they had a motto of never being played, always being players, so that if they went to a party together and had sex with other people, they would recount their episodes to each other afterward, bragging about how they got the person they were after that night. They also had sex themselves, sort of in an instructional way at first, and later, sort of for fun. Francesca never developed a crush on him, but became more his buddy, or, as he liked to call her, his little sister. He also suggested a pact—that whenever either of them wanted to have sex, the other had to come over and comply. And it would work both ways. That would help them not to get dependent on other people (which he called "weak"). To be a player, you'd never want to be in the position of needing to see someone or wanting them. People were dispensable, to be played; but he and Francesca were buddies for life.

When I met Francesca, she was focused on another boy whom she really liked but who did not return her interest. She had flirted with him, had occasional sex, and constantly wrote to him on AOL's Instant Message system. She had never had a boyfriend and really wanted one, but Andrew, her "big brother," had told her that boyfriends are for suckers. He would say to her, "Do you really want to be a pathetic girly girl? Waiting around for some guy?

Giving him all the power? That's for wimps. Stay a player." When I suggested to Francesca that it sounded like she really did want a boyfriend and she really did like this guy, wanting a real relationship instead of playing him, she said, "Yeah, but that's weak." She would also give a little shudder of disgust when she said the word *weak*, like she was embarrassed to want the things other girls wanted and to be that vulnerable.

As a new therapist to this 17-year-old who had been in an arrangement with Andrew for three years, I was not going to attack his solid place in her life. After all, in spite of this odd and, to my mind, exploitative relationship between them, they had a connection that went back to early childhood and I feared if I challenged that too early, she would reject me. But as therapy progressed, I began to question her obedience to Andrew.

Francesca: Andrew called and needed sex so I went over to his apartment.

Therapist: Did you want to go?

F: No, not really, but that doesn't matter; we have a pact.

Th: So, how long does this pact go on for, indefinitely?

F: I don't know. I never thought of that.

Th: What would happen if you ever said no, you didn't feel like it tonight.

F: I couldn't do that.

Th: And why not?

F: Because he's done everything for me. I owe him whatever he wants. He made me who I am. You should have seen me before he helped me out. I was a nothing. I was still not shaving my armpits. I wore baggy clothes. I was a science nerd. I didn't know how to wear makeup.

Th: To me, you sound like a lot of girls.

F: I was ugly. I wasn't popular.

Th: I understand that it was really important to you to be popular back then. Does a real friend exact a price for this kind of help?

F: I like it better that way, cause I know exactly what I owe him.

Th: Forever?

This was how these conversations went. I would poke a little bit at this strange conception of a friendship and she would defend it. We would talk about what friendships were like and what mutual relationships were like, and she would question the "weakness" of it all. I would point out how in spite of her fear of being weak, it sounded like she really desired something more mutual with a guy, something more romantic. And eventually, in time, she said no to Andrew. It wasn't that Andrew asked for sex that often, maybe once every few months, but it was indeed momentous when she said no, because when she did, she also said to him that she didn't want to have sex with him anymore. He blew up at her, called her weak, spit at her, said he was disgusted—anything to manipulate her back into his control. But she quickly left him that night at a party and she didn't hear from him for a long time after.

This was a girl, in my mind, who had developed her adolescent worldview about relationships from a very jaded, self-serving older guy she looked up to. She needed him as an escort and a protector into this scary but exciting world. But she wasn't his puppet. She had her own views, her own desires, and that made my work easier, because I could reflect these back to her, affirm them. She merely had to stop putting down her own wishes and views in the voice of Andrew. My therapy encouraged her to express these views and consider what was hopeful and good about her desires, how she hadn't become completely jaded about male-female relations and wanted to have a sincere and honest relationship with a boy. When I represented that perspective, she would represent Andrew's, that hers was a stupid girlish fantasy, but as I began to honor that side of her and talk about how one enters into a relationship with a guy that's both romantic and mutual, her desire for it grew, and she was able to pull away from Andrew. She never saw Andrew as anything but a good friend who took care of her, and yet, she did make the decision to separate from him and his very harsh worldview of female-male relations.

FROM PASSIVE TO ACTIVE

Andrew taught Francesca to take an active role in her sexuality, but it was a pseudoactive, aggressive role. He laid out for her an important dichotomy for girls' sexuality—far too many take up a very passive sexuality, not only becoming sexual objects, pretty to look at, desirable, but giving up their sexual subjectivity, their desires, their interests. The self-objectification that we see in many teen girls comes from more than just the media. There are a hundred ways girls are told that they have no voice and that their self-worth is wrapped up in their sexuality. Andrew, it seemed, had taught Francesca how to use that sexuality instead of being used, using her in the process. A student of mine saw a girl who also attempted to turn the passive into the active, taking on the role of sexual object.

Toni saw herself as sexual, but her sexuality was wrapped up in being admired and desired. She had developed a crush on the landlord of her building and fantasized about him. Toni was long, lean, and gorgeous at 14, and she wore clothes that made people stop on the street and stare. She would laugh in therapy at all the men who tried to pick her up on the street, obviously getting a sense of superiority over them as she strutted by in high-heels, short skirts, and stomach-revealing tops. But she wanted none of those guys, nor the guys in her high school. Instead, she seemed to want only the attention of her middle-aged landlord. At home, she would dress up, put on makeup, and go up the back stairs of her apartment building to hang out on the porch with her land-lord, Dennis, a guy in his 50s. Her mother, an alcoholic, didn't seem to mind and thought it was good for Toni to have a "father figure" since her own father had abandoned her. Toni told her therapist about her visits and the thrill whenever he looked at her in "that way." She told her therapist that for Dennis's birthday she got dressed up in a new dress and went to visit him with cupcakes she had baked for him. She described herself in the summer, lounging on his porch in a bikini as he was drinking a beer or making himself dinner, and they'd talk about her day and his.

As her therapist, my student worried that this man would take advantage of Toni or was already crossing boundaries and that Toni was smart enough to know that her therapist would need to report this if she told her. Why didn't he turn her away? We were sure it was clear to him that she was presenting herself for a relationship and sex, but he seemed to resist and just looked and talked. Her therapist had asked Toni if she would like to have a relationship with him and she said yes. Although it was important to talk about the issues involved with her having a relationship with someone so much older, the risks to her as well as the legal risks to him, she only half-listened. She could only see the up side. Her therapist reminded her how Dennis could go to jail if he ever took her up on that and how if anyone knew that he had taken her up on that, they would have to report him, including the therapist. But she didn't care. She was in love and seriously didn't want to think about those other problems. While she never touched him to seduce him, it was clear that she was making herself a very tempting cupcake.

What did Toni and her therapist talk about? My student, who was a young woman at the time, just beginning to do therapy, would ask, "Is this what you want? You talk to me about how hard it is for you to live with your mom. It seems you are searching for a man to take care of you, but that you're trying to seduce him into doing that." She pursued a direction that spoke to the deeper need of having attention from a man, someone besides her alcoholic mother to depend on. And they talked about how this landlord seemed like a stable man, not a boy, someone who would take care of her, maybe even father her. If Toni's therapist had been a man, how might this conversation have differed? If her therapist had been a young man beginning therapy, and I had been his supervisor, we might have wondered together if another kind of displacement was taking place, that she was taking the feelings she had for her therapist and displacing them onto the landlord. I might then have asked the male therapist to try to have her bring these feelings into the therapy session, not by being seductive but by talking about her attraction to older men in as neutral a way as possible, what it was like for her to sit with him and tell him about her exploits, whether she sometimes wished to be seen as a sexual object by him instead of in a deeper way that showed her vulnerabilities. These questions would be meant to help her explore what kinds of feelings about herself she got when she presented herself as a sexual gift to this older man. Perhaps those feelings of being desired and desirable helped her not to feel those other feelings of being unwanted and uncared for. But without allowing for discussion of desire in therapy, there might not be the opportunity to examine other more painful feelings.

GIRLS GONE WILD

There's another kind of "active" sexuality that's not about finding one's own desires or interests (a healthy active sexuality) but about becoming a powerful sex object. I once saw a beautiful young woman who came from a horrible childhood background with an abusive father who also criticized her and put her down relentlessly. My client wanted to become a prostitute in order, in her view, to have power over men. We discussed this choice extensively, as well as her feelings about my belief that this was not a positive life choice. So, instead she became a nude dancer. As a nude dancer, she felt she was in control of the gaze of the men watching and even their judgments. We never agreed that this was the right path to power for her, but therapy ended before the issue was resolved.

We as therapists can't deny that there is some power in being a good object, in making men watch you, want you. Why else might all those young women on beaches pull up their shirts for the cameramen filming the *Girls Gone Wild* videos? Well, yes, alcohol plays a part. But, for the moment, they feel powerful and hot and devil-may-care. It's not just about being wanted but about being a good object for a moment, idealized, sexy, desired, and unjudged.

Even though it's somewhat of a pornographic urban legend, there are teen girls who are doing a lot of sexual things at parties and making their therapists mighty uncomfortable with talk about it. Much of the time, these girls know that what they're saying to the therapist is shocking and that she or he probably disapproves, and so edit the stories before talking. Others don't censor themselves, like Valerie, who came in week after week talking about how high she was on the weekend and relating tales of whom she fucked and whom she blew in a way that emphasized not the sex but how out-of-control things were. Valerie's therapist listened week after week with little judgment getting the feeling that Valerie was testing her: "How much can I shock you? See how bad I really am?" What Valerie's therapist did was to stick with her feelings rather than the acts, to continually ask her: "How are you feeling about what you're doing?"; "Do you check in with yourself about how you're feeling during the evening? Are you sober enough to do so?"; "What would it feel like in the moment to you if you knew you wanted to stop? What would you be saying to yourself?"; "What would it feel like in the moment if you knew you wanted to go on? What would you be saying to yourself?"; "Do you have a sense of control over the evening? Do you want a sense of control? Why or why not?" No therapist will be successful barraging an adolescent with these questions. But listening to the story of the evening's events, exploring moments of choice, of ambivalence, of control, helps an adolescent to be more self-reflective in the moment, if not before. And there are times when some of those questions can be reflections: "Yes, there you were making a decision to stay, weren't you? And it sounds as if you felt powerful in that moment, making that decision, even if it was just the power to screw yourself over."

No matter how much the media presents girls in these kinds of situations as powerful or in power, as exercising their sexual freedom, therapists know better. Adolescent girls do not feel very good in these situations. Such situations are rife with sexism and objectification, and although it might be nice to be looked at and desired, objectification leads to lower self-esteem, the lessening of choice and awareness of feeling, not the development of those things. And this objectification can lead to more risky and exploitative experiences at a party, as when my client Tanya was led to a couch in a side room, undressed by a guy she had just met, and raped in front of party guests who watched. Why was it rape if she didn't protest, which she didn't? She was drunk. She was numb. She was, in her words, "totally out of it," and she thought, "Just lie there and get it over with." She was so out of it that she was going in and out of consciousness, but alert enough to hear some girl at the party say, "I think he's raping her" in a tentative voice. But nobody did anything about it. In school, however, several guys began to harass her, calling her "ho" and "slut" in pretend coughs as they passed her in the hall. She internalized their view of the event, saying to me in therapy that she must have been a slut if she let this guy do this to her, and proceeded to the age-old hardened adolescent defense of "I don't care."

Some girls use their sexuality to feel powerful, and why not? The media has taught them that their sexiness is a way to power, that being looked at and admired is tantamount to having power for a girl. Shows like *Sex and the City* sell a kind of sophistication about sex and "doing it" that some teen girls buy into. But using sex to feel powerful can backfire, as it did for Tanya. She, like many others, turned the experience of exploitation on its head and began to have sex with as many guys as possible to prove that she was a slut and wanted it. She would purposely get drunk at parties to see who would do it to her and who would take care of her. Where was the power in this? In her confused mind, it was in the not caring, and in laughing at them. "They're fools. I can just wear a hot outfit to a party and see them all slobbering about me, 'Oh you're so sexy.' But I don't care, and that's my revenge." It was difficult for me to see the power in this except to think of it as a mastering of a trauma. She was inviting the sex and the raping and so it was in her power. She was saying, "Yes I'm a slut, so now that I've taken on that identity you can't call me that and hurt me."

It's hard to break through this kind of denial when it appears in milder forms with so-called party girls who say, "I'm having lots of fun, a good time" and in scarier forms with girls who are reenacting more traumatic experiences. Tanya, who dressed like she was in an MTV video when she went to a rodeo, was furious at a man who was harassing her to come over and sit with him. He was drunk but also telling her how beautiful and sexy she was and that she should come sit by him and talk. Rather than ignoring him, she chose to "take him on," in her words, separating from her friends to go over and talk to him and inform him that he was harassing her. In her rendition of events in therapy, it was unclear how she went from "informing him" to having sex with him in his car, but that's what happened next. When I heard her tell the story, I couldn't figure out how it was that she was furious with him at first, feeling objectified and wronged, and then would agree to go to his car. It didn't sound like a rape but felt like one to me, a self-induced rape, if there could be such a thing. She couldn't explain it to me either.

Tanya: He just told me "Let's go to my car," so I went.
Therapist: Did you want to have sex with him?
T: No.
Th: Did you think you probably would if you went to his car?

T: Yes, but I didn't care. So what if he wanted to? It didn't mean anything to me.

Th: This was rape then.

T: No, I went with him to his car and let him fuck me.

Th: How did you feel?

T: Fine. This is what he wanted and this is who I am, a slut, so I just let him.

Then with a wry laugh she added, "He was such a jerk. He acted like this was his lucky day, and he actually wanted my phone number afterward to call me again for a date! Like I'm going to go out with a 50-year-old man!"

Tanya insisted that she didn't feel that bad about it, but she revealed that she had cut herself that same weekend.

Th: You feel good but you cut yourself afterward?

T: I know what you're thinking, but I just cut myself because I hate myself; I don't care about that guy or any guy.

Th: So why go with him to his car?

T: Why not?

Th: Because it's not what *you* want to do.

T: Who cares what *I* want to do?

Th: I care. [*I think therapists ought to take a stand on these sorts of questions.*] I want for you to have caring relationships with people and I want for you to have sexual relationships that are pleasing to you, where you enjoy sex and feel cared about and respected, and feel that it's the right thing to do.

T: Well, I don't care about that. (then attacking me) You're getting off on these stories anyway.

I always perk up when a client addresses me directly about the therapeutic relationship. I love it because something that's been influencing the sessions underneath it all is finally brought to the surface. Many beginning therapists are afraid of this, preferring in the beginning to hide behind the professional aspect of the relationship, worried about the tricky waters when the relationship itself becomes the focus of the therapy. I like when teens "make it real" because it gives us a chance in the moment to work with them on projections as well as their real experiencing of other people.

Therapist: You see me as just another person only interested in you for your sexuality, as someone who also is ready and willing to exploit you.
Tanya: Yeah, so what? You don't care. You get paid to do this.

Rather than defending myself, pointing out how little the state actually paid me to see really difficult kids like her and that I actually looked forward to seeing her every week, I discussed process.

Th: It seems to me that when I told you what I wanted for you in a caring way, you accused me of only wanting to exploit you. I wonder if it was hard for you to hear my caring about you.
T: (well-defended) Yeah. So care! Good for you!

Caring for a teen like Tanya is hard and sometimes is a struggle. She felt so bad about herself and those feelings were so hard to sit with that she needed to defend against them. And yet she brought these horrible stories into therapy, so that I could reflect on them with caring for her. As she couldn't yet care for herself, and having no internal voice that went beyond calling herself "bad" and a "slut," I needed to be that voice for her, even when she pushed me away with accusations and hostile remarks.

Other girls, less troubled than Tanya, try to find power through sex, assuming a more masculine role. Hillary and her best friend Jeanine thought themselves a mighty duo who would try to have sex with as many cute guys as they could, compare notes, make lists, and compete. They were *Sex and the City* girls who were proving their independence and assuming power by taking a notch-in-the-belt attitude, defying cultural standards that girls should be modest, pure, and wait for a boy to choose them. Later Hillary confessed to having a few bad feelings about this time in her life. As she moved beyond it, looking for more long-term relationships, she remembered the fun she had with Jeanine around doing this, but that she also felt kind of "yucky" about the sex. She didn't feel horrible about herself. But she didn't enjoy herself either. It was really about playacting a kind of role with her friend and talking about it afterward. And, as it turned out, she really did want a relationship with a guy. I saw Hillary toward the end of her period of sexual bravado and so got the benefit of her hindsight. But had I seen her during this period, again I would have asked her what she was getting for herself out of this, and whether there was something in using guys and spitting them out, (in "typical guy fashion") that spoke to larger issues, issues with her dad for example, who left the family when she was young, rarely making contact. Did she have issues with the vulnerability of the passive role, the waiting, allowing guys to be the choosers? Did she want the rush of always being wanted, if only for sex?

While Hillary didn't feel bad about her "bad girl" sex, other girls have felt enormously guilty. One therapist I worked with saw a girl named Ali who, as it turned out, had anal sex with a guy she hardly knew at a party. She was drunk and had been doing drugs all night. Same with him. They ended up together. He asked. She was game. But afterward she thought this made her perverted. How did she even tell her therapist? Her therapist had a feeling that she was hiding something about that evening that she was ashamed about and pursued it. When Ali told her that she had "done anal sex," my colleague didn't bat an eye but pursued it by asking Ali how she felt about it. Ali said she felt like she must be a pervert. The conversation that ensued was more about her drinking and drug use and how it led to her doing things that she didn't feel comfortable with. But this therapist also thought it wise to throw out information to Ali that some people enjoy anal sex and that it is part of a repertoire of things some people do in relationships, and she did this simply to normalize the act as one that a sexual adult might *choose* to do with someone they trusted or cared about. Would it be better to let Ali sink in her shame about how perverted she had become? No, because shame usually doesn't lead to self-reflection—more like self-loathing. It was more important to help Ali to understand that she was in the process of developing and understanding her sexual self and that doing so with some commitment, forethought, and choice would help her to feel good about what she was doing and learning about herself. The conversation was tailored toward her feelings as well as her judgment: "How do you feel in those situations?" "Can you trust yourself to have good judgment in those situations where you have been drinking?"

Some teen girls like Ali hide the things they think are most disgusting and perverted about themselves. Others will throw it in your face, as if to ask, "How much can I shock you?" These girls already feel disgusted with themselves and seek to have their therapists reflect back disgust, confirming that they are horrible creatures. What sorts of acts do they throw out, hoping for and fearing rejection? Having sex with a friend's boyfriend; exposing themselves on the street, pretending it's by accident; having fantasies about their female teacher; having the little boy they babysit touch their breasts in a game they made up. Where do therapists go with information like this? In the same direction as always: How do girls feel about themselves? What were they thinking at the time? How did it come to be that they did something that they feel bad about, and what, from their perspective, was wrong with this? How can they restrain themselves from doing things that are illegal and can harm other people as well as themselves? Empathy for their underlying feelings, worry about their own welfare, sharing their concern for what's wrong with these feelings and, when appropriate, sharing with them what's normative can help teens to process these experiences for more than a few minutes in a session.

TEEN GIRLS AND PLEASURE

Sometimes we therapists talk only to teens about sex as a responsibility, helping them to become the kinds of people who will make choices with a lot of reflection, understand the consequences, and use caution or precaution. We're concerned with girls having a voice in what they do and knowing what's okay with them. It's more difficult to talk about sexual pleasure and especially desire. And yet, especially for girls, it's important to let them know about the potential for sexual pleasure and their right to it. One of the ways we can bring up the whole idea of pleasure is by simply asking a girl who is having sex with someone, "Are you enjoying it?" And if they say yes, a therapist can then go on to ask, "I mean, not just do you want it and like the person, but are you sexually enjoying it also?"

Some girls feel nothing but love for their boyfriends. While willing to talk about having sex, they feel unsure and embarrassed in talking about what might be going on "down there." Words like *stimulated* and *aroused* sound technical to them. *Horny* and *hot* sound too raunchy for a therapist to use. My strategy for these kinds of girls is to simply tell them what I know, that many girls don't ever get in touch (so to speak) with the pleasurable aspects of sex, beyond the holding and the kissing, afraid to get to know their bodies or explore with their partner what feels good. Knowing that there is the potential for sexual pleasure is important for girls.

Others have known the thrill, but feel that it is only okay to feel this excitement at the hands of someone else. Gabrielle came into therapy complaining, "I have so much sexual energy all pent up. I need a boyfriend!"

Therapist: (straightforwardly) There are other ways you can handle that . . .
Gabrielle: Eeeewwwwww. No, that's gross.
Th: Why is that gross? It's *your* body. Don't you want to know how it works? How to make yourself happy?"
G: I just couldn't. It would be so weird. It would be like I'm a lesbian.

Gabrielle had so objectified her body that to touch it would automatically put her in the position of an "other," an onlooker. When she felt aroused, she believed that the only action to be taken was to find a boy, a boyfriend, to please her—that could mean trouble. "What if you looked at it from this perspective? It's your body and you should understand it, and if you know what is pleasing to you, you'll know how other people can best relate to it and you." She didn't buy this philosophy in the therapy room, but often, with teens, they do "go to school" on what you say, the results of which will be revealed later.

A female suggesting to a teen girl to masturbate is akin to presenting her with a role model. "Do *you* do it?" one cocky teen might ask. To which I'd reply, "Many, many women masturbate. I know that teens are shy about it, but in my experience, all the women friends I know have and do and all the research I've read says it's normal and common." You don't have to get personal to give her the information she needs!

Could a male therapist suggest to a teen girl to masturbate? This is trickier. But if he comes from the perspective that she has a right and an obligation to know her own body, and he expresses this in a caring voice, as if this is a very important goal of her growing up, he can get around her suspicions that he's got a fantasy or two on this very subject.

Most of the therapists I know take a very liberal view of subjects such as masturbation, that it's natural and part of getting to know your body and how it works, and also that it's a resource, a means of coping with feelings that arise. We need to remember that many kids don't come from homes or peer groups with similar perspectives. They might have seen some joking about it on TV, making them feel like it's something embarrassing that jerks or nerds do, or they might have gotten the message from their parents that it's something shameful to do. Without you knowing, your earnest and accepting attitude about it can be a revelation.

* * * *

Many therapists will see adolescents for long stretches of time in which no sexual issue will emerge; others will encounter sexual issues in their first session. It's our obligation to separate in our own minds the cultural image of the teen girl from what individual teen girls really know, care about, think about, and do. But it's not always easy. Teen girls themselves are influenced by the culture's projection of them and their beginning sexuality, and understanding of themselves as sexual beings is deeply influenced by these images. If a therapist can see what's dangerous and unhealthy about parts of that image, and what's healthy and safe about alternatives, then she or he has a perspective from which to view it all. While supporting a teen's growing autonomy through connections to those she loves or want to have sexual experiences with, a therapist can help a teen develop a more true autonomy, help her make choices that are free from the influence of damaging images and expectations. Supporting autonomy, helping a teen make healthy connections, and, for girls especially, finding a way to have an active sexuality—these are great goals for teen girls in therapy.

CHAPTER SIX

Teenage Boys in Therapy
Sexual Concerns and Issues

The developmental task of boys in the adolescent years plays out differently than the developmental task of girls at this time. Both boys and girls are influenced by the culture, but in different ways, and boys don't necessarily have it easier than girls.

Several developmental issues are at work in the transition boys go through from boyhood to adolescence. The first is that boys have to work with a narrative of masculinity (and images of manhood) that is stereotyped. This narrative of the independent go-getter, the player, is at odds with intimacy goals. It represents a shallow, action-oriented sexual ideal that gives little room for relationship, self-understanding, and passivity. The second issue is that in addition to incorporating and working with these representations of men, boys have to learn how to integrate very real feelings of aggression and competition with their sexual selves. Another issue at play in boys' sexual development is that they have to find a source of self-esteem that can carry them through adolescence while their fear of rejection can interfere with their ability to open up and be close to anyone else, boy or girl; so self-esteem is more easily gained through nonrelational means. These issues can all be discussed explicitly with boys, especially those willing to come into your office and discuss sexual feelings, fantasies, and relationships. But there's a whole different cadre of boys who are going to be more comfortable sitting beside a therapist at a computer, playing wastebasket basketball, or going to the machines to get a soda—hanging—while they find a way to ask or express what's eating them.

MASCULINITY IDEALS

Up until adolescence, boys have been encouraged, trained, provoked, and humiliated into being ready to compete, up for action, and comfortably loose with their aggressive tendencies. This is not to say that they all end up in this stereotypical pattern, but that this is a pattern they play against, a narrative of boyhood that they form their identity against. It's a narrative that describes boys as aggressive and competitive, as moving away from mothers and dependency feelings, and toward a mock masculine world of harder competition that purportedly describes manhood. This narrative requires that they negotiate between media images of manhood as independent and cultural expectations that they also have a girlfriend, an intimate partner. How confusing.

They might join the stereotypical world of boys in preadolescence, competitively sharing knowledge and information of a sexual nature without quite understanding what they are talking about. Participating in a boy culture that bonds and delights through the sharing of the forbidden, the racy, and the disgusting, they exchange dirty jokes, definitions, and observations long before their sexual feelings have arrived in any significant way. This is the mold the culture sets out for them and whether or not they conform, they are made aware in hundreds of ways each day, through TV sitcoms, movies, cartoons, and adults' reflections and suspicions, that this is what it means to be a boy. Unfortunately, in far fewer ways does the culture lay out for a boy what it means to be a man and how to integrate sexual feelings into sexual development, feelings of competition and aggression into real and caring relationships.

Thus adolescents begin to integrate sexual feelings in their lives in the form of conquest and bravado. Other feelings regarding insecurities, vulnerabilities, and worries, as well as relational feelings that connect sex with love are suppressed or, if not suppressed, relegated to very, very private areas of their lives. Rarely are these discussed with friends and sometimes not even with their girlfriends or first loves. In this way, they grow up to be "masked men," as the psychologist Joseph Pleck (1981) called them. And in therapy, the therapists I know who work with teen boys tell me that they won't let themselves feel very much. Those who are hurting, and seem to be feeling a lot, often don't have the words to describe these feelings very well. Still, as the authors of *Raising Cain,* Dan Kindlon and Michael Thompson (2000), wrote, boys want to be loved and to love, only it feels too complicated. Many need help making the journey from the simplicity of sex to the complexity of relationships, from aggression and competition to love and caring.

What that means is that in therapy with teen boys, a male therapist may hear more about relationless sex (sex that does not occur within a relationship), tales of sexual bravado, jokes about sex, sexual pranks in groups of boys, and stories about other boys, than about their concerns about their sexual development or sexual relationships. A female therapist may not hear very much at all. The more experienced therapist will realize that these jokes and references are a way in, indications that a boy has some concerns about sex and sexuality but does not want to appear vulnerable or unknowing or like a wimp.

FANTASIES OF AGGRESSION AND FEAR OF REJECTION

Given that boys are permitted more aggression, adolescence then becomes a time of integrating this aggressive/competitive side with a new sexual identity, and, more important, with intimacy. Not an easy task. They may worry about their competition and aggression and become passive around girls. Their sexual fantasies may contain images of aggression and competition that disturb them. They may worry that they could be rapists or sex offenders, that they are perverts, that they could get carried away, and so withdraw from the world of real relationships.

Other boys may need to objectify girls to allow for the expression of aggression and the suppression of more intimate feelings because these kinds of feelings make them feel dependent and vulnerable. Such objectification of girls keeps boys in a preadolescent boyhood phase of joke-telling, pranks, and buddies that doesn't make demands on them to integrate or inhibit aggressive feelings in a relationship. It's an easy way through adolescence and one that the culture supports in many ways. But it doesn't afford boys the opportunity of working on this issue in a real relationship.

In real relationships with girls, boys can enact these feelings of aggression and competition in problematic ways such as jealous possession. Possessing an object rather than loving it is one way boys inject aggressive feelings into a relationship. The madonna/whore split is another. They can control girls by labeling them. This tactic also permits boys aggressive feelings in relation to some girls while preserving intimacy with others.

Girls sometimes are not very real people to boys. Some see girls simply as objects or playthings, hot bodies to conquer. But objectification of girls can serve a different purpose. Sure, a boy might protect his self-esteem in a culture where intimacy is seen as a weakness by talking about and treating girls as objects. But doing so also protects a boy from investing in a relationship that makes him vulnerable to rejection.

VULNERABILITY IN RELATIONSHIPS

Some boys do deeply depend on their girlfriends as transitional figures away from their home and mother, talking to them nightly on the phone, but sequestering this relationship from the rest of their world. Unable to have this kind of relationship with their parents or other boys, they need a girlfriend to help them sort through the vicissitudes of high school life. The gay male teens that I have worked with seem to have real friendships with girls. It's harder for gay males in high school to keep their old friends once they are out because of homophobia, and gay male teens miss the experience of being buddies with their old guy friends, playing video games or going to the movies, sometimes fearing their attraction to them as well as their buddies' reactions to their sexuality. All kids, straight or gay, who can hang out in a group of kids are lucky enough to get the advice and encouragement of both female and male friends and have a cushion against the rejection that can come with real relationships.

Boys who fall in love may not be prepared for the feelings that come with it and the intensity of the sexual experience. Jealousy can overtake them, and it may be difficult for them to negotiate their other friendships around this love interest. To protect themselves from the vulnerability of love, some boys become "drifters," in the words of Dan Kindlon and Michael Thompson (2000), half-heartedly in relationships, asking for little and giving little back in return. Still others go the road of exploitation, pursuing sex without any conscious or acknowledged interest in love. This lack of awareness can leave them in a cynical, exploitative place.

Adolescent boys often feel that girls have all the power in sexual relationships because they have the power to say no. And part of doing therapy with boys is helping them understand the *no* from the girl's perspective. Rejection is emasculating to boys; girls, by saying no with hurtful comments or humiliating remarks, can really wound a boy. But if boys can be helped to understand that *no* as less personal, and see it from a girl's perspective, then they won't feel so vulnerable and rejected by the many *no*'s they get, and won't need to lash out at girls or super-size their fantasies of domination.

Those researchers who have interviewed boys about their first sexual experiences and romantic relationships, Deb Tolman at San Francisco State and her colleagues, have described many of them as yearning for intimacy, not just a "make-out body." She warns that it is important to remember that boys' longing for closeness and curiosity about sexuality has to be integrated with a public world that asks them to demonstrate their masculinity (Tolman, Spencer, Harmon, Rosen-Reynoso, & Striepe, 2004).

ANXIETY ABOUT SEX

Most therapists who write about "real boys" agree that boys are very easily aroused and sexually aroused quite a bit through their adolescence. One approach in therapy to this topic is lighthearted. Many a boy may worry that he's a pervert for thinking about sex too much, so a therapist's humorous comments, careful not to brush off serious worries, can provide enormous relief. A colleague told me about a science teacher in high school who began a talk to an all-boy class about sexual functioning by describing a "very serious disorder" that afflicted adolescent boys. The boys squirmed in their seats, thinking that they might have this disorder, the symptoms of which were easy arousability, excessive masturbation, difficulty concentrating, and persistent thoughts about sex. Then the teacher said, "Professionals refer to this disease as 'boobs on the brain'!" and all the boys broke out laughing in relief.

Most parents talk about arousal too late, after a boy may have begun to wonder if he is different than other boys, a "sex fiend," a pervert, or uncontrollable because he masturbates "too much." When therapists try to talk about a boy's inner life with him, they should take heed of the warning from Dan Kindlon and Michael

Thompson that sometimes it seems to a boy that his inner life is all about his sexual fantasies. It's also interesting to note that boys sometimes have their first sense of being a private, separate person through these fantasies and thus sex is wrapped up in their understanding of themselves as separate beings apart from their parents. As Michael Kimmel (2005) argued, boys tend to keep private their experience and have few skills that enable them to share. While we may assume that kids in this culture today know that masturbation is fine and will not cause disease or blindness, kids may still need to know how frequently is fine, what fantasies are fine, how hard is fine, what objects are fine, and what length of time it takes to reach orgasm is fine. It's incredibly difficult to find that information in books, and not many teen boys seek out book information. It's also somewhat difficult to find this information on the Internet without wading through a lot of porn sites to figure out which ones give real information for teens. Those that do give sex education often merely say that masturbation is fine and normal and don't go into the specifics a teen really needs. There is way too much vague reassurance out there with very little information for the nervous kid about the specifics.

That's why it may be important for therapists to provide an adolescent with books, education, and resources for his own investigation. Having a list of therapist-approved Web sites is likely to be a more successful approach than handing a teen boy a book to look through. Most of the teen boys I know would rather get information from the Web than a book. Some, though, may not have the privacy to search the Web at school, the library, or home, and a book in this case can be useful. Talking about sex in the movies is also a very good way to share information with boys in a therapy session. This kind of conversation is less dry than Web or book sex education, and enables a therapist to integrate talk of relationships with how people feel and what they do.

Boys' fantasies are influenced by the media, the same as for girls. What becomes arousing to them is heavily influenced by what they've been exposed to as well as by more psychological issues they are dealing with. And a therapist ought to ask about fantasies. Some boys appreciate the opportunity to check them out, no matter the embarrassment. If their sexual arousal initially comes in school in relation to a girl or boy they have crush on, all well and good. But sexual arousal can come to be associated with the porn they've perused or with the hyped-up sexually exaggerated women with plastic breasts they've seen on TV. For most boys, a variety of images will become sexually arousing. But Patrick Carnes (2001), the leading researcher on sexual addictions and an advocate of the addictions model, wrote that sometimes early exposure to some kind of shocking pornographic image can lead to a feeling of that picture being burned into one's brain, with a corresponding inability to remove it.

Fantasies of domination and exploitation of women are not uncommon among boys. They reflect a more immature self still preoccupied with competition, aggression, and conquests. Many come to feel ambivalent about these fantasies, knowing they're sexually exciting yet thinking that they would never do something like that to a girl. Fantasies of women being tied down or forced to perform sex acts speak to larger gender roles that have become eroticized. Playing out these roles in their extreme while fantasizing makes men feel more like men and women feel more like women, and their enactment on TV and in the movies helps to instill an erotic tinge to these roles. On TV and in the movies, men are constantly pushing women up against walls, forcing them to do their bidding; women are constantly being killed in seductive poses or prancing around in front of men in high heels and sexy lingerie. But we should also keep in mind that some of these fantasies of domination come from a fear of rejection, of not being good enough to have a woman. Boys can denigrate girls and women to not feel anxious about them (Kindlon & Thompson, 2000), and if a boy can dominate, then he's in control, and no girl tent, or unmanly. No girl can make

[handwritten notes in margin: - No penalty / - Summer $50 penalty / - 41 for 1 year / 1787]

TO COUNSELING BOYS

ritten about counseling boys around re, there's quite a bit of work on sex- sexual offenders, but what about vho are in psychotherapy for their om death of a loved one or divorce, ieir depression? Wouldn't one think e now and again? There are only two n the *Handbook of Counseling Boys* ne & Kiselica, 1999). And while in contribution to a 1995 book, *A New Psychology of Men,* authors Gary Brooks and Lucia Gilbert pointed out that a consistent issue in men's literature is the hidden confusion of men in the area of sexuality, only about 10 pages of 400 are devoted to adolescent boys.

In this chapter, I picture the therapist treating the adolescent boy as a male therapist. Generally, I refer adolescent boys to male therapists. I've seen a number of adolescent boys, successfully I think, and I will write about the difficulties of talking about sex with them, but I think the bulk of adolescent boys seen in treatment do see male therapists. I don't refer these clients to men because I think men can do a better job; in fact, when it comes to talking about sex, I think teen boys can have good conversations about sex with female therapists. I refer them to men for another reason. Many adolescent boys in our culture are dealing with a profound sense of loss at adolescence and there's something in me that wants to give them a real man to look to for modeling when many of them see so few real men in their lives. They may have lost a dad through death or through divorce or even abandonment when they were small. But they also may be feeling the loss of a real relationship with a father who's rarely around, an alcoholic, or a dad so critical that the teen would never approach him. And with that loss comes a longing. Sure we female therapists can get there. My colleague Sally has seen a boy throughout five years of his adolescence, carrying him through his father's suicide and his stepfather's criticisms and rejections, sticking with him when his mother could not. And this boy has done well, graduating high school, in a solid relationship with an empathic girlfriend, working an after-school job, and applying to technical college. Sally's work with this boy was around loss, and the two of them never talked much about sex.

In my experience, teen boys do not ask to go to therapy. A great many of them are brought in for acting-out behavior, from inappropriate outbursts in school to actual sexually aggressive acts. Others are brought to therapy because adults have identified anxiety, depression, loss, or loss of connection to others. It's beyond the scope of this book to deal with severe sexually acting-out problems of boys, and I refer the reader to experts in this field. But within the "normal" population of teen boys in therapy, there are still incidents of angry acting out expressed in some kind of sexual aggression or objectification of girls, and the safer the therapy space, the more likely the boy will be able to discuss them.

In Chapter 1, I discussed how to create a safe space in which boys can discuss sex seriously, respecting a boy as someone who may have a lot of sexual knowledge already and even allowing some locker-room talk. Therapists may need to talk about masturbation directly so that they can provide some relief from fears.

Conversations about sex work best using what Mark Kiselica (2003) called "male-friendly practices": flexible time limits, informal settings, humor and self-disclosure, rapport-building, sports, and electronic games. Kinseylike interviews face to face in an office are likely to make a kid feel abnormal and uncomfortable. Kiselica also wrote that "many young men use humor as a vehicle to achieve intimacy" (2003, p. 1227) and that a joke, even if it's a sexual one in bad taste, may mean more than just disrespect for girls and women. It's true that for ages men have bonded over their disrespect of women, allowing them to be close without fear of homosexuality, because they're achieving that closeness by talking about the "bazoombas" (a word a therapist may want to use for humor) of some girl. This is tricky, though, when a therapist doesn't want to join in disrespecting and objectifying girls but realizes the kid is trying to bond with him.

It's important to remember that many guys want to make the transition from fantasy to real girls, and may be eager to have meaningful sex with a girl they really like, but none want to do this if it means humiliation or rejection. The more a therapist can help a guy read girls realistically, see them as people too, and understand the difference between his fantasies and the real world, the more competent he'll feel out there negotiating sex and romance.

LOCKER-ROOM TALK IN THE THERAPY SESSION

If a male therapist sees a teenage boy in therapy, the boy may attempt to bond with the therapist or prove his maturity and masculinity through engaging in some locker-room talk about women and girls. In choosing how to respond, there are a few things to understand: First, this cocky conversation may be a way of showing competence in an area a boy feels very incompetent in; second, he may have learned this talk about disrespecting women to earn respect and feel powerful in front of other boys. This will mean that he wants his therapist to know that nothing the therapist says can make him feel incompetent or disrespected. A therapist may need to respect his need to talk that way in front of his peers but help him understand that the relationship in therapy is different. A therapist can support him without putting him in his place, and reflect on the meaning of this kind of talk by allowing it.

Mannie was seeing Jerome, a boy who was sexually inexperienced but would bring up all sorts of sexual interests in session. Hyperactive and with somewhat of a developmental delay, he saw sex everywhere and wasn't shy about sharing it with Mannie. He fantasized that Mannie and his wife would have sex sometimes in the office, and this was exciting for him to think about. He wanted to enter Mannie's wife's office down the hallway, where she also saw clients. "Can we go in there and get some things?" he asked, which Mannie recognized was a question about a boundary. Jerome wanted to know whether he could enter his therapist's wife's space. Could he enter his therapist's wife? Jerome added, "If she was there, you two would be doing it right now. I know it." Mannie brought this kid to reality: "We work together every day. We talk together about what's for dinner. We share stories we heard on the radio driving here. We live together. Why would we be doing it here?" This indicated to Jerome that there was more to their relationship than sex and that there's a time and place for sex with one's wife. But Jerome would have none of that. "If it were me I'd be screwing her all the time." Totally overstimulated about the thought of a husband and wife, for Jerome the whole meaning of getting married was sexual—when men and women get together, that's what happens.

Jerome also used the telescope in the office to see if he could look into the apartment buildings across the way or view the people in the cars in the parking lot below whom he imagined were having sex. Two people got into a car below, and Jerome offered to Mannie nonchalantly that they were probably doing it right now.

"Do you really think so?" asked Mannie.

"Yeah, they probably couldn't wait until they got home."

Calmly, Mannie would reflect that this was exciting to Jerome but that in his experience, people weren't having sex that much in the world around him, mostly in bed at night, and that most of the time they went to they were probably just going to sleep. To illustrate, Mannie pointed out the window and said, "Those people look like they were coming from the dentist's office. See? Maybe they were talking about having to get a filling or needing to floss more." In saying this, he was trying to help Jerome see a boundary around sex, as a private activity in one's bedroom and not something that spills over into every interaction, and also to imagine more mundane interactions between men and women.

Jerome had boundary problems in several areas, not just sexuality. They had been playing aggressive soldier play with some toy soldiers and tanks in the room, Jerome setting up war scenarios. Sometimes these aggressive feelings had been so overwhelming that Jerome would try to hurt himself in the session by ramming a tank into his arm over and over again, or, on the way out, spontaneously try to destroy or knock down something in the waiting room. And it was in this atmosphere that he started teasing Mannie about not knowing anything about sex. Jerome had been on the Internet and had seen quite a bit. He had also talked to a lot of teenage girls online about sex, talking dirty and telling them what he was going to do to them, and though inexperienced, he defensively presumed he knew more about sex than Mannie. This was a dilemma for Mannie, because to engage in this sex talk with Jerome would be to enter an entirely overstimulating world where relationships were only about sex, and if he were to share his knowledge, he also risked entering a competition over sexual competence and knowledge, one that Mannie was certain to win and that could make Jerome feel humiliated. At the very least, such a competition could reinforce the idea that knowing about sex was a way to feel more masculine. Instead, Mannie addressed Jerome in this way.

Therapist: You're right. I may not know that much about sex. Kids try to keep up with all the things that are new and different, don't they? And I bet kids you know compete to see who knows the most

Rather than asking Jerome if he wanted some information, which surely Jerome did want, Mannie allowed that Jerome might be an expert of sorts.

Th: (continuing) It seems so important to boys that they know a lot about sex, as if that makes them more powerful and manly.

Jerome: Yeah, Ted didn't know what 69 meant. What an idiot! Everyone was like, "You jerk!"

Th: (incredulously) A jerk because he didn't know something? Wow, that sounds cruel. It seems like nobody can ask questions or get information without feeling like a fool in your crowd. (pause) [*Then Mannie made a kind of proposition.*] You know, you may know a lot more about what people do nowadays when they have sex 'cause I don't keep up with that stuff, but I do know what's typical from the kids and grown-ups I see in therapy. You could tell me something you heard of people doing, and I could tell you how typical that is for people to do, if I've heard of it. And I could also tell you about girls and what they might think and feel about that.

Jerome was all ears, and he was able to show his competence by talking about all sorts of weird sex. Mannie was able to address how common some of those things were in as humble and "old man" a way as he could, acknowledging that he might not be up on everything, but as far as he knew, that wasn't so common. He could also bring in the feelings of a girl about those acts, which was a kind of social skills and empathy training that Jerome sorely needed.

Another therapist friend of mine, Paul, worked with a boy who would brag to him about what he was doing with a girl in the neighborhood. As Bradley reported what they did, it seemed as if he were a boy bragging to a man, "I touched this," "She touched that," "I was so big!" and so on. As he related each little act he looked to Paul to get a reaction, wondering if he was impressing him. To Paul, it seemed as if Bradley wanted to be seen as a big guy by him, as macho, as a man. He had to be careful not to shoot him down. Bradley was a boy without a dad to support his growing up and becoming a man. But Paul wanted to confirm Bradley's maturity in a different way and simply asked, "Do you know how to be safe?" He brought up the issue of contraception but also tried to tie that in with being macho and grown-up, making it seem as if a real man would know that kind of information. Bradley bragged that he always carried a condom around. And Paul told him that he could really impress a girl by showing that he knew that condoms were only effective 87% of the time if a guy didn't know how to use one properly. Then he could tell the girls all the stupid mistakes that guys make by taking it off too quickly or not putting it on early enough or using one that's not made of latex. And he could let his friends know that they could get 100% effectiveness if they used a jelly or cream with it that killed the sperm, not the kind they put on the condoms but the kind you have to buy in the store. Paul also modeled that he found all this out by reading about it in a book. He said, "I didn't even know all that until I read about it. I'm sure they have all those statistics on the Internet too if you can get to a good site instead of all the wacko porn sites!" This condom talk was not very successful. Paul seemed to be turning Bradley off. Being a man by using a condom was a very hard sell. But Paul hoped that at least Bradley knew he could look up information on the Internet.

Paul tried a different topic while still trying to be influential.

Therapist: Girls can be hard to read. It's hard to let them know you respect them. [*Bradley seemed interested in this line of thinking, so Paul went on.*] Okay, let me tell you. Don't do anything she doesn't want. And make sure you know what she wants and doesn't want to do by checking it out with her. Do you know how you might do that?

Bradley: (seeming mature) Yeah, I can ask.

Th: (tentatively) I wonder if it would be nice to have a real girlfriend. Someone you feel comfortable asking questions, some you can talk to about the things that happen to you every day as well as someone to hold and to explore sex with.

For many boys it is impossible to have both, too threatening, but a good thing to consider. And it was Paul's feeling that Bradley really would like someone like that, but it seemed too over-whelming a task, so far beyond him socially just yet to relate to a girl that way. But that was part of the work ahead.

The whole idea of girlfriends can be confusing for some boys, especially those coping with the serious loss of a parent. Their attempts to keep girls at a distance through objectification are often coupled with a longing to have someone who cares about them. And yet for immature kids this fantasy is rarely articulated. Daniel worked with a boy, Sam, who had lost his mother when he was very young, and although he talked the locker-room talk with Daniel, his sexual concerns and interests were always tinged with a feeling of vulnerability and loss. The fragility he showed when working on issues of loss and relationship arose around feeling rejected or criticized in any way by a girl. Sam talked to Daniel about the "girlfriends" he had. But he called a girlfriend someone he had only talked to a couple of times. This very act showed the desire to have someone, an intimacy reached too soon, as well as a kind of defensive bragging to Daniel as in "See how many girl-friends I have? See how easy it is for me to get one?" After a year of "girlfriends" whom he "went with" and "broke up with," he talked about wanting to have sexual intercourse with someone. Knowing Sam to be somewhat fragile emotionally, Daniel saw his talk about wanting to have sex not merely as bravado or simple lust. He seemed to want a real girl and yet was conflicted about it. Daniel asked what he had been doing with girlfriends so far. And Sam said they would lie together on a couch in his basement, sometimes sleeping together. Daniel assumed they were doing other things besides intercourse but didn't ask. He asked, "Do you enjoy this or is it excruciating because you want to have inter-course so much?" "No, it's okay," Sam replied. And Daniel noted that Sam did not say he enjoyed it. Using the words of pleasure might sound too unmanly.

One session, Sam walked in and announced he had had sex. Daniel did not react as if this were a triumph—no high fives or "that a boy." Nor did he reflect that Sam looked proud or happy.

Therapist: (simply and directly) Tell me about it. How did it feel for you?

Sam: (laughing) Good.

Th: So it felt physically good. What were your feelings about it during and after? Sometimes a kid can feel weird or even kind of, what's the word, *naked* emotionally?

Sam knew what he meant and told him that he didn't feel weird at all because it was a one-night stand. Daniel then pursued a safety conversation with Sam, and Sam had been safe—in fact, he had been wanting intercourse for so long, he carried a condom with him at all times.

Daniel let go of another conversation that could have happened, one about why the first time was a one-night stand. Sure, it could just be because that's what came along. Opportunity knocked, right? But this important event happened with someone Sam didn't care about. Could there be a meaning to that? Was it a way of protecting himself from having to care about someone else? Someone else's feelings? From having to connect and be even more vulnerable? Perhaps. All of these questions could be expressed to Sam in one question: "Did you feel at all odd doing this with someone you didn't know very well?" But these are incredibly difficult conversations to have with boys. Boys can hide behind the culture's view that of course all boys want to have sex all the time. It's tough to go there. And most therapists I know who work with adolescent boys are afraid that the wrong question will shut them down for the rest of the session.

SEXUAL HARASSMENT AND BOYS

Calvin had been in therapy with my colleague Don for about a year when a sexual issue came up. Calvin had been "sexually harassing" girls in school. He stormed into his session with Don, furious at the school. He had been brought to the vice principal's office and made to sit there all day until the "jerk" had a moment to talk to him and explain the new Vermont laws about sexual harassment, about respecting girls, and about their plan to get a one-on-one paraprofessional to follow him in the halls and cafeteria if he didn't refrain. "Refrain from what?" asked Don. "From asking girls out. That's all." "Huh?" said Don, suspecting there was more to it than that. "Gosh, that doesn't sound like sexual harassment to me. We've been talking about you asking girls out."

As it turned out, Don figured out that Calvin had been asking girls out constantly and he was bothering them. The hall monitors had told him to cool it because he tended to get into people's personal space and he was rather relentless. Don and I pictured those guys from *Saturday Night Live* who were clueless, the guys in the movie *A Night at the Roxy* going from dance club to dance club trying to pick up girls by rubbing up against them and not understanding the girls' disgust and rejection. Don understood where Calvin was coming from. His obnoxious begging was coming from a combination of neediness and social awkwardness. He was one of those kids who just seemed more socially immature than most. Calvin was cute and boyish, but also big and somewhat overweight. When he got too close, he was a presence, a big boyish fidgety presence. And Don thought it could be really annoying if he was hanging out where he wasn't welcome, trying to insinuate himself into girls' conversations.

Therapist: What behavior exactly do you think they're calling sexual harassment?

Calvin: They think I'm bothering the girls because I'm hanging out at their tables and walking after them when they go to class, but they don't mind. Lots of people do that. They just pick on me. I hate Mr. S. He is such a jerk.

Th: Do you think any of the girls felt more than bothered? I mean, sometimes boys can really get into their space without realizing it.

Don put the thought out there, hoping that it would increase Calvin's awareness when he was with girls. If Calvin had managed some good peer relations by now, other guys might have told him to hold back. But as a bit of a clown and a loner, the other guys egged him on and laughed *at* him as well as *with* him when he irritated the girls.

Don saw Calvin as "developmentally desperate." He wanted a girlfriend. He saw other boys with girlfriends. Yet he appeared to have a nonverbal learning disability that interfered with his social perceptions and judgments—he was unable to figure out how to get a girl. Working at the level of pulling a girl's pigtail in second grade, he was physically more mature, but interpersonally not, and really unable to control his impulses in school.

The next week he came in even more furious. The school had actually given him a paraprofessional to accompany him through the halls. He was not in a special class for learning disabled or emotionally disturbed kids, but they were treating him like a "retard," as he put it. This was incredibly humiliating. Don didn't know how to find out what incident had provoked the school's decision. Finally, Don figured out it had something to do with a girl named Alissa. Calvin and some guys had been hanging around a lunch table of girls, and Alissa was eating some ice cream. She called Calvin a "retard" and he dumped the ice cream down her shirt. He swore to Don that Alissa didn't mind and was laughing and so when one of the guys told him to go in her shirt and get the ice cream out, he reached in. Alissa screamed and the cafeteria monitors came over and took Calvin to the vice principal's office again.

As Don worked with Calvin around this incident, it became clear that he was very overstimulated by the girls and their shirts and their joking and maybe could use some assistance in controlling himself around them, but they could never work on the sexual issues because Calvin's humiliation and defenses were so great. He could never admit to sexual harassment, and even the guys thought that his punishment was way too severe.

So Don took a different tack, supporting his goal to have more contact with girls, hoping for a girlfriend. He looked for areas in which Calvin could practice. One successful way to practice in the therapy session is to work with a kid using computer games involving the SIMS families and dating scenarios. These are simulated computerized images of people that the kid can control and several versions explicitly enable users to create dating scenes. Conversations about what they're doing and how they're reacting is a wonderful way to work with kids on social relations. Don also suggested that Calvin start to try to talk to some of the girls on AOL's Instant Message service or MySpace. It's a great place where kids can figure out what's offensive. A girl will just block or warn someone who annoys her. Don knew that kids could warn each other on IM and if a warning level got up to a certain percentage, a kid would get kicked off AOL for some time. What Don wanted to do was to help Calvin learn some social skills without over-stimulating Calvin or hurting a girl. Instant Messenger is a bit removed and would give Calvin practice to be around girls without offending them, but if he did, he would get instant feedback about it.

WHEN IT DOESN'T WORK

Teen boys as well as grown men occasionally have problems with keeping their erections. From the number of Viagra ads I get in my e-mail every morning, I would guess 9 out of 10 males are worried about this. But seriously, boys do bring into therapy concerns about whether their penis "works right" or whether their attractions are real, letting their penis decide for them. More than a few have wondered why, when they finally have the opportunity to have intercourse, after waiting so long, with someone they were initially so attracted to, why oh why would they suddenly lose their erection? With girls there may be an issue about desire and arousal, the desire there, the arousal not, more frequently than the opposite. For boys, the desire is there and the arousal is lost, and they compound the problem with their fear that something isn't working physically because the idea that the brain is the most important sexual organ is a little too complex for them at this point in their lives.

An early psychoanalyst wrote about impotence in very narrow terms, describing the boy or man as either wanting to punish the woman by teasing her or fearing loss of control over his own masculinity, devoured by the threatening female. He was working from the false assumption that men have grown up in a female-dominated society that is hostile to their manhood and that the root of many problems is a domineering mother. They then have an unconscious wish not to gratify their mother and act this out by becoming impotent at the moment of intercourse with a girl or woman. Impotence was seen as an unconscious devaluation of the other sex.

William Pollack, author of *Real Boys* (1998), wrote that it's common for boys to worry that they simply aren't capable of having intercourse. The only way they can know that they can do it is to have it, but this puts a lot of pressure on the act. Sex means a boy is a man, he's mature, he's capable. With so much hanging on it, it's no wonder that fear of impotence "runs through every boy's mind." And why? He may feel intimidated with a girl who matured several years earlier and seems to know her way around the social aspect of the sexual games they have been playing. He may also simply care too much, so that the worry about it going right or working well interferes with arousal. Could it be that he didn't feel ready? Or could it be that having sex all of a sudden felt so much more intimate than he thought it would feel and he suddenly looked down at her and thought, "Who is this girl?" One college-age student seemed to lose his erection with a particular girl because he wanted her so much and was overfocused on pleasing her, wanting her to like him. Another lost his erection because the strangeness of having sex with someone he barely knew hit him like a ton of bricks in midentry.

A different psychoanalytic way of looking at this is that the adolescent may be anxious about a female's arousal. Fears of fusion, of dependency, of intimacy may cause a boy to lose his erection. Fears of rejection may be just as common as feelings of self-worth and competence. Fear of his own aggression being too much may also cause an overreaction in the form of inhibition.

The point is that, as with most issues relating to sex, we therapists have to put aside the technical for a moment, trust that the apparatus is intact, and look for the emotional side to sex that could be hard for a boy to talk about. Reassurances that this happens to a lot of guys could be met with a question to a male therapist, "Did it ever happen to you?" Be prepared. Reassurances from a female therapist may not mean as much to an adolescent boy who thinks that what happened to him makes him less of a man in the eyes of other guys. I might say something like, "Boys don't often talk about this with each other, but it's way more common than you think. Somehow boys feel more comfortable sometimes talking about this with a therapist than with the other guys. Everyone's so afraid of not looking tough enough, right?"

One client, Guy, just beginning his sexual explorations with other adolescent boys his age, discovered that he could perform oral sex on others, but when a boy tried to return the act, Guy would freeze up. He was excited thinking about it happening to him next, but then would lose his erection when the other person began. Not a guy, and not gay, I tried to put myself in his situation and asked, "Do you think you feel a little more self-conscious just standing there or lying there, with nothing to do, and that maybe the self-consciousness gets in the way?" He admitted that he did start thinking about things like what his penis looked like close up and whether the other person really wanted to be doing what he was doing and . . . pretty soon he would lose his erection. Together we came up with situations in which he thought he would feel less self-conscious. "I can't do it" became "I can't do it this way" or "in this situation."

Lyn Ponton, in her wonderful book *The Sex Lives of Teenagers* (2000), wrote of a boy who was worried that his penis didn't work right, not because he would lose his erection (he hadn't actually had any sexual experience with a person yet), but because he thought he wasn't getting hard enough or large enough with an erection. He began masturbating with all sorts of contraptions aimed at making his erection larger and ended up "jacking off" with a vacuum cleaner. As the therapist tried to get more information from him, he called her a pervert. Over time, she came to see him as an anxious boy, whose physical touching of his penis soothed him when he felt anxious about other things, and could share that interpretation with him as they explored his world together. The symbolism of a very large penis soothed him also, making him feel less vulnerable in a world that could make him feel very small.

As we move on to look at boys and pornography, it's important to remember that it's not just society that emphasizes size. Size and strength, signs of masculinity, reassure a boy that he's not vulnerable, not vulnerable to teasing, to harm, to emasculation, to rejection. These fantasies of size, strength, and endurance seem to pervade pornography even when looking at porn seems to be simply about getting aroused by a sexy woman.

AM I A RAPIST?

My colleague Gary worked with a boy named Adam who revealed to him that he liked to draw pictures of women being raped. He told Gary that he was upset with himself for doing so but that he was intensely interested in these pictures and felt that he was wrong and perverted for this. Gary asked him what exactly about the pictures did he dwell on and what did he think about when he drew them. Adam said that he worked hard at the facial expressions of the women and liked to stare at them once the pictures were done. He also was interested in the positions he would put them in.

In real life, Adam desperately wanted a girlfriend but he was very passive around girls. He was able to identify a couple of girls in his high school that he was interested in and denied drawing them in his rape pictures. But he was afraid to approach them. His passivity seemed to be about his own aggressive feelings, although he didn't make the connection. He was afraid of the aggression and the pictures upset him, and yet he was fascinated.

Gary decided to pursue what it was that upset Adam so much in looking at the drawings. And Adam was able to identify that it was that he had the potential to enjoy or feel excited by such horrible acts. While they spoke of the drawings on and off in therapy, Gary was also able to identify other aspects of Adam's life in which he was afraid of his own aggression and carried a belief that his aggression could destroy others. It was easier at times to discuss aggressive feelings, such as his hatred toward a teacher in school and subsequent guilt feelings, in nonsexual terms, and then later, when talking about the sexual drawings, to draw parallels for Adam.

Over time, Adam's interest in these drawings diminished. This happened via multiple strategies. As in all good therapy, reflections by and bonding with a therapist that approves of the teen and sides with him gives him a feeling of having a basically good self, one that can withstand flushes of anger, hostility, and aggression. Also, the simple revealing of his fantasies in a comforting and friendly environment took some of the edge off how guilty and bad Adam was feeling about them; and the lack of secrecy made the compulsion less forbidden. Finally, Gary encouraged Adam to get some experience with real girls and come back and report to him how it went. Playing through possible humiliating failures and possible successes made it easier for Adam to approach the girls he liked. And he was able to introduce some teasing and aggression into one of these relationships with a girl in a fairly adolescent way, competing with her on an academic quiz team and verbally teasing her about small things she did, which seemed to go over fine with her, according to Adam.

PORN ADDICTION AND BOYS

Pornography is one of those social issues that produce deep ambivalence in most people, including therapists. It's difficult to get a definition of porn that adults can agree on; nevertheless, whether you can define it or approve of it, porn can be arousing, and many male therapists and some female therapists have fond as well as shameful feelings about a particular magazine pinup or porn image that was a part of their fantasy life when they were younger. While our goal in working with boys is to enable them to have real relationships with partners, whether female or male, that include sexual pleasure, that doesn't mean that they will no longer have a fantasy life. And a person's fantasy life is one of the most difficult things to discuss in therapy. It's a place where some of one's most unacceptable longings get played out, and thus a site of tremendous ambivalence and privacy. The therapist who can discuss with a teenager the teen's fantasy life has an entry into some of the most important material that defines the teen as a person to himself or herself.

Porn introduces material into a kid's fantasy life that might not have gotten there in the normal course of events. But the porn that stays as an image that's useful or functional to a teen most likely has some meaning, meaning that only the teen may understand. If a teen can say, "I like S & M," "I like men all wet and oiled up," or "I like to look at women with big boobs" in therapy, these interests may reveal more about him than his sexual orientation and may produce some good discussion about why those images are salient and arousing and how they make him feel (other than aroused).

Porn for boys can be something akin to the crushes that pre-teen girls get on movie stars. Girls can develop quite involved fantasies about their relationships with Orlando Bloom or Brad Pitt or even their high school tennis coach, only half remembering that it's only a fantasy and there is no possibility for satisfaction. They can develop intense longings to meet or see their "crush." As such, they are practicing romance in a very mediated way, through a fantasy figure that can't talk or touch back. And they are safe from any real confrontation or any real sex. With porn, boys are practicing sex and sexual feelings toward a partner who is a piece of paper or a photo on the screen, a mediated woman or man, not a person in the flesh, someone who allows them in. In this way the Internet (as was the phone) may be a way of practicing relationships.

The relationships created over the Internet have a mediated quality that make them not quite real and yet real enough so that a boy can get blocked if he's too offensive or hurt by someone else who's careless about typing. One of my teen boy clients had a "girlfriend" he had only seen twice but with whom he talked on the phone constantly. Another client I see had a "girlfriend" in Switzerland. Both were working out the difference between fantasy and a real relationship, perhaps frightened or not yet ready for the real thing, but struggling to make this developmental shift.

In this mediated world, sometimes a kid can get "addicted" to porn. I put the word *addicted* in quotes because I don't want to biologize the behavior. All too often, the public is convinced by doctors and the pharmaceutical industry that addictions are not our fault, that chemicals in the brain or biological mechanisms have such enormous control that a person is helpless. Paradoxically convincing oneself one is helpless to fight alcoholism is exactly the first step to not drinking that Alcoholics Anonymous suggests. My friend, writer Rich DeGrandpre, who coauthored with Stanton Peele the brilliant piece, "My Genes Made Me Do It" (1995), pointed out that if smoking is so addictive, how come so many people are able to quit?

Porn addiction is getting more and more common as a presenting problem for teen boys coming into therapy. Parents may have discovered a massive collection or constant Internet viewing; librarians may have discovered a boy who won't stop downloading porn from the school's computers; occasionally a boy himself will ask for help because he feels ashamed of his problem. And there is very little literature, if any, that shows therapists how to work with teens with this problem. One issue that continually arises, though, is whether or not the therapist ought to look at the porn with the teen.

In short, the answer is no. It's not the same as play therapy where acting out the issue through dollhouse or dramatic play helps children express themselves. And even so, if a child were being aroused by dollhouse play, a therapist would stop it immediately. Teens can talk, even if they won't, so the modality for working on these issues has to be talk. If one is a behaviorist, there can be homework assignments, but not in-session Internet porn viewing. So, why are therapists getting in trouble with ethics boards for watching Internet porn with their teen clients? How is it that fine therapists, who want to help kids, step over the line and believe it could be helpful to peruse the material together?

And what is porn? Although most all of us can recognize it, we have a difficult time agreeing on what is harmful. In 1992 the Campaign Against Pornography defined porn as anything that is "graphic, sexually explicit, and subordinates women (or people). . . . It must also contain one or more specific conditions of harm in the form of sexual objectification or sexual violence." This is a clear definition of porn as harmful material to be distinguished from erotica.

It's sometimes useful and ethical to use pornography in treatment, according to those who treat sex offenders. The National Association for the Development of Work With Sex Offenders Policy and Ethics Subcommittee (2000) permits the use of porn in treatment and assessment and details how. For example, the committee asserts that porn can be used to assess progress related to arousal and reconditioning. Porn can also be used in therapy to help offending adolescents and adults form appropriate nondeviant fantasies, especially material that conveys mutually consenting sexual activity. Those who use it write that for some adolescents with no real life experiences, such material can be helpful in formulating real-life mutually consenting fantasies. The catch is, this organization writes, that the materials should only be used in the context of a program and not individually by practitioners, and proper consent from parents and the client needs to be obtained first. Further precautions are having a manager at the clinic approve the use and keeping the materials at the clinic itself.

We know very little about cybersex porn addictions, but those who have interviewed adults speak of a rapid escalation toward compulsive use, and one research study showed about 5% of adults who have visited porn and cybersex sites find themselves compulsively going back (Schneider, 2000). Many preteens have visited a porn Internet site, and many of them have returned to seek out other sites. Those who speak of their Internet use as an addiction talk about the detached emotions with which they seek out material and about the constant footage running through their brains. One doesn't get the sense of real pleasure, only arousal and compulsion.

Is Internet porn educational? There are some teens who simply want to see sex and body parts, wonder what certain terms mean, and want to be knowledgeable. And it's a sad day in the United States when they have to turn to porn for sex ed. because other material is so inaccessible. Gay teens may find that the only images of people like them having sex (because their family doesn't get HBO or Showtime) are to be found on porn sites. For them, porn may be one of the only ways to see themselves sexually.

But dealing with a kid who's into porn is trickier than one would think. Unlike that crush on Orlando Bloom, porn may not be harmless. Sure, it's possible for guys to grow up sexually healthy and respectful of women even having overdosed on *Penthouse* and *Playboy* images that subtly degrade women by objectifying them, depicting women as offering themselves up as sexual servants to guys. Why? Because fantasy and reality are different. And as stimulus to one's imagination, a naked woman on a page can be just the beginning of a whole scenario, no longer based on the actual photo itself. A therapist wants to tread carefully before invading the fantasy life of an adolescent boy, creating more guilt and shame than might already exist. But there are also images that have potential to harm, ones involving violence and graphic degradation. And I suppose there's also the harm done in the amount of time spent in this activity rather than other activities important to development. This perhaps is one of the primary problems of a porn addiction in adolescence.

Like cautions about safe sex given out like condoms in therapy sessions, a few words of advice to boys about porn might also be wise. These can come out naturally in a therapy session as a discussion about what's fake about porn, and what's fun. A therapist can probably elicit from a kid the fact that fantasy women don't often look like real women; they're airbrushed and have had breast implants. A therapist might also point out that the guys in porn don't look like real guys, and their penises are enhanced through digital photography methods. Therapists might also want to look forward into the future with a teen to point out, "You want to make sure that when you finally get a real girl in your bed naked that you won't be disappointed because she doesn't look like a porn photo." A therapist can also point out that in porn sex, what women do and do to men is the focus, while in real sex, what men do with a particular person they like and feel attracted to is the focus. "You realize you're probably not seeing a whole lot of images of mutually consenting, mutually satisfying sex on the Internet, right?" A therapist could ask, "Is that hard to picture?" Suggesting that an adolescent evoke such a fantasy, even as a homework assignment, could be helpful, just in terms of helping him see what gets in the way when he tries to picture that. Michael Kimmel (2005), a leading sociologist on masculinity, pointed out that porn pretends that men aren't interested in stories or narratives about sex, which is untrue. To ask a boy to imagine a narrative, to put in the details, to develop particularity, is to ask him to develop a more rich internal life around his sexuality. The more porn is used at one level, simply looking and masturbating, not fantasizing and imagining what could be, the less arousing it becomes, and the need for newer more explicit material becomes a problem.

And then there's the issue of sexism. The therapist must always take the perspective that girls and women are people too and refer to the images of girls serving guys as images. The Internet is more likely to contain violent themes (Kimmel, 2005) and boys should know that. In my experience, guys who have satisfying relationships with girls, who like them as people, and who've had nurturing family environments growing up—did you think I was going to say don't use porn? Ha! The truth is that these kinds of guys use porn but are very aware that these women aren't real, still get enjoyment with real women, prefer real sex even though sometimes it seems too complicated and difficult, and realize a fantasy is a fantasy.

What about the truly addicted, if there is such a kid? There are plenty of cognitive-behavioral methods out there for all sorts of compulsive behaviors that work fairly well. But if a therapist uses any of these techniques without a discussion of mutuality, sexual pleasure, excitement, and the idea that fantasy is fine but reality can offer so much more, eventually, then the management of an addiction is only a preliminary step to a sex education and a self-exploration with regard to oneself as a sexual being with enormous potential.

ACTING OUT BOYS AND SEX

Sexually acting-out boys often have done more minor acts that went unnoticed earlier. This means that once caught, a slew of behaviors and incidents that led up to the offensive act may be revealed. While we tend to picture sexually offending boys as aggressive types with anger management problems, there is a variety of sources for sexual problems that may not be about sex or sexual offending. There are boys who have a nonverbal learning disability who can confuse sex and aggression when angry at girls and women, have very poor boundaries, and act impulsively. And there are boys that may be having a psychotic break, holding it together and then bursting at the seams, their acting out technically classified as sex offending. There are also healthier boys who are struggling with inhibition of aggression and issues of trust.

For therapy with adolescent boys who have committed sexual offenses, I refer people to a chapter by Jolliff, Newbauer, and Blanks (1999), *Handbook of Counseling Boys and Adolescent Males*, which emphasizes moral education regarding responsibility, apology, and forgiveness along with social skills and cognitive therapy. Teens targeted as sex offenders will end up in group therapy, group homes, and individual therapy with a specialist who is usually a cognitive-behaviorist ready to work on cognitive distortions. Still, occasionally, a sexually acting-out kid presents himself to us in psychotherapy.

Doug, a talented young therapist I supervised, saw one boy, Vince, who continued to bring up scary issues around sexually acting out. In therapy, he wrote long drawn-out stories about how he would date, and marry, and then have kids with Holly, a girl he was infatuated with. Socially awkward and with no friends, Vince created a fantasy life around this girl Holly—their first kiss, their dates, their potential intercourse. And he would discuss this with Doug, my supervisee.

At first Doug and I agreed we should treat Vince like any client. Though Vince was somewhat developmentally delayed, Doug spoke to his feelings: "Boy, you really like this girl Holly" and "You really would like a girlfriend, wouldn't you?" But Vince would not be swayed from his fantasy.

Then it was discovered that Vince had been following Holly and coming to her workplace. The stories in therapy that he sometimes presented and wrote within the sessions turned into stories of rape. Doug and I became increasingly uncomfortable with them and felt that Doug's empathic responses were no longer appropriate. We decided he ought to take a very direct approach with these rape stories and talk about how horrible and harmful that would be to Holly, the girl Vince purportedly loved and wanted to marry, and that he would be arrested and sent to jail if he ever were to do something like that. Vince replied, "I was just kidding," an odd response to say the least.

Doug began then directly addressing the compulsion to see Holly and to talk about her. He pushed the reality at Vince: "Holly said that she doesn't want to see you." And later, "There's a restraining order against you going near Holly, so you simply cannot see her again." "I know," Vince would say, "but someday we'll be together."

This gentle therapist who could reflect feelings and show caring to all his other patients was becoming the most directive therapist you've ever seen. As soon as Vince mentioned Holly, Doug would say, "It's not good to talk about Holly. You have to put her out of your mind because you can't see her." Vince would say he had a dream, and then the dream he described would be a thinly veiled story about a girl, presumably an unnamed Holly, and what Jack the Ripper did to her. Doug would respond by saying, "We need to work on how to stop scary dreams like that from developing in your head." But they weren't scary to Vince. And Doug began to realize that Vince didn't have the appropriate emotions around the sexually violent scenarios he was laying out. They were getting all too common, as if he felt a need to bring some in every week to Doug.

Doug experienced this not as a call for help but as a torture. He was forced to listen to horrible stories of abuse and rape or he was forced to be the kind of therapist he never trained to be, one that said, "No. Stop. Don't talk about that. Don't think about that." When Vince started asking about Doug's wife, identified her in a photo on Doug's desk, and pointed out that he could read the address number on the door she was standing in front of (something so subtle in the picture it was freaky), Doug got scared and started to take action. We understood this as a boundary problem, but what did it mean? Could Vince have been threatening Doug? It seemed unlikely. But it may have been that the idea of using the therapy room as a container for Vince's obsessions was too threatening for Doug. Not trusting that this room and session could actually contain the strange fantasies, Doug became scared.

First, Doug consulted a sex offender expert in the area. Then he called a meeting with school personnel, a psychiatrist at the clinic, parents, and social service agency caseworkers to say that he thought this boy was a walking time bomb. Vince was, because shortly after the meeting he broke his restraining order by coming to Holly's house and leaving a dead bird at her doorstep. He was placed in a home after that and Doug could no longer be his therapist. That was fine with Doug, but we both wondered how Vince was going to be helped, who would be able to fix that broken record, and how.

Pleck, Sonenstein, and Ku (1994) argued that adolescent boys' problematic behaviors stem from their adherence to traditional masculinity ideology. Boys who adhere to this ideology are more likely to be sexually active earlier. Pleck (1981) wrote that those who adhere to norms of aggression and emotional constriction are more likely to get in trouble; this may be because of responses to their aggression and their inability or unwillingness to communicate with important others around them.

Some boys are mandated by the court for therapy, but this kind of treatment is tricky. Most resist it. Psychotherapy calls for a vulnerability and emotionality they may be unwilling to commit to or may even be incapable of. That's why many who work with sexually acting-out boys provide interventions that are explicitly educational—sex education, relationship education, dating education, education about sexual orientation or masculinity. David Price, the assistant clinical director at the Devereux Foundation in Rutland, Massachusetts, found in his work with sexually offending boys that their sexual difficulties were "not the development of a deviant or self-destructive arousal pattern" (2003, p. 225). Rather they had been derailed developmentally from healthy sexuality and development. After they were helped to give up destructive sexual behaviors, they asked him, "What do I do now?" He called them "sexually vulnerable youth" who have developed barriers to development of healthy sexual identity—lack of social skills, lack of healthy peer relationships. They are lonely with poor social skills, few intimate relationships, passivity, confusion around self-image, and inadequate sex information, and are unable to delay gratification and have poor control over sexual impulses, deficits in empathy.

One thing to remember about sexually acting-out boys is that many of them present with shame as well as compulsive or impulsive behavior. Even though practically all make excuses for themselves, spend a little time with them and you can feel their shame. In a group home, they are often given treatments that focus specifically on their sexual compulsions, but an environment where a kid can talk one-on-one about his feelings of shame without being treated punitively for his feelings has, I think, the best chance of helping a kid to not offend again.

* * * *

Therapists assume that boys know all about sexual pleasure and have known about it ever since they began masturbating. Unlike girls, who need to be told that it's okay to feel pleasurable sexual feelings and pursue them, boys need no instruction there. Or do they? Boys, too, need to know that seeking sexual pleasure is fine. But they also need to distinguish sexual pleasure from the pleasure (and anxiety) that comes from acting out masculine narratives of power and aggression.

Both male and female therapists can provide something that parents have a difficult time with—approval and acceptance of their teen sons as sexual and sexually sensitive creatures, beings with longings as well as interests, with fantasies of domination as well as longings for intimacy. They can help with the transition from the jokester, the competitor, the player, into the little man who can integrate sex and relationships. The boys we see in therapy are faced with a culture that depicts them and grown men as almost depraved in their constant needs and orientations toward sex. Therapists can present a fuller, broader view of what male adult sexuality might be if they can avoid joining these kids in their titillating talk of sexual innuendoes, escapades, fantasies, and competition. If they can unmask the boy, they might even evoke a longing to be that adult man who connects to his partner through sex and sensuality—connects, not conquers.

CHAPTER SEVEN

Working With Parents of Teens

Therapists who work primarily with individual teens and children often still have the aim of bringing families closer together. Although eager to supply information about sex to the teen who needs it, many therapists wish they could help parents have these conversations about sex with their children instead. In some ways, it's parents' right and responsibility to convey their values around sex and sexuality. By values, I mean so much more than their opinion about when it's right to have sex; they ought to convey a host of values about male-female relations, about self-care and self-love, and about the future for their child. Support around these areas at home is worth more than the 50 minutes a week we can give.

Many families don't enter therapy ready and willing or even expecting to have this kind of talk. If a family comes to therapy to work on issues regarding an adolescent as the identified patient, the therapy tends to focus on the teen's behavior, the lack of communication between the teen and the parents, or the parents' marriage.

In the course of treating a family, it may be that sexual issues, fear, or concerns arise, and therapists are called upon to do some education around these issues in a session. This can also occur when parents come in to speak to a therapist when their child is seeing the therapist in individual therapy. When working with parents of younger children, therapists generally want to help parents feel comfortable addressing their children's questions and supporting their explorations, setting limits in a way that doesn't make children feel guilty or ashamed of their bodies or their urges. When working with parents of an adolescent, therapists want to help parents express their concerns and hopes directly to the teen, to enable them to provide information, and even to ask their teen questions they know full well they may not get answers to. Parents can come to therapy with sex-negative ideas, afraid to communicate with their children about sex and wishing only to prevent them from having it. But others can come to therapy with sex-positive ideas. Even if they do, they still might not have the ability to talk to their kids about sex for a variety of reasons. Both sex-negative and sex-positive parents (and many parents lie somewhere in between) may not have clear boundaries in their house around their own sexuality or the sexuality of their kids, even if their beliefs might warrant such boundaries. And both types of parents can be too lax when it comes to setting restrictions around the kinds of material children are exposed to as well as their children's behavior. I've seen teens of quite liberal parents trying to set limits for themselves in household atmospheres with no limits. And I've seen teens from quite conservative households struggling with how to limit their exposure to overstimulating material.

HELPING PARENTS TO COMMUNICATE

Many parents want to talk to their kids about sex but feel incapable, embarrassed, and incompetent. With little ones, they are unsure about what to convey and how much is too much. The topic of sex also introduces into their communication a seriousness that for many families is just not a part of normal communication patterns unless someone has died or gotten into trouble.

When a child has been showing a lot of interest in sex in my office, in conversation, or in play, it's almost always the case that the same has been happening at home. Some parents tell the therapist and hope she'll take care of it. Others ignore it.

Some attempt conversations with their children. These parents often feel that the way to discuss sex with their children is to sit down and have a full-fledged birds-and-the-bees talk. Thinking of it this way, the task can seem daunting. But this is how TV and the movies present sex education by parents; rarely is it presented as bits and pieces of conversations integrated into an ongoing relationship. Mothers often feel that for boys, this information ought to come from the father. But research shows that very few boys get their sexual information from their father. It's much more frequently the mother (if any parent) who does "the talk" or provides the information (Holland, Mauthner, & Sharpe, 1996; Rosenthal & Feldman, 1999). This is fine and although it would be nice for a father to be involved, it's also fine for a mom to talk about sex with her son. She's just as invested in his having a responsible and healthy sex life as an adult.

I let parents know that "the talk" is out of fashion anyway. It sets up too awkward a situation and puts a lot of pressure on the parents to make sure they include everything they'd like to include in the 30 minute space allotted for their daughter or son's entire childhood! Instead, I ask parents to be aware of the questions behind some of the behaviors, the curiosity behind some of the questions, the sideways remarks, and the small observations their son or daughter is making. Instead of following the child's lead through his questions—for he may never ask the big question, "Where do babies come from?"—parent can follow his eyes and ask him if he ever wonders about that.

The following are some thoughts and strategies I have used with parents around talking to their kids about sex. Some come from simple conversations I've had during parent meetings. Others come from my early training in family therapy, which focused on structural family therapy à la Minuchin, paradoxical approaches à la Watzlawick, narrative family therapy coming out of Australia's Dulwich Centre, and feminist family therapy à la Hare-Mustin, a brilliant thinker and my first teacher of family therapy.

First, we need to emphasize to parents how important it is that the child hears from them about sex, not just me and not just peers. Sure, there will be other sources of information, but it's very helpful to know that one's parents are open to talking about situations and to know where they stand; more than just helpful, it provides a foundation. This approach with parents tends to empower them and de-emphasizes the role of the therapist as a substitute parent.

Second, therapists also ought to try to normalize fears about broaching the topic. Most parents are petrified of talking to their kids about sex, afraid they'll ask questions that the parent will feel uncomfortable answering and maybe about which the parent has little information. Some parents may even be afraid of what terms to use. Normalizing this feeling and externalizing the blame outside of the family (it's the culture that separates kids from their parents on such an important issue) helps a family to come together to combat unhealthy trends that keep teens getting their misinformation from peers.

Third, a therapist also should provide parents with some information about normative behavior from a developmental view. None of us knows exactly what's normal, but in talking about it we can try to figure out what each individual child needs to know and what may be harmful to that child. If I end up telling parents that it's natural for a young child to be curious about his or her body, about romantic relationships, about sex in general, I say this in a way that makes me less of an expert and more like a person conveying "what we all know" by now, information that can be gotten from any book. I try to empower the parents by indicating that a few questions may help parents know where that curiosity is focused. For teens, I tell parents it's natural and common for them to have masturbated, to have fantasies, to be sexually attracted to someone, and even to be sexually active.

Fourth, parents have their own stories to tell. Many parents have lived with shame from another generation. Their own parents might have made them feel dirty or anxious about their sexual interests. Make room for these stories. And sometimes a therapist can reframe these stories. That is, parents might think that their history would make them less able to judge what's right or wrong, what's normal and healthy, less able to speak openly. Often they are embarrassed by their lack of experience or their problem behavior in adolescence. A therapist can turn this around to indicate that such experiences help parents know what good parenting ought to be around these issues. For example, a mother might explain in therapy why she feels incompetent, for example, "My mother never talked to me about sex. I didn't even know what my period was when I got it." And a therapist might respond by saying, "Let's think about what you know now and what you wished your mother had said to you."

Fifth, in discussions with parents, I want to help them clarify their values and not just state their positions. Whether it's natural, common, or frightening for teens to be active sexually, parents have a right to their views and a responsibility to convey those views. But too often parents simply lay down the law about sexual activity without explaining to their kids their moral view behind it. Even when their views or restrictions come from a religious perspective, it's important that they be able to convey the reasoning behind their or, in some instances, God's view. I've rarely worked with religious adults who reduce their values to a literal reading of the Bible such as "the Bible forbids it." All were able to express the reasoning behind their moral outlook, whether it was a philosophy of the body as a temple or reasoning that had more to do with sex being an expression of God's love and thus only for marriage. An adolescent should be able to say after talking to his or her parents, "This is what my parents believe and why." The truth is that sometimes teens will do things that disappoint their parents or demonstrate a different perspective, but disobedience out of hostile rebellion instead of consideration of one's own values in relation to one's parents' values won't lead to healthy choices.

The sixth point is that it is wonderful when parents can discuss sexism and homophobia that their children hear around them; I encourage parents to do so. But sometimes parents themselves are the source of these comments. If I know that parents are making these kinds of comments at home, having learned this from individual sessions with their child, for example, a father making nasty comments about girls to his son (thinking it doesn't hurt anyone because he doesn't have any daughters) or nasty comments about gay men or lesbians (thinking, once again, that it doesn't hurt anyone because he doesn't know any gay people except for Uncle Josh and he doesn't mind homophobic jokes), I try to explain to them how such comments influence their kids and contribute to their anxiety and insecurity. I tell parents that kids hear a lot of put-downs about other kids' sexual behavior and so little about what is good, meaning morally good, sex and people's values. In my opinion, whether it's wrong or not to talk like that, it makes kids and everyone else very anxious that sex and sexuality can be such a source of bad feelings and humor. Taking a perspective that promotes tolerance, being the kind of parent who rises above sexism and homophobia, along with giving positive messages about sex, can help teens feel more confident in their bodies and in their romantic relationships when moving forward into the world.

Seventh, so how do we help parents to instill positive messages about sex when they don't want to talk about sex or even acknowledge their child's interest? One way is to talk with them in session about what they feel and think, and a good way to start is to ask them what they think about all the sex in the media. Most parents have strong opinions about this, and it's a common way discussions between kids and parents get started. I remember a time when a commercial was on TV with a beautiful model dancing around singing the Right Said Fred British pop song, "I'm too sexy for my shirt, too sexy for my . . ." And I started singing, "You're too sexy for my son, too sexy for my son!" which cracked him up. And I added that I really wished they'd show girls who looked real on TV so he didn't learn to be all into fashion model types and not be able to enjoy a real girl's looks and sexiness. Saying this, I tried to convey that it was all right to enjoy a girl's sexiness but that I hoped it would be a real girl and not some plasticized version of what a sexy girl ought to be like.

If parents say that they have strict boundaries around TV watching, I ask them, "And how do you convey the reason why to your daughter?" They usually make some statement about why they don't like TV and I will help them to reframe that as a concern they have for their daughter's sexuality and sexual feelings and then as a wish they have for her to grow up to be healthy. In my experience, parents need some space and help to clarify their hopes and wishes because they have been so wound up in saying *no* and *don't*.

Point eight is that sometimes parents have disagreements about this. Mothers who live day in and day out in the world of relationships with their teens frequently have a more liberal view. The stereotype is that Dad's view will be more liberal, pushing his son to "get some," but women in our culture have been so inundated with relationship and sexual advice via magazines, *Oprah*, and other "female" sources that they have become more expert and perhaps the more liberal parent in families. A father might lay down the law about his little girl and a mother will tell him that's unrealistic. An all-too-typical family situation is one in which the mother keeps secrets from the father that would upset him, for example, allowing their daughter to stay out late after the prom with her boyfriend, but indicating to the father that she's at a sleepover with girlfriends. I don't think this pattern is indicative of a bad marriage or a dysfunctional family. Rather, it's a typical American middle-class familial pattern where the father is allowed to believe he has authority over the family and his teenage daughter but where the mother actually has the authority. She props up the father as a figurehead and to avoid confrontation and maintain her own covert sense of power and connection to her kids, lies to him, and makes the real rules and regulations. We ought not to blame the mother for this because obviously, if the father wanted to be there in the trenches, he wouldn't accept this position as figurehead. They both are in collusion to keep the father blind and to give the mother responsibility for raising the kids.

Keeping himself at a distance from the daily ins and outs of his kids' relationships, a father might have quite unclarified views about what he wants for his son. I normalize this kind of interaction and tell parents that it's quite common for parents to have disagreements. I also tell parents they do not always have to present a united front as long as they explain their disagreements rationally and don't constantly fight about them right in front of their child. It's actually paradoxical if you think of it—telling parents that they don't have to be united and then helping them to be united in the way they convey their lack of unity to their child.

Jude's father was firm, saying that no way was she allowed to be alone with her boyfriend in the house. Both Jude's mother and I knew that Jude had already spent time alone with her boyfriend in the house quite frequently, and I knew, because I was Jude's individual therapist, that Jude was having sex with her boyfriend. I had a confidentiality agreement with Jude that took priority in a meeting with her parents; that is to say, I could only convey to them what Jude and I had agreed beforehand that I could talk about. So I asked Jude's father for his reasoning behind this rule.

As he spoke, the rigid rule-maker father seemed to melt away, and the thoughtful and reflective human beings we all can be shone. He said he guessed he thought Jude needed to know that he didn't approve of premarital sex because he didn't think a teenage boy would really appreciate her or respect her enough and he would hate to see her used and spit out. He added that he had done some of that in college and felt kind of bad about it. He knew that there were a lot of guys out there who could be totally one way with a girl and then disrespectful behind her back. I asked, "Have you shared your experiences with Jude?" "No," he answered. "If I were to ask Jude why you had this rule, what do you think she would say would be your reason?" He realized then that Jude would probably think that he thought that she was untrustworthy, a "slut." That was indeed what Jude thought but it wasn't necessary for me to confirm that with him in that moment. My goal wasn't to get him to loosen his rules for Jude, but instead to open the door for communication so that Jude wasn't acting and making decisions in the world without benefit of her parents' real opinions and experiences.

William Pollack, the author of *Real Boys* (1998), suggested that parents acknowledge the complexities of adolescence with their kid, saying sometimes, "It's hard being a teenager." This is the ninth point I want to emphasize. It *is* hard, given all the media messages about what it means to be a woman or how to be a man. If parents talk about sex within this framework or what it means to grow up with certain gender restrictions, it gives their talks about sex a different meaning and puts sex in the context of what it means to be a responsible adult in a world that creates images of adulthood that are gender-stereotyped and very narrow. Parents are aware of this as you point out the messages and I encourage them to have gender talks with their kids: "You're getting a lot of messages about how to be a man—messages, about being tough and macho and always wanting sex, and then messages that you have to be respectful and loving with your girlfriend. It must seem like you have to be a different kind of person wherever you go." Or, for a daughter, "You're getting a lot of messages about how to be a woman, about how to dress up and act sexy to be appealing to boys and yet at the same time messages about not crossing over the line into becoming a slut. It must be confusing about where the lines are drawn and what is expected of women today, how much assertiveness, how much girlishness."

Finally, Pollack (1998) has reminded us to "provide frequent affirmation" to teenagers. Pollack also wrote, "Make your home a safe place" using the metaphor of the revolving door. I use that metaphor with parents. Sure, teenagers may not be home a lot, but you want them to be able to whiz by and refuel, feel safe, and pause to check out any ideas. If you're standing inside the house when they zoom by, they may step out of their flight pattern for a moment to stop and talk.

PARENTS ARE HELPLESS BUT INFLUENTIAL

The Bishops were in my office to have a regular parent meeting about my individual therapy with their 14-year-old daughter, and they brought in a crumpled-up note that they found on the floor of her room, a note that missed the wastepaper basket. The note insinuated that she would give a boy a blow job if he were to come to a certain party. They weren't sure whether Katie actually would do this or if this was just a way that kids joked around with each other, but most important, they had no idea how to talk to her about this, so they asked for an appointment. If they were to bring it up to Katie, they knew they would be accused of snooping, and the conversation would probably end there, with her storming off to her room and slamming the door. Their inclination was not to let her go to any more parties until she was older. I joked, "Maybe you'd better first take away her pens and paper!" just so that they'd entertain the possibility that the problem was in the writing and not in the behavior.

Together we went over the possibilities this note conveyed: (1) Katie wrote pretend notes to boys with her girlfriends, laughed over them, crumpled them up, and threw them away (not an option the parents had thought about); (2) she wrote notes to boys to joke around in a sexual way, probably following up on lots of pretend Instant Message conversations about the same; (3) she was actually promising something that she wasn't going to deliver to get this boy to go to the party or to convey how much she wanted him to go to the party; and (4) she was willing to perform oral sex with this boy at the party. If a journalist got this note, there'd be seven news stories about teens and sex, but parents don't have to go the route of sensationalism. And we all ought to realize that the constant harping on teen sexuality in the media makes us all believe too much too soon is going on everywhere. Still, their daughter could be among the few who do extend this "benefit" to boys in their social groups, and there are very few parents I know who want their daughters feeling free enough to perform oral sex on acquaintances at parties—even among the most liberal. And the Bishops were very liberal.

I shared with them that it is a different world out there for teens today. Lots more sex joking and sex talk between boys and girls, talk that mostly leads to nothing but is a way of acting sophisticated, knowledgeable, hot, or tough. I also explained that I had recently come to understand this whole oral sex phenomenon in a different way—when we were growing up it was thought of as something more intimate than intercourse, a fifth or sixth base, not a stop between third and fourth to use the age-old baseball metaphor. Bill Clinton shaped (or expressed) what was on the minds of American youth when he said, "I did not have sex with that woman." Teens don't always see oral sex as sex. Girls also tend to think of it as something that's easy enough (no big deal!) to do though a bit gross at first. It doesn't feel intimate to them because their own private parts are not involved. And it's something about which they can get praise and attention from boys while feeling sophisticated, like a *Sex and the City* woman. Girls, as always, have to walk a thin line between slutty and sexually assertive, and they're trying to walk it.

At the end of this session, the parents had clarified that what they wanted to convey to Katie was that they wanted sex for her to be something mutual and special, and not something casual. They decided to tell her they found that note on the floor and while they didn't take it totally seriously, they thought they should share with her their feelings about sex. I encouraged them to tell her how they know that it's unfair to girls that they have to walk such a thin line between skanky and sophisticated, and that they wanted to protect her from the judgments of other people and support her to make her own decisions based on her own sense of self and desire, not other people's judgments. They decided to tell her that they didn't want her to grow up thinking that sex is something you perform on people or that they do to you, but acts to express something special, a special feeling. They wanted to acknowledge that they like sex jokes too but that they thought that too much in society cheapens sex and makes it a joke.

I took the perspective that whatever they decided to convey was fine, as long as they were able to speak honestly about their concerns in a nonjudgmental manner. It wasn't that they shouldn't have judgments, but strategically speaking, expressing judgment instead of values often ends the conversation or begins a fight. I paradoxically tried to convey to them the double message that they had no control but enormous influence; they couldn't control Katie and she was going to do what she wanted to do, but what they said would have enormous importance to her. And I didn't take a stand about parties or blow jobs.

When Katie came into her next session, she was "onto" the next big issue in her life and didn't even ask what her parents had talked about with me. I asked if she wanted to talk about that.

Katie: Oh. Yeah. So what did they say?

Therapist: They basically had some concerns about your growing up sexually, and I basically told them to think through what they wanted to say to you about that and say it.

K: Cool. (pause) Yeah. We had a good talk. They're totally hyper about parties now but that's stupid. I'm not going to do anything stupid there. It's way too public. And other kids can be so immature.

Kids often need to dismiss their parents as being out of touch and wrong in their perceptions about them, but they take in what their parents say.

HELPING PARENTS SET THE RIGHT KINDS OF LIMITS

One of the funniest things I've noticed in therapy with teens is that parents are constantly setting limits around one area in which their child is totally innocent and in no danger, while not setting limits in another area where I'm petrified their kid is going to go out and really hurt herself. For example, one set of parents prohibited their daughter from going on an overnight camping trip, thinking for sure there would be boys and drugs there. Actually, it was going to be quite an innocent outing where two best friends really wanted to get away from it all on a nearby mountain; for whatever reason, my client was unable to convince her parents of that. These same parents didn't know that the weekend before, when their daughter slept over at a friend's house, after the parents went to sleep, they all got in a car and were driving around drunk.

The other frightening aspect about all this is that a teen feels totally justified in getting angry about a punishment, restriction, or suspicion raised by a parent that is wrong in one context, when the teen is doing exactly the thing the parent is afraid of in a different context. Teens never seem to see, unless I point it out, that they're furious about being misjudged, thinking the parents are totally paranoid, although they may be being judged (or worried about) correctly except that their parents got a somewhat irrelevant detail wrong. "What fools parents are" is a common theme when parents restrict. They do it wrong. They miss all the important stuff. And yet, I say, "Hey, the bigger message is more important. They're worried about you and given the other risks you're taking, shouldn't they be?"

In a parent meeting, parents want to know if their limit setting is on target and if their son or daughter is doing something unsafe or irresponsible. They've been accused by of not trusting their teen. They want to trust but are afraid. I reaffirm their fears to a certain extent if it's warranted. I tell them straight on that most parents miss the mark. They are too strict for some activities that are innocent, and not strict enough for others. And I tell them that they may never know which are which. However, I also tell them that their message can still be clear even when it's misdirected to an innocent activity—they're doing this for overall safety. They may be wrong sometimes, but they're doing the best they can to help children get through their teen years safely.

One teen client, Kayley, whom I saw for a couple of years, had had to take care of herself for a long time. Together we understood her mother as totally overwhelmed by her divorce, continued threats by her ex to take her to court for custody, several jobs, and longstanding multiple sclerosis that sometimes left her weak and tired. When Kayley's mother started feeling better and began setting limits, without practice, she wasn't doing it perfectly, restricting, according to Kayley, stupid things that she had done already many times, and not seeing other important areas where she needed more parenting. She not only mocked her mother but was furious. Although for a long time she wanted her mother more involved in her life, when her mother set a limit, her attitude was "How dare she!" Kayley had been competent enough to take care of herself last year, so why did she have to listen to her mother this year? Besides, her mother was such a novice. She couldn't even see that it was stupid to restrict Kayley on Friday night when Kayley was just going to go out and do the same thing on Saturday night. I sympathized and said it would be hard for Kayley as her mother tried to be more of a mother to her, perhaps inadequate, yet she was trying, and not leaving Kayley alone to fend for herself.

When a therapist is seeing a teen individually and not doing family therapy, the therapist's allegiance lies with the teenager, but the situation is a tricky one. It's important not to replace the parent and be the one to set restrictions when the parent is too lax; but a therapist ought not be just another friend who sympathizes over difficult parents. When alone with the parents in ad hoc parent sessions, a therapist will want to help parents to be parents, without betraying how much and in what areas their daughter or son needs one. In this case, when I spoke with Kayley's mother I complimented her on her efforts to set more limits and sympathized with how hard it was to set the right kind of limits. I also told her that even though Kayley might put up a fight, in the long run, if her mother could convey to her the reasons for these restrictions, she would understand it as caring. Back in the office with Kayley, I told her that I needed to support her mother in her setting of limits and staying involved. Kayley began to go on about how pathetic her mother was whenever she tried to set a limit. I told her that I thought it was for both their benefit if her mother kept trying, even when she failed at getting it right. She accepted that.

I was once consulted on a case in which a family was seeing their son's therapist for twice-weekly family sessions in addition to the once-weekly sessions for the son. It seemed to me that this therapist was making a mint on this overly intensive focus on family issues at a time when this 15-year-old boy's task was to separate. However, separation was more difficult given that this boy, Drew, was coping with his parents' divorce and subsequent remarriages. At his father's home, his new stepmother was better at limit setting than his father; however, she clearly did not want to be the bad guy. At his mother's home, Drew hated his mother's new hus-band and wouldn't accept limits from either of them. An issue arose when the therapist brought in the father and stepmother and asked that Drew speak to them directly about something he had brought up in individual therapy with her. Drew asked for permission to have a girlfriend sleep over at the house. His par-ents hadn't even met this girlfriend. The therapist then urged the parents to say yes to this request, as it would indicate to Drew that they accepted his becoming a sexual being and would show sup-port. I was quite shocked that the therapist argued on behalf of her client for this. Such a statement demonstrates the problems that arise when an individual therapist begins to do family therapy. Her position is to support her client, and in that position, family therapy becomes problematic. She put the father in a very difficult position. Because his new wife didn't want to have girls sleeping over in the house and because he was told that allowing that would show support of his son, he was then asked by the ther-apist to choose between wife and son.

I asked the father, who consulted with me, whether or not he thought it was okay for his son to have sex at this age. He answered that he did, but that his son might not even have a girl-friend yet. If he had a girlfriend, then maybe, over time, they would get to know her and maybe they would find that it would not be so difficult if she were to sleep over. But right now, it seemed so abstract and sordid. The fact that they hadn't even met this girlfriend struck me as very important information. I asked a few more questions and discovered that this girlfriend was prob-ably a very new thing in Drew's life and that he had never had a girlfriend before. I then advised the father and stepmother to come up with rules that they both felt comfortable with and to share them with Drew, but also to tell him that they were open to change in the future. They could encourage him to explore having a sexual relationship and still say that they were uncomfortable with having a girlfriend sleep over at the house at present. I also then instructed them to tell Drew that his sexual life was a private matter, and that while they wanted him to be responsible as far as contraception and relationships go, and could give him condoms and information if he asked, that his sexual life was his business and that he would know when he was ready and when he was, it probably wouldn't become such a public family matter then.

My take on this was that Drew was making his sexual activity a family problem because he was ambivalent himself. The whole idea of becoming a sexual person was probably a bit scary for him, although exciting, and he wanted his parents to hold onto one side of the ambivalence so he could feel like he was a man raring to go. The fact that he made this such a family event was indicative that this was about separation and not sex. His father needed to support Drew to make his own decisions about this, just as the father and stepmother were making theirs about the house and their need for privacy and comfort.

Sometimes a therapist, when working with a teen, hears about all sorts of problem sexual behaviors that the therapist dearly wants the parents to know about. But while some girls seem to get off on telling therapists about their escapades, it's not always a good idea to join in with the excitement and collude with the secrecy from the parents, the excitement, the adventure. Lynette, for example, was sneaking boys into the house, using drugs, having sex with boys she didn't care about, and not using any contraception. But over time it became unclear if she was talking about a lot of activity or just a little bit that she found so exciting that she built it up for her therapist, Anne, into tall tales. She would tell Anne, a young woman I supervised, about all the things she was planning to do—stay out all night, meet up with this guy, "he was so cute," and so on. But as Anne was relating to me what the girl was doing or said she was doing, there were parts of the story that didn't match up. We wondered at first if Anne was just getting the story wrong, so she went back to sessions with a keen ear for inconsistencies and reported back that she thought Lynette probably was glamorizing her adventures for Anne's sake, and maybe to evoke Anne's motherly cautions.

Lynette's mother had abandoned her when she was six because of severe drug problems. She remembered her mom well and even though she had been the parent-child in the household, she still felt, as kids do, complicated feelings that she was bad and deserving of such neglect and that she was to blame for her mother's drug addiction. The caseworkers all liked her and wanted her to do well. They thought they had found her the perfect preadoptive home, with Andy and Bonnie, a couple who couldn't have children of their own and were committed to helping a child in need. They thought they could handle a difficult teenager because, put simply, they felt like they had a lot of love to give.

Anne began seeing Lynette alone, but after many phone calls from the preadoptive parents about Lynette's sneaking out of the house in the middle of the night, she asked for a family meeting. As is common among therapists of teens, she knew a lot more than these parents. She knew that even though Lynette was a big talker, she probably really had been sneaking out of the house and sneaking boys in. In fact, Bonnie and Andy had caught her sneaking back into her room at five in the morning twice, and told Social Services and Anne, but were committed to keeping Lynette and working on these issues. In therapy with Anne, Lynette admitted she was worried about her own drug use and about sneaking boys in. But Anne felt there was also some excitement about the chance of being found out by these parents—that they would discover in some dramatic scene that she really was a slut and decide they couldn't possibly keep her.

I had initially understood Lynette's sneaking out of the house and sexual behavior, whatever the truth was in her stories, as representative of her desire to act out how bad she thought she was and to test these preadoptive parents. But when Anne told me what the parents were like in session, we formulated a different idea.

These parents wanted to see her as younger than she was; they loved her and had missed out on her earlier years. They were gung ho about this adoption, but they saw her as a younger, more innocent child than she was at 13. Her features supported this—petite with long dark hair and big wide-set eyes that revealed some of her Native American heritage. Anne had asked Lynette before the session if she was willing to talk to them about what she knew about sex and drugs and let them learn how mature she really was, but she said no, they wouldn't adopt me then. Anne said, they need to know that you're a teenager who needs their protection."

But part of Lynette didn't want to be prevented from doing what she wanted to do; having lived in a house where she was the parent to the parent, she was used to making her own choices. Part of her didn't want them to know the real Lynette because knowing that she wasn't as sweet and innocent as they thought would surely lead to them abandoning her. But she also was still sweet and innocent in some ways and wanted them to baby her. When Anne suggested this might be the case, she looked at as though to say, "Are you kidding? Who in the world wants to be babied?" Anne stood her ground and said we all do and that maybe Lynette still had a side of her that wanted to be someone's baby, and that she didn't have to give that up or make that part of her fake.

Many teens lie about sex and drugs, and so it was normative for her to be doing some of this with her preadoptive parents. But it was still dangerous. She sorely needed overprotective parents, parents who were savvy about what to watch out for and who would sit on her rather than let her sneak out at night. She needed to bring some conflict into the relationship instead of showing them only her little-girl side. If she integrated that at home, then perhaps she wouldn't need to be so slutty and tough with the boys she snuck out with.

I suggested that Anne start to work for a little bit with the whole family while she was working with Lynette separately and that if things seemed to be working, she could find the family or the parents their own therapist. This would be tricky, because she'd really have to be careful about keeping confidentiality with Lynette, but it seemed important to reinforce the trio rather than the separate adult self of Lynette. I suggested a paradoxical treatment session where the parents would grieve the baby they lost and ritualistically welcome the teenager they had. This took a few sessions to achieve because it became clear these parents weren't ready to do the difficult parenting required by a teenager. They wanted to "cure her" with love and care. Anne noticed that together in the room, Bonnie teared up when she talked about Lynette's early childhood and what she must have missed, while Lynette stared at her intently. Systems theorists have shown us how one family member can do the feeling for others, and this family was a dynamic system already. Anne asked Lynette to tell her parents if she felt like crying sometimes about her childhood and what she missed. On cue, she told them that she was "way past that" and that she also felt that she had learned a lot by having to take care of herself and that it didn't really bother her anymore. Bonnie and Andy said that they understood her to be saying it was too painful for her to look back. But Anne asked if there were other possibilities. Andy suggested that maybe she really didn't feel that bad about her childhood (Lynette lit up at that). Bonnie said maybe she wasn't ready to look at the pain. Anne could see that Lynette was paying attention and considering all these possible selves. She added that she never saw any grief or sadness in Lynette. Then Anne said, "Do you think that it's possible you two need to grieve the baby you didn't get to take care of? You obviously love Lynette so much, it must be hard to think back about the times when she was hurt or alone and you weren't there to comfort her, and hard to accept, as she says, that she may be way past that." Anne and I didn't really think Lynette was way past that, but we had talked about the need to reflect back what Lynette said to her parents and didn't want her to have to own any feeling she wasn't ready to accept. The parents were sent away, with Lynette, to think of a way that they might, in the next session, create a ritual where they grieved their lost baby, symbolically. Anne told them what she knew of the power of rituals.

They returned the next session with a baby doll. Lynette proudly said that she made them buy one because no way was she going to be part of any ritual. Anne smartly said that she didn't need to play the part of herself as a baby; that this was about the baby in Bonnie's mind that she lost, who sometimes she saw in Lynette. Rather than coming up with a funeral or eulogy, Bonnie and Andy had decided that they would ritualistically go through the stages of child development. Playful and yet serious, knowing all the while that Lynette was watching them, they talked and walked through the earliest stages of raising a child, from pretending to breast-feed the doll, to toilet training (at which point Lynette entered the conversation with details from her own past, telling them that her mom said that she was really good at toilet training and had always been very neat and folded her toilet paper into smart little squares), at which her adoptive parents marveled at how fast the doll learned and told her it was okay if she still had accidents or if she wanted to crumple up the paper. A few tears were shed at the beginning because this ritual had enormous meaning to Bonnie, who had suffered many years trying to conceive, and yet it ended very playfully with Lynette a participant, giving advice about how the baby Lynette would have responded and teasing them to keep an eye on the baby doll when they put her down.

We asked them to go away and come up with a ritual for adolescence, knowing this would be difficult for them. I had suggested to Anne to tell them that she didn't think of adolescence as a time of letting go, just of renegotiating the relationship, acknowledging that a child was almost adult but letting the child know that there would still be direction and guidance. They came back empty-handed but talked about all their images, such as letting a bird out of its cage, which didn't seem right. Lynette was quick to point out that the bird could get eaten by stray dogs or cats. They also thought of planting a rosebush, but then they'd have to wait to see what would happen and roses didn't really mean that much to either of them. So Anne posed the question a different way. If adolescence wasn't about separation, and if Lynette had had too much independence in her life already, what did it mean for her to become a teenager? Andy laughed, "Sex, drugs, and rock and roll?" "Perfect," said Anne. "Let's think of a ritual where you join her in guiding her through sex, drugs, and rock and roll." The parents were sent away to think about what they wanted to share with her about each of these important adolescent issues. Anne asked them to make a list that talked about both the risks and the pleasures of each, and to say how each could contribute or influence Lynette in becoming the adult they saw blossoming in her.

Our goal was to enable Lynette to have her new parents be players in her life, to have them understand the extent to which she was involved with some pretty risky behaviors and a fast-moving crowd. But while Andy and Bonnie were ready to share their dreams and fears, it was much harder for Lynette to share what she knew and did with her crowd. While our plans were for Anne to work with this family so that Lynette could eventually use her parents as a resource and so that these parents, who were innocents of sorts, could get scared enough to set appropriate limits and provide consequences for this behavior, Lynette ran away. She didn't actually run away; she stayed out all night for two nights while her parents and the police combed the streets looking for her. The Department of Children and Families then placed her in a home for adolescent girls and stopped their adoption talk with Bonnie and Andy. Bonnie and Andy continued to visit her but were told that they probably wouldn't be able to adopt Lynette when she came out of the home.

This was a very sad ending to what seemed like an interesting family therapy exercise. But that's the way it goes sometimes. Not all cases end well in spite of our best intentions. A child with attachment difficulties or ambivalence is one of the hardest children to reach. And sex may seem to have little to do with it. But for so many teen-age girls issues of feeling bad and dirty inside are wrapped up in their issues of attachment. Sexual feelings in adolescence get played out as evidence of their badness, their worthlessness. They're unlovable because they're dirty, damaged goods, throwaway children. They may also go after sexual experience in a counterphobic way, just as sexually abused children try to master their abuse by sometimes putting themselves in situations of danger. But sex brings up other issues too. Being wanted, whether for sex or love, can momentarily answer deep feelings of longing, and sex is a way to have fleeting moments of being wanted and desired. Finally, sex can be a way a teenager reenacts her own abandonment from a powerful position, using others and then rejecting them, sometimes in humiliating ways, to make them feel like the unwanted one, not good enough.

ACKNOWLEDGING THE JOY AS WELL AS THE DANGER

One of our hopes with Lynette was that if her mother and father could talk about the joy they wished Lynette would have in the future and not just the risks of the present, Lynette might be able to see herself as a sexual person in a different way, and understand the excitement as part of the sex and not as part of the rebellion. Most parents feel that the reason to discuss sex with their teen is to keep them from danger, but therapists can help them to understand why it's important to also talk about fun and pleasure.

I once wrote about a conversation I had with a mother and her two daughters about sex. The girls were identical twins and in the eighth grade and had heard about my recently published book on girls' sexuality, *The Secret Lives of Girls*, and wanted to talk (Lamb, 2002). Jessie told me how in her junior high, some girls were "giving head" to boys at parties. They spoke of one girl who, with a friend, found random "cute" boys at the movie theater and offered to do the same there. Coming from a feminist perspective, I casually asked them if the boys ever did something back to the girls. Jen said sometimes a boy would offer to "finger" a girl, then looked at her mom and said, "I don't think that's fair. Don't you think that a girl would feel more pleasure if the boy gave her oral sex?"

Wow, I thought. Could this mother rise to the occasion? And she did. She said, "Yes, one would think so. But perhaps a girl feels more uncomfortable with that. What do you think?" We don't have many opportunities to have sex-positive talks with teenagers, and so one needs to grab these moments and hold on. Same with teenage sons. Sure the culture supports their need for pleasure, but joy? I think not. Joy and lovely feelings quickly get turned into bragging bravado and snickers about sex. Feeling happiness about sexual pleasure may be too vulnerable an emotion for a boy to share with his friends. And yet it's so important for parents to acknowledge the sweetness of this. With boys, parents will talk about restraint, respect, and protection. If you think about it, this starts with the premise that a boy is going to be a harassing irresponsible animal. Yet what we know of boys is that they can be incredibly sweet and good to their partners, that they feel thrilled when they can do sexual things with a girl they have strong feelings for, that they don't separate lust from love.

It is sometimes difficult, with parents, to get beyond a response of restraint. Some parents will want restraint for religious reasons, advocating that their daughter or son (if they don't have a double standard) should save sex for marriage or save sex for when they are older and more mature or for someone they love. But parents need to place these values in a conversation about joy and pleasure, not only because they're more likely to be able to have a conversation that way, but also because that really is an important focus of sex for teens. When parents can talk about pleasure and the body, then the underlying message to their teens is that it's *their* body and they need to know it and make sensible decisions regarding the feelings this body is capable of.

To only advocate restraint with teens is misguided for other reasons. First, most responses that focus on abstinence or restraint indicate to teenagers that the parents define sex as intercourse. This focus on sex as intercourse actually has the paradoxical effect of setting up a goal or endpoint of sexual development—losing one's virginity, as in the very popular teen film *American Pie*. In this film, boys try to lose their virginity before graduating high school, and having intercourse is glorified as the be-all and end-all of sex, one more must-have in our material culture, next to the iPod. Judith Levine, in her controversial book *Harmful to Minors* (2002), has reminded us of the exquisite sensuality of teen petting, those hours on the rec room couch when kissing and some touching seemed to go on forever. She worried, as do I, that today's teens are being taught that intercourse (or oral intercourse) is all there is; that teens are trying to get there too soon.

Therapists can tell parents that if they're going to promote a "wait until you're older" perspective, they can also follow up by pointing out that there's a whole lot more kids can do sexually before they have intercourse (including masturbation). Instead, parents say "Wait until you're ready, until you're mature enough to handle all the complicated emotions, until you're old enough to be sure this is it, until you're in love, until your body has stopped changing, until you're out of the house and not under our supervision!" It's as if parents are saying, "I'm not ready, this is emotionally taxing for me, and I can't handle it." I believe that part of parents' fear about the repercussions of sex is fueled by their own fear of their child's sexuality. We know that in countries like the Netherlands, France, and Germany, kids generally have sex at the same age as those in the United States without many negative repercussions because they're given great sex education, use condoms, and are very positive about the whole thing.

Both fathers and mothers can acknowledge their teens as sexual beings in proud and loving ways rather than through wisecracks. Mothers play such a crucial role in sex education that it may be worthwhile to have a mother-daughter session, no matter how full of conflict it might be. I've found in practice that daughters are desperate to have their mothers give them permission to be sexual. They tell me how they wish they could speak to their mothers about what they do. They want to be known for who they are. It's mothers who need to help their daughters understand that being sexy is not the endpoint of a developing sexuality.

How does a mother do that in a therapy session? Many will need the support of the therapist to feel okay about discussing this taboo subject. Some may need individual work with the therapist to understand what kinds of sexual pleasures they have given up as they have grown older and more complacent in marriage, less likely to ask for what they need, and less playful sexually. I would start by asking the mother to talk about her own sexual education with her daughter. It's helpful for the daughter to see the mother as someone who has grown up with certain criticisms and restrictions, as well as support. Making sure to tap into all sources of sex education, peers, parents, religion, media, and school, I would then ask the mother to talk about how her sex education affected her as a sexual person. How old was she when she had her most pleasurable experiences? What gets in the way or has gotten in the way of her loving her body, respecting her body, or experiencing pleasure?

While kids really don't want to hear about their parents' sex lives, and the therapy session should avoid that kind of conversation in front of kids, these kinds of questions are different. Note that they ask parents to share not what they do, but how they reflects on themselves as growing sexual people. Through these questions, the therapist can help parents convey to their teenage daughters that parents are still sexual people, and that her parents are people who know something about sexual pleasure

* * * *

It may be that in a therapist's work with families, sexual issues never come up, not for the parents and not between parents and kids. It could also be the case that many therapists are not alert to sexual issues or are afraid to ask. Hopefully, if we take an attitude that sex is a part of life, and acknowledge with parents that their teens are developing into sexual beings before the parents' very eyes, we'll begin to hear family talk a little differently. Even those therapists I know who do couples counseling feel nervous when talking about sex and sexuality—wanting to help couples who struggle with these issues, but never feeling quite knowledgeable enough or clear enough themselves to lead the way. But in a session with parents, when therapists are a little more alert to these issues and parents' concerns, they can help parents address sexual issues and values more directly with their kids and teens, convey a sense of what they hope for the future and well-being of their kids, and make important statements about the kind of sex education their children are receiving from the media.

CHAPTER EIGHT

Coming Out During the Teen Years

With Glenda M. Russell and Janis S. Bohan

When a teenager self-identifies as gay or lesbian, talk in therapy need not include talk about sex, but it frequently does, if not with the teenager, then with parents, who may consult you with questions and concerns. Same-sex sexual attraction is indeed one of the reasons teens begin to self-identify as gay, and a therapist may need to make a concerted effort to move beyond the safer talk about identity and ask about sexual feelings and attractions, if only to let a teenager know it's acceptable to give voice to these thoughts and feelings to someone. In fact, when first meeting with a teen who is in the process of coming out, a therapist can signal that it's okay to be out in therapy, that there's space for what the client may think of as unacceptable feelings and talk.

This chapter presents issues for therapists when an adolescent is considering coming out. Other parts of this book present clinical case material (see Diane in Chapter 5) and guidelines for adolescents who are confused, questioning, or even just wondering. Some of the principles for working with these adolescents are the same, whether they are coming out or just questioning.

First, acknowledge that what makes working with this youth different is the homophobia and heterosexism in our culture and the world. (Homophobia is wide-ranging and although most therapists are not overtly homophobic, we all harbor some of these feelings from living in a culture that denigrates same-sex attraction. And many are heterosexist, presuming heterosexuality in their clients and the world in a way that may feel homophobic to their clients.

Second, Remember that contexts differ radically for each client. Individual adolescents differ in terms of their sexual, cognitive, and socioemotional development. Perhaps more important, they come from different families and different communities. It might be quite different to come to an awareness of same-sex attraction in the rural South or the Midwest than it does to come to that awareness in San Francisco, Western Massachusetts, or any large city with a prominent and active gay community. Also, adolescents come from different religious perspectives that express support or condemnation for being gay. And history plays a part in this. Is a youth coming out in the middle of a community-wide or statewide effort to legalize gay marriage? Youths that come out today are coming out into a very different community than youths who came out 20 years ago.

Third, therapists always ought to be aware that the kid who is considering coming out is also an adolescent. This goes for working with teens who are questioning their sexuality. Sexual orientation is one part of their identity and does not have to be a master identity for them or the people around them. Some therapists forget that there are other issues going on in a teen's life that have much more to do with being an adolescent rather than being a gay adolescent. It's a therapist's responsibility to avoid an overfocus on this one aspect, to view teens as adolescents with adolescent issues, and to encourage adolescents to maintain and develop activities and supports for all aspects of themselves.

Fourth, it's important for therapists to note when lesbian, gay, or bisexual (LGB) teens have other intersecting identities that should be discussed. For example, when a Korean American girl who is discussing coming out to her family talks about the issues, a therapist who is not Korean might ask what sorts of issues there might be in the Korean community about homosexuality and whether or not her family might be influenced by them. But it is also the therapist's responsibility first to do some research and talk to this client about how this might play out in her life.

Finally, therapists need to provide resources or talk to teens about how they might access resources for further knowledge. Helping a teen to connect to a community group is one way a therapist might intervene. Also, sometimes it is good to have some simple pamphlets in one's office. Even knowing that there are resources out there counteracts a feeling that the world is uniformly homophobic and that one is alone.

These same guidelines work well with families too: (1) acknowledge the homophobia in the child's world and talk about heterosexist assumptions; (2) discuss the child's environment, the context in which he or she is coming out; (3) help the parents see their child as an adolescent first, a gay adolescent second; (4) address other group identities that the family has, racial, religious, and ethnic; and (5) give parents resources (the PFLAG Web site is a good one).

This chapter explores sex talk in therapy when a teenager has announced she or he has come out to someone—his parents, her friends, even to himself! But "coming out," now a somewhat celebratory phrase for the act of telling friends and family that one is gay, deriving from the phrase "in the closet," denoting that few if any people know about one's sexuality, even that one is hiding it, also suggests several narratives about gay and lesbian identity. In familiarizing ourselves with these stories, we as therapists can recognize when we are buying into them over a different reality that a client presents. We also can help our clients understand that their experience may be very different than what they have come to expect.

NARRATIVES OF COMING OUT

The first narrative about gay identity and coming out is that it happens in one big dramatic moment. We may get that idea from TV and the movies, where such experiences are portrayed in dramatic ways following traditional plot narratives where the coming out is either the beginning of a series of problems or the climactic moment after a series of problems. In today's society, in liberal families, and in urban environments, to name a few contexts, the idea of coming out may be less salient. Teens' families may have already come to see them as gay or lesbian, or, in some families, albeit the atypical ones, teens' sexual orientation may not have that much importance.

Inherent to the "dramatic moment" narrative is the idea that one comes out once. While this is a good climactic moment for TV, typically there are many first times in a teenager's life: the first time she told her family, the first time she told her friends, when she came out to her grandmother, when she came out at school. In one's life, there will be continuous choices to make about whether or not to self-identify as gay or lesbian in describing oneself to people or in one's interactions. At different moments in a teen's life, not identifying oneself as LGB may feel like a betrayal of the self, like closeting one's identity, or as if one were ashamed. At other moments, it may just not seem relevant and a teen may ask, why does my sexuality have to be an issue all the time? Of course, the feeling that it *is* an issue with other people can be a teen's accurate reading of a homophobic culture. It can also be based on fearful expectations or projections of the teen's own self-criticism or insecurities. Therapists will need to explore these as both realities and projections as the therapy progresses, keeping in mind that homophobia still exists in even the most liberal of communities.

As an aside, it's important to note that there may be times when it's dangerous to come out. Naive therapists can be too paternalistic about this, worrying that the world is a dangerous place and that every teen must be absolutely sure the person to whom they come out is safe to talk to. Other therapists might feel as if it's their job to help the teen come out, assuming that disclosure is healthy for everybody, not taking into account the specific circumstances.

Another narrative of coming out suggests that LGB identity is rooted in biology. This is a moment when a person discovers his or her "true self." It's a narrative steeped in biological assumptions—that one's sexual identity was there, from birth, waiting to be discovered, that it's fixed, permanent, unchangeable, simply there. A therapist may truly believe that his or her sexual identity was present at birth, but it's wrong to make the assumption that the client feels that. Also, it's wrong to conclude that simply because something is biological that it can't be changed, and simply because something is a product of socialization, it can. Socialization goes every bit as deep as biology. Most complex human characteristics do have components that are biological and social. And if a teen is exploring the reason why, therapists ought not to jump to biology but wonder why this question is important to the teen and what different explanations might mean to him or her.

Coming out also suggests a third narrative, a story of shameful secrets made shameful by cultural institutions like the family, religion, the law, and psychiatry. In coming out an adolescent joins a group of oppressed individuals, sufferers of sorts, in a society of the hurt. Made-for-TV movies, magazine feature stories, and popular novels of the 1970s and 1980s created a master story of painful oppression and victimization by a cruel culture. But things have changed somewhat for some people in some places. A therapist may believe deeply that a youth is coming out into a hostile culture, and perhaps she herself experienced her own coming out in this way. But quite a few LGB youths today tell researchers that they don't feel oppressed and that they don't feel quite the same need as their elders did to fight homophobia in the culture. While we know that homophobia still exists, we need to be open to youths' experiences and not simply think of their more positive outlooks as defensive.

These three narratives are grounded in reality for some, but there is a sea of stories about knowing, discovering, unfolding, and unveiling LGB identity they don't express, and it would be wise for gay, straight, and bisexual therapists to wade in the water. Even therapists who identify as LGB can also be drawn to these major narratives as shapers of identity, especially the narratives that reflect their own experience. For example, the idea of sexual identity as something more fluid and less fixed and as something less identified with a history of oppression and more identified with hope and possibility, seems to be capturing young people's imaginations today as a way of viewing sexual identity. This has caused tension between older and younger LGB communities. Narratives that spoke to a biological inevitability and included histories of oppression may have been useful to the older LGB community in the shaping of identity, and they may be invested in continuing to see the world in a way that reproduces the truths of their own coming out. But they, as well as straight therapists, need to be open to cultural changes and a variety of narratives.

COMING OUT DEFINED

There are four ways to look at coming out when teens come to discuss this in therapy. The first is coming out to themselves. How and when did they come to acknowledge and name certain feelings as gay or lesbian? When did they say to themselves, "I have experiences suggesting I might have same sex attractions." A therapist might be there in the thick of it as a teen explores these feelings, or there after it all happened, ready to reflect back on the process. In the latter case, the teen will often present this as a discovery of their essential being, something that was always there, perhaps hidden. Knowing that the narrative of biological inevitability is at work here doesn't bring a therapist to challenge it, but alerts a therapist to pay attention to how that biology narrative is working for the teen. Does she use it to defensively claim this is the way she has to be, protecting herself from the possible wishes and disappointments of parents and friends? Does he use it to describe giddy feelings of lack of control, something that may lead him down dangerous paths in his sexual explorations later? Just because this is a typical narrative of identity formation in our culture doesn't mean it has no personal meaning in the way it's used by teens.

A second way that kids come out may be to specific people. Research shows that after acknowledging something to themselves, they might typically come out to a best friend, maybe a couple of friends, or a sibling. Sometimes the therapist is the first person a teen has told, and the therapist can be a conduit to the community, particularly when a teen doesn't know how to find that community.

A specific person or couple in the next group of people that teens come out to is a parent or the parents. While coming out to a parent can be a big deal for an adolescent, some describe a process of letting it happen, coming to see their parents as acknowledging that they are gay without ever talking about it with them specifically. Kids who are out but didn't need to come out with their family don't usually come to therapy to discuss issues regarding coming out. There is more of a natural process akin to how a heterosexual child develops and interacts with parents around that specific teen issue—a parent observes the teen is interested in someone else and lets it be, watching and waiting to see what develops. By the time something has developed, a parent doesn't need to ask, "So are you dating John?" It's already clear.

It is often coming out to a parent that brings a teen into therapy. Either the teen has come out and the parent is worried, or the stress and anxiety around not coming out in the family have led to some blowup that results in the teen being brought to therapy. Whether or not a teen comes out to a parent depends a lot on the relationship he or she has with that parent, whether the relationship might be threatened by coming out or by keeping it a secret, and whether or not it's safe to come out to the parents.

A third way a teen may use the term *coming out* can refer to finding a community of "people like me." The community could consist of a small circle of friends, a support group at a downtown association, or some other place where the teen feels safe to show, talk about, and be himself. In many rural areas, teens begin to come out on the Internet. There's lots of reasonable information on the Internet and in chat rooms with like-minded kids; but they can also find gay porn and porn chat rooms. Within this intermediate category, between coming out to oneself and coming out to the world, there's a whole range of experiences. And sometimes kids are making really major decisions in that area—coming out to friends, at work, at school, to one's family, to one's extended family. A child may be out at summer camp but not at home. In fact, when schools start clubs like gay-straight alliances, they enable a kid to be out at school but not at home. These are all separate decisions. So indeed, when a teen says he's out, a therapist might wonder, out to whom, when, and where, and not assume that the teen is out in a public way.

A fourth use of the term *coming out*, coming out in a public or political way, could still mean to teens that they told one person. They may have blurted something out in a class discussion that they assumed was now all over the school or they may have walked in a parade with a local organization and feel that this announced to the world that they identify as lesbian, gay, or bisexual. A good way to figure out what the teen means by the phrase is to ask.

Coming out is different from being out. And the teens who proclaim they are out may reveal to the therapist that there are situations in which they hide their identity. In fact, coming out may itself be an old-fashioned notion, relevant only to some kids who have to break the news to family and friends. Being out may happen gradually over time, with varying awareness of friends and family. And for the teen who may need to come out in order to let other people know, there may be continuous decisions to make, continuous coming outs.

One thing therapists ought to remember is that the whole idea of coming out is a function of homophobia and heterosexism. It speaks to the assumption that teens are heterosexual. And the process of coming out indeed announces that one is dealing with what may be an unacceptable or stigmatized identity to some.

IDENTITY AND ADOLESCENCE

The idea that adolescents are shaping their identity is an old one. Erik Erikson saw identity as an intersection of self, biology, and society, and all three should be considered in helping teens or their families through a period of what they may call coming out. An adolescent can come out or be outed, can struggle with being labeled and hurt by those labels before he or she has identified as gay or lesbian, can have either a clear or murky sense of sexual identity, can identify with the politics or inner life and subjective realization and yet have very little experience, or can have had an erotic experience or two but little inner life or reflection about his or her sexuality. A teen can come out in a loving family who say they somehow knew all along, or a family who has trouble under-standing and sees this as a phase. A teen can come out only to a best friend in a religious community where the reactions threaten to be incredibly hurtful or at a parade in a liberal town in New England.

Some kids have been identified as gay by others even though they identify as heterosexual. The usual basis is violation of gender norms, and parents may have brought their child in for therapy because of this. A boy who loves musicals and spends time in sedentary activities rather than sports, if he's also small and delicate looking, gets labeled a fag. A girl who's interested in sports and not interested in dating, if she's also strong and ath-letic, gets labeled a dyke. The best predictor of gay bashing is gender violation, not gay identity. There may be no positive draw toward romantic relationships with same-sex peers, but they've heard it so much from other people that these teens might begin to think it's true.

When does coming out turn into an intake for therapy? When parents need reassurance. When parents believe that this identity is harmful. When a teen is at risk for doing harmful things to him or self. When the teen has been hurt by a homophobic act or remark. When the teen thinks being gay is horrible. When there's depression. When there is conflict in the family. Remember, too, that when parents first hear about sexual identity or sexual iden-tity questions, they sometimes realize that there is more to their adolescent that they don't know. Caring parents want to make sure their child really is all right. And we should give them the benefit of the doubt, believing that they sincerely want to know if there isn't more the teen is hiding that he or she needs to talk about, and whether or not their child will be okay in the world. I'll talk first about therapy that is a result of coming out and then later in the chapter about teens who come out to you in a session. Keep in mind that sometimes therapy simply helps a teen make a life transition, and long-term psychotherapy isn't needed. In any case, identifying as gay is not itself a reason for psychotherapy.

ERIC AND HIS PARENTS

Eric's mother was the one to call me after Eric came out to her. Eric's mother is the one I presented in the introduction, the one who was incredibly upset. She asked, "Couldn't this be a phase?" Is he confused because he hasn't had a girlfriend yet and other boys have? Everyone in her family was a late bloomer and couldn't he just think he was gay because he hasn't had any experience yet? She also wanted to know what I knew about the organization SafeReach. He'd been meeting with them, and could they be "recruiting him" to become one of them? If they are giving him lots of attention for this, would that mean he could never turn back? She had forbidden him to go until he agreed to meet with a therapist to talk it out. She also was concerned about the smaller children in the family. What if they found out? Would they be teased at school by other kids because their brother was gay? Would this confuse them? Would this be a bad influence on them? Might they turn gay too? And then there were the neighbors. Why did he have to go around announcing it all over the place? Couldn't he keep it a secret? What would happen if people in town found out, his teachers? His employers? Didn't he realize that this affected the whole family and not just him?

Believing as I do that sexual identity is not as fixed, as many people would like to believe, I felt inclined to support her views that this might just be experimentation. And yet to call it "just" experimentation seemed to confirm to her that anything that wasn't heterosexual was experimentation, and heterosexual teenage activity was the real deal. Teen sex is either the real deal or experimentation, but whatever it is, it cuts across all sexual identities. We like to categorize anything teens do as experimental, but it feels real to them, and who's to say we adults aren't still experimenting as we pursue our own experiences?

I also felt critical of her using the term *recruit*—this has been a stereotype of gay men for a long time, and every liberal bone in my body wanted to argue this one out. But when she said that in the SafeReach group for teens, there were college students and even guys out of college, I too began to worry. As a mother of a teenage son, I wondered how I would feel about his struggles and anxieties about his identity being responded to by these older boys and men. I also know that sometimes in self-help groups older members are so eager for younger members to see it from their perspective that they can be quite persuasive and might not realize the power they have to shape younger members' thinking. This isn't at all like the concept of recruitment, but I did wonder if such a group could provide the support for Eric to be where he was at this moment in time with regard to identity. Could he be a teen and be there? I told her I knew of this organization and the people who had worked there in the past, and that I would find out more for her.

I knew that there are books and Web sites with statistics and other helpful resources that answer these kinds of questions for parents. So I set to work in finding these for her and for my own benefit.

I agreed to see Eric and see what I thought, but I warned her that what her son and I talked about would need to be confidential and that I would only be able to share with her what he and I agreed would be good for me to share. As a child and adolescent therapist, it wasn't hard for me to see that Eric was my client, even before I met him, but that garnering the support and understanding of his parents would possibly be very helpful to him in his struggles through adolescence as well as in allowing him to use therapy over time.

Eric was a cute blond 15-year-old who seemed happy and eager to see me. Open and talkative from the get-go, he announced he was relieved that he had finally told his mother, but that he only wished she could accept it. He told me that he was so close to his mother that he couldn't bear lying to her and presenting a false self; it was coming between them. His father knew too, but they hadn't spoken much about it, nor did Eric want to talk to him about it. It seemed that his most important relationship was with his mother, and if she accepted him as he was, all would be right with the world. The urgency in his voice was clear. He needed his mother to accept him today. I began to see this teen as someone not only dealing with issues surrounding coming out, but that coming out to him might have something more to do with his feelings about normal teenage distancing from one's parents, creating a separate identity, dealing with the loss of a certain kind of relationship with one's parents—in short, growing up.

He found great support from a couple of kids at school and at the SafeReach group. He was incredibly upset that his mother wouldn't let him go to it and he had lied to her and gone there anyway when she thought he was at a school band rehearsal. Lying to his mother made him feel awful. But part of why he liked to go there was that he found his first boyfriend there, a man in college, about seven years older than Eric. He didn't like lying to his mother, but he didn't want to stop going, and he didn't want to stop seeing his new boyfriend.

I found it unnecessary to talk about sexual identity with Eric. He wasn't asking me about his sexual identity; nor was he struggling, questioning, unsure, experimenting, or confused. This didn't mean that he wouldn't change or question someday. But I had to meet him where he was, validating a sense of who he was. As a phone call to Glenda Russell and Janis Bohan confirmed for me, validating who he was at that moment was different than confirming his identity, and distinguishing between the two might also be helpful to his mother. Janis and Glenda suggested that I might even offer the following interpretation to Eric: When people have been sitting on a suppressed feeling for a while, they suddenly may find themselves so relieved and feeling so free that they overidentify with what is now out in the open, making it seem and often feeling as if it's confirmed for life—this is the real person. Some choices and identities that begin in adolescence develop into lifelong identities, but others don't. He would see what was ahead but it wasn't my place at that point to try to raise confusion and doubt, just to keep an open ear for his confusion and doubts if ever they arose.

I had called Glenda and Janis (who have coauthored this chapter) for help talking with the parents. While I was more critical of the mother, on behalf of her child and because of my own liberal views, their empathy toward her experience gave me pause. They saw her as someone who all at once believed she had lost her son, a son she had been very close to. And they emphasized to me how important it was to help this mother see that this was still the same boy she loved. Gay identity was not his master identity now, but just one among many other identities, identities she was familiar with. He still played in the band, was still a wonderful babysitter to his younger siblings and a great camp counselor, still a smart student, and still a hard worker. He was also still his parents' boy, a boy who felt deeply connected to them and didn't want them to feel hurt.

Although critical of the mother on the phone, I had also gone along with her views in a way in which I now felt uncomfortable, perhaps supporting her homophobia; and I felt rather ashamed. She was worried about the men in the SafeReach group, and gay men in general, being predators of younger men, like her son. I told her that as a mother of boys, I would be worried too about the older men in the SafeReach group. And I had to admit to myself that I did kind of worry that way and hadn't ever reflected on my own stereotypes and homophobia. With several gay men in our extended family and my close relationships with friends and colleagues who are LGB, it was hard to recognize at first that I might have some prejudices. But I had to come to terms that I had a homophobic view, separating in my mind my LGB friends from a generalized other whom it was okay to suspect.

Janis and Glenda said that this was an understandable response given that we have all grown up in a homophobic culture and all need to work on this—everyone needs some help coping with homophobia. I could help this mother see that she could be worried, as any mother would be, about her child being influenced and sought after by older people, and I imagined how I would feel if a 23-year-old woman was interested in my 15-year-old presumably heterosexual son. Not very happy. I also imagined how I would feel if a senior boy in high school were interested in my freshman daughter. This led me to put aside the homophobic underpinnings of my joining with her (to be examined on my own) and to then help her without joining with her on those issues.

Looking back, though, I wish I had taken the next step and helped her to unlearn this homophobic response as I was unlearning it. Maybe we could have done that together as I explained from a sympathetic viewpoint that heterosexuals can make assumptions that simply aren't true about gay men and lesbians. But I think that I was a bit ashamed and so lost this moment of coeducation. Active unlearning within a therapy session is so important. If we can name these assumptions together, we can challenge them in a safe place. While being good-hearted to all people is a wonderful value, it doesn't do the whole job. There is education that needs to take place. Does that make therapy political? Well, yes, but doesn't a lot of therapy have more political components? When we help a girl to not value body images she sees on TV, we are teaching an antisexism agenda as well as healthy body image.

My work with the family was fourfold: (1) giving them real information in the face of fears and prejudices; (2) helping them to see that Eric's gay identity was just a part of who he was and that he wasn't now an entirely different person; (3) reassuring them that he was making healthy choices which would be a concern in therapy too as in any therapy with a teen; and (4) helping them to understand what role the community played in terms of their own community and the community their son had found. I also worked on mutual empathy. Eric was to come to understand that just as it may have taken time for him to claim being gay as his identity, it would take his mom and dad time to "accept it." And even though he felt a need to share his life with them right now and be accepted for it, they were asking him to keep them from knowing too much. Their desire not to know more was an example of homophobia and I wish I had gone after that, providing these parents with more information about the homophobia many of us have learned.

Working with this homophobia may have given Eric more tools to deal with the times that his mother and father used language that was rather hurtful to him. They would say, "just don't flaunt it" and "don't throw it in our faces." They were also incredibly concerned about public opinion. We had a discussion about gay men and "flaunting it," and Eric joined with his parents in a bit of homophobic putting down of gay men who flaunt it. I mentioned that oftentimes heterosexual people believe gay people are flaunting it when they are simply doing what heterosexual people do, such as walking down the street holding hands, and I told them the idea that gay people should have to hide their feelings comes from the assumption that what they feel and do is wrong.

We also talked about a more exaggerated version of flaunting it, because Eric had a friend that was clearly "in your face" with his gay identity, provocatively trying to hug and kiss straight boys at school to make them uncomfortable. I tried to contextualize this notion of flaunting it for them by talking about the many ways kids can manage owning a stigmatized identity. One way of facing the world is what's been called "minstrelization," exaggerating the stereotypes. I also contextualized this as a part of adolescence; we knew of lots of ways adolescents create in-your-face identities, performing exaggerations as a way to become visible and to try to prove to themselves that they don't care what others think and especially that they are separate people, separate from their parents.

Eric and I had decided it would be good for his mother and father to meet with me alone so that they could ask questions and gain reassurance on issues that they would be uncomfortable discussing with him. He wanted me to "fix them" and make them accept him as I did, and thought I could achieve that better on my own. We also had two family sessions in which Eric was present. One stood out in particular.

With Eric in the room, his parents were generally cautious about what they asked and how they asked it, trying not to anger their son. Eric's father, though, who had been primarily silent and rather accepting, hurt Eric deeply in one session when he told him that he thought he needed to tell the camp counselor Eric assisted in the summers that Eric was gay. His insistence that this was something she needed to know felt to Eric as if his father thought that he had a disease that might spread, that he could harm the young children he worked with, that he would be asking them for sex. Eric pointed out to his father that the camp director had a gay sister, that she was a very liberal woman and that he couldn't imagine any possible scenario in which he would just come out and tell her this. They just didn't have that kind of relationship. His father argued with him, saying that he had some kind of obligation to tell the camp director, implying that Eric was a danger to have at camp. His mother argued on behalf of Eric, but it was difficult to know if she was taking his side because she thought the father's views were extreme or because she simply didn't want Eric to tell anyone else, supporting her own view that this matter should be kept secret until he discovered that he actually was heterosexual.

This was a moment when more education about homophobia may have been useful. Labeling the hurt Eric was feeling as the hurt that comes from being confronted with homophobia may have helped toward making the family a safe place. This was in part our goal, to make the family a resource to him so he had the strength to confront homophobia in the outside world. Asking his father questions about his assumptions, why a camp director would need to know, would have modeled for Eric how to ask questions about assumptions people are making.

My work with Eric alone was different. From session one, I asked if he was interested in anyone at present, letting him know that it was fine for him to talk about same-sex attractions and relationships. Eric seemed rather happy, but he worried he had lost a part of his life that he treasured, his fun with the boys. Most of his straight male friends knew that he had come out or suspected he was gay, and he felt strange among them. He started hanging out with his female friends more but missed his "guy activities" of watching action movies and hanging out playing video games. Could he still be the same person among them? Just one of the guys? Or would they feel that he was interested in them sexually?

He confessed, he was kind of interested in one of them sexually so, in his mind, maybe they would be right to suspect that he was not just one of the guys. I had to point out that there was nothing in the way of his still being one of the guys, even if he had an attraction to one of them. But could he still be one of the boys with the feelings he had? It was important to realize that a worry about the homophobia "out there" was in part a projection of his own worry about whether he was too different to still belong.

A second issue for Eric was whether or not he could tolerate lying to his mother, and this was most salient in his dating the older college student from SafeReach. In family sessions, his mother told him very directly that she was working on accepting this and that she would prefer that he didn't tell her all that much about his life. Eric couldn't understand this. He felt as if not telling his mother about certain things was the same as being closeted, lying to her. He wanted to share more with her and have it be okay.

This was clearly an issue of adolescent separation. What was Eric protecting himself from by making up some rule that he needed to tell his mother everything in order to feel all right? Perhaps he wanted to restrain himself and take things slowly with his new sexual relationships but was unable to own that and wanted his mother's worries to restrain him. By making his mother the brakes, he could slow himself down. Truth was, he was pretty scared as well as excited about kissing another boy and moving forward sexually. Above all he wanted a boyfriend, someone whom he could develop a relationship with slowly and trust before he did some of the making out he was eager to try. He wanted safety and he wanted to discuss relationship issues with his mom, just as if he were a heterosexual teen seeking out his mom's advice. The work that continued was typical adolescent work with a healthy teen. He needed to make his own decisions regarding relationships and sexuality and feel good about them, and he used therapy to figure out his feelings about guys and anticipate choices he would have to make about how far he wanted to go and with whom. And he worked on tolerating the anxiety of not telling his mother everything.

I only saw Eric for about six months, but when he left therapy he had begun to conform to his mother's way of looking at guys, which I thought was a regression and an internalization, temporary I hoped, of cultural homophobia. He "hated" the guys who "flaunted it," he had dropped that gay friend who was "too in your face," and he had started a long-distance relationship with a friend of a friend over e-mail, taking it slowly as a way to cope with his own anxieties about starting intimate relationships outside of the family. He had come out in the family and the younger siblings seemed to have accepted it without concerns or questions. Bringing a boyfriend over to the house was something he could never dream of doing, and his parents seemed to prefer to drift into the parental fog where many parents of adolescents find themselves, not knowing exactly what their teen was doing, worrying, sending out vague messages about safety, but separating themselves from what was too anxiety provoking at the time.

Eric was colluding with his mother's homophobia because he wasn't quite ready to separate. Beyond his mother's homophobia, he was awash in the homophobia everyone's awash in. This kind of rapprochement is not uncommon in adolescence. And homophobia is something that gay and lesbian adolescents are learning to deal with through a variety of coping mechanisms, some healthier than others, and internalizing it as a way of controlling and avoiding the hurt is simply a way of coping. Of course, down the road this way of coping leads to self-hatred and he would have done better to deal with his anger and sadness toward his parents for their views, but I felt rather confident that eventually he would.

JEFF: SEEKING DANGER

When an adolescent is doing dangerous things, you want the parents to be watchful, involved, and informed. But you have a rule of confidentiality and so mostly you can only encourage the adolescent to talk to his parents. Many therapists think that their work is done after the 50 minutes spent with the adolescent, and if he's not intending to commit suicide or murder someone, then what's said in that time stays in that time. Of course it stays in that time, but any therapist who has worked with children is familiar with bringing in the parents to enlist their support in any number of ways.

Should a therapist ever encourage a kid to come out to his parents so that the therapist can enlist them in protecting this teen? How do you know if that would actually be helpful to a kid? It may not be, but whether or not a teen discusses his or her sexuality with the parents will almost always be part of your conversation.

Teens who are not out to their parents have to mature sooner; they have to take on more of a parenting function for themselves. Sometimes this makes the therapist the parent. But that's not unusual for any teen who is underparented for a variety of reasons. They'll sit there telling you they took their parents' car over the border to Montreal, drinking and driving all the way, and you sit there petrified for them and what they have done and what they might do in the future. You walk that thin line between wanting to be their therapist and wanting to be the parent who says, "My God, what are you doing? Do you realize how dangerous that is?" In actuality, I've often said almost that. Many a time I've said in a rather neutral and inquisitive voice, "Let's explore together what you're doing. Do you realize what's dangerous about it?" Usually teens will either explain all the precautions they took that made it less dangerous, or so they thought, such as, "I didn't have any of the beer, and when we got to the border we hid it under the seat and I made everyone in the back pretend to be sober." Or they will admit to the danger: "Yes, that was so stupid."

Now, I had been seeing Jeff for quite some time before the idea came up that he might want to come out to his parents. He initially came to therapy because of depression and we had been talking about his issues with his father and stepmother and his loss of his mother at an early age long before he began talking about his sexual attractions to other guys.

Having met his parents at the beginning of therapy, it was clear that his father's overbearing style, strong opinions, and excessively controlling actions would make him a hard father to come out to. With me, Jeff seemed to talk naturally and openly about his attractions and early sexual activities. It was when he started doing more dangerous things that I wondered how and if

I could enlist his parents' support. Although only 17, he'd been going to gay bars to meet older men, and had had unprotected oral sex with two different men in their cars.

Why did I think this was dangerous? Sex with strangers? Lack of protection? I didn't need to answer that for him. He knew that what he was doing was dangerous and so we spent considerable time discussing what exactly this behavior meant, what he wanted from these experiences, how he felt going into them and coming out of them, and whether he could make a decision to pursue more healthy avenues of experience, even if that meant being patient for a while.

Jeff said that it was gross and that afterward he felt gross. I asked, "But exciting too?" letting him know that it was okay to speak about the arousal and the sexual feelings involved. He said yes but that he almost instantly felt strange and not that into it. He felt really scared that someone would catch them. I asked him about the "grossness" and he clarified that he didn't think it was because he was gay but because these were older guys and he didn't really want to look at them much. In my mind I wondered if he was responding to a stereotyped image of a lonely old gay man and thought this was something we might need to work on later. For now I said, "So this was not really the kind of person you wanted to be doing this with." "Right," he answered. "How do you imagine it better?" I asked, and he replied that he imagined there being a club with kids his age who might be gay and that he might meet someone and talk and go home with them and talk some more and then mess around. We talked about how that might really eventually be possible for him when he went to college in a year or so and that it was great that he knew how he wanted things to happen.

What was drawing him to gay bars though? Was it the riskiness too? Did the fear of getting caught also arouse him? "No," he said, but I was unconvinced. I could have dwelled on the problem of AIDS or other STDs, but I knew that he was aware of this and worried. So I said, "Even with your awareness of AIDS and other STDs, you still seem to want to take this risk." He replied he didn't but he did it anyway. We then explored the scariness of the older guys whom he seemed to allow to take control of him. When I said that I thought he felt overwhelmed by the experiences and that he might need to make decisions that would keep him from getting overwhelmed, he seemed to agree. There was something in our talk that day that led Jeff to make a decision not to go back. Perhaps it was too close to home to recognize that there was something arousing about being controlled, but he decided in that adolescent way that he needed to take more control of his life. I didn't know that at the time, though, and felt a need for a parent meeting.

In the session with his parents, alone, I let them know that I thought their son was depressed. They knew this and easily placed the blame on the death of his mother. We spoke of Jeff's sexuality because I had permission from Jeff to do so, and they had a fairly liberal attitude toward it, perhaps exaggeratedly so, indicating to me that they would give him no trouble about his explorations and process of self-discovery. But they asked point-blank whether Jeff was doing anything dangerous that they should be aware of. I was trapped. I wanted to let them know that they should be keeping a more watchful eye on their son, and yet to do that would lead an already controlling father to overcontrol some more and may even produce rebellion.

Therapist: (generalizing) It's always a good idea to keep in mind that a teen may get into situations that are difficult and may prove dangerous. (pause) Sometimes I worry about this with Jeff and yet I too want to support him in his process of self-discovery.

I felt a bit as if I was betraying Jeff and sleazing around the confidentiality issue by talking about myself. But the parents heard the ambivalence rather than just the fear.

Parents: (together) That's exactly how we've been feeling.

Father: Should we prevent him from going into town? Would you suggest that?

These parents were smart. I had to pull back Dad's reigns and remind him that prohibiting things never seemed to work with Jeff and seemed to contribute to an already difficult relationship. At this point, I threw it back on them as a question all parents of teens have: "How do we keep teens safe when they are out there in a pretty dangerous world with lots of temptations and messages about sexuality?" We all sat there in silence as we thought about all the negative social messages about being a sexual person or how to be one, the homophobia, the drugs, the hurt that was bound to come.

Th: (breaking the silence) By talking with them. However awkward it may be for you, it's going to be really important for you to talk to him about sex. Don't feel as if you have nothing to say because you're straight or that you need to leave the issue alone because it must be so different for a boy growing up gay. Instead, let me remind you, kids are aching to hear meaningful talk about sex from their parents. Meaningful talk and not proscriptions and warnings. Can you talk to him about what you want for him as a sexual adult?

F: What exactly do you mean?

Th: What do you want for him sexually?

F: (laughing) I guess I want him to enjoy it and not feel guilty but to not do anything stupid that might put his life at risk. [*We were all thinking about AIDS though not mentioning it.*]

Th: (enthusiastically) Yes! He needs to hear that from you, particularly the part about enjoying it and not feeling guilty. That will make him also be able to listen to the other part about the danger. What about *who* you want him to have sex with?

P: (reaffriming) We're really, not upset that he's gay; he can have sex with whoever he wants.

Th: Whoever?

F: Well, not whoever.

Stepmother: I guess we'd want him to be experimenting with friends. Kids we know, kids from other schools are fine. Not a teacher in the school, any older guys.

Th: That's also a good thing to tell him. Can you explain to him why that's important to you?

P: It's more mutual.

Th: (rephrasing) You'd like him to enjoy sex, but there's also a moral dimension to what you'd like to advise him. You'd like him to be in a relationship, however briefly, with someone in which the sexual experimentation would be mutual. (pausing then asking) Loving?

P: What do teens know about love? (pausing then adding) I'd like it if he had a relationship with someone. I don't think it's good for anyone to have casual sex.

Th: Then tell him that. You're sharing your values with him, and that's what parents do. That's what he needs. He may not follow your advice or adhere to your values, but he'll know them. More important, he'll know that you care about the way he's learning about sex and experiencing it, and that you want him to be a sensitive and aware person in his sexual relationships as well as in his other relationships.

Parents: Absolutely. *[feeling empowered to go out and speak to their son]*

I only knew that the talk went well because of what Jeff said indirectly. In that adolescent way, he complained that his parents didn't really like it when he went into town alone at night. Although complaining about their limits, he seemed to feel protected by them. They didn't lay down the law, but over the next few sessions I heard him internalize and repeat to me some of the things that might have come out of his talk with his parents: "I don't want to do things I'll feel guilty about afterward," and "It's too hard to sneak around behind their backs." He was doing what a lot of adolescents do, putting the control on their parents and obeying them, before internalizing that as self-control. I didn't feel a need to push him by saying, "And what do *you* feel" because I wanted him connected to these parental voices and worries.

VANESSA IN VERMONT

It may seem odd to some folks that some teens don't need to come out to their families. Historically, we're living in a period in some areas, some families, and some communities where plenty of people are out and where heterosexuality isn't always presumed. Vermont is one of those places where, although there is still plenty of homophobia and even some violence against gay individuals, there is at the same time quite a bit of acceptance and integration. Vanessa came from a family in which she never had to come out. Her parents and sibling understood her to be gay when she and her girlfriend appeared to be more than friends. Vanessa was quite open with her family about her relationships and couldn't remember exactly when she or her parents became aware of her orientation. If this seems idyllic to those who have suffered through the anxiety of living in the closet, perhaps it was. But it all came crashing down during the civil union fights in Vermont.

Vanessa's father was the one who called me to set up an appointment. She had agreed to talk with someone once but told him that he had to check out whether the therapist was the right kind of therapist. On the phone, he asked if I ever worked with lesbian teens. From that question alone, I couldn't tell whether he was checking out my politics or wondering if I could help change his daughter into a straight teen. I told him that I was familiar with the issues lesbian teens might have living in this culture and had read and taught about adolescent sexuality in my courses at Saint Michael's. I added that lesbian teens often had issues to talk to a therapist about that were simple issues of adolescence and not related to their sexual orientation. It was important to say that in the beginning so that a parent wouldn't expect that the focus of the therapy would be sexual orientation if that wasn't what

Vanessa wanted to talk about. Although not irrelevant, it might be unimportant to the issue at hand. Little did I know that Vanessa was the one who had given him that question to ask to ensure that she would not be confronted with a hostile therapist. She had also wanted her father to ask potential therapists if they were gay, but her father drew the line there. He didn't feel comfortable asking that question. She did, and asked me within minutes of starting our first session.

Before that question, she came into my office and did a little stroll around the room before plopping down on the couch. "Nice office; do you see kids too?" This was not an unusual remark for a teen to make. My office is very large and divided symbolically. In one half there's a couch and a cushy chair; in the other half there's a super-sized beanbag chair, a smaller cushiony chair for me, a small table and chairs, a sandbox, bookcases filled with toys, and large colorful boxes of Legos and figures. My answer to teens and adults alike is, "Yes, and if you think you'd like to talk over on the other side of the room on the beanbag chair, we can move there." That way they know that they don't always have to be adult; they don't always have to communicate through talking. I've had some teens ask to use the sandbox on occasion, creating scenes with the sandbox figurines.

But Vanessa stayed on the adult side, as most teens do, and before proceeding with the story of why she came to therapy, asked me, "Are you gay?" and then added, "Not that it matters." I thought immediately that it probably did matter to her. But should I answer? I could answer with a reflection: "You'd like to know if I am gay." I could answer with a reflection and interpretation: "You'd like to know if I am gay, like you, maybe to know if I will be able to understand you?" I could simply ask the question, "How would it matter to you if I were or if I weren't?" This would, of course, be an important question to pursue; however, to ask it without answering her question might feel very evasive and off-putting.

But even if I answered, what would be the right answer? Clearly she would categorize me as heterosexual, and perhaps in her world people were either heterosexual or straight. If I answered something more philosophical, about the way I think of these issues, I would be raising interesting points to discuss that might move us away from her in the present. For example, I could say, "I think of myself as bisexual but primarily my experiences have been heterosexual." That's a complicated one to mull over. Or, "I think of most people as bisexual who have leaned in one or another direction, and I've leaned toward heterosexual." More personally, I could tell her that when I think of my younger self, I see experiences and potential to have identified as a lesbian, but recognize now that not only sexual attraction but fear, homophobia, and a heterosexist culture helped push me in a different direction. But then we'd really be into talking about me. And I needed to answer the question where I thought she was.

I answered that I identified as heterosexual but felt an alliance to the lesbian and gay communities in Vermont. Thus I was trying to contextualize where I was in the world of sexual identity. I used the word *identify* to avoid the biologism of "I am" and I used the word *alliance* to sound a bit cool to her and let her know I knew of communities of support called *allies*. She didn't ask anything more after that short answer. She didn't even seem relieved or to reflect an "I knew it!" Instead, she launched into her story.

Vanessa grew up in such a liberal town and family that there never was an official moment of coming out for her. As far as she could remember, she had attractions to other girls and the transition from playing games with other girls to best friendships, to romantic girlfriends, seemed to pass smoothly, unannounced, and unnoted in the family. It wasn't that her parents held back from asking her or commenting on it. Instead, they had raised their kids believing that the possibility for same-sex attraction was there and that it was a natural part of adolescent development on the way to a more confirmed identity. Sound unbelievable? Well, it is Vermont, and these families do exist. Sound healthy? Actually it was. As I grew to know her, Vanessa seemed like a very psychologically healthy individual in many ways. So why therapy?

During the civil union battles in Vermont, things grew tense in many quarters even though Vermont has a live-and-let-live tradition and neighbors who are friendly and respectful. As one 90-year-old dairy farmer told me, "There were some women who owned the farm next door and lived together there all their lives. They were just our neighbors. Nobody asked questions. Nobody thought about it much. We knew they were probably together like a husband and a wife but that was their business." That attitude changed when people began putting up signs on their property proclaiming their views: "Take Back Vermont" from those against civil unions, and "Take Vermont Forward" from those who supported them.

It was during this time when the high schools led students in debate about the issues. Vanessa, who had been neither out or closeted, just "herself" as she put it, was placed in the situation of representing LGB people in class discussion after class discussion. Not identified with a larger community of support, and just living her life as a lesbian teen, she did not have a supply of information nor a guidebook through the mines of homophobia. While white, Christian, heterosexual kids are rarely asked to be experts on their whiteness, their Christianity, or their heterosexuality, teens whose identities seem marked or outside the norm are frequently asked to be representatives, to reveal what it's like to be them.

Vanessa was completely thrown by the hurtful remarks in class and the offhandedly stupid statements by some of the kids there. She had never thought of herself as deviant and that word made her cringe. During one classroom discussion, one boy had asked, "Why don't they just try to be normal?" She became so furious that she couldn't speak. At the time the boy asked that question, all the other kids' eyes quickly shifted to her to see her response. She felt frozen in their glare, a glare that suddenly seemed to tell her that she was different and unacceptable. She told me, "I just felt out of control, like breaking something. How dare he? I kept asking myself." Feeling suddenly unsafe and too visible at school, this girl who generally liked to fly under the radar withdrew and stopped going to school, getting behind in her homework. She wanted to drop out of school and just get a GED. The teachers tried to talk to her on the phone after her parents contacted the school, and although they seemed friendly enough, she couldn't help seeing them differently and worrying that they too might come out with some nasty remark, even if by accident.

Vanessa talked about her girlfriend too in a pained way. This relationship had changed. She had discussed her feelings with Mikalah but when they were alone, Vanessa no longer felt comfortable with her; she got this strange feeling of being watched and felt kind of miserable and depressed. Mikalah, who went to another school, just blew off the incident as something that the "creeps" do. But Vanessa liked some of those creeps and felt awful that behind that veneer of friendship they could be judging her and seeing her as abnormal. Homophobia hit her hard. Her parents saw this once chipper and engaged kid dig her heels in and become inflexible, something she had never done before. She refused to go to school anymore, so her parents said they wanted her to talk to a therapist about this decision before it got too far and she missed so much homework that she really would have to drop out.

As Vanessa related her story, I responded with disbelief and disgust each time a teacher asked her to speak out. She felt bad that they had, but somehow believed they had a right to do that. "Why are they forcing you to educate the other kids?" I asked. "That's so unfair that they ask you to speak!" Vanessa at first defended her teachers saying that they asked everyone to speak about themselves and that who else could they ask about sexual orientation in the classroom, and that it wasn't their fault, just the fault of "those assholes" in the classroom.

Therapist: Did she ask the others to explain their heterosexuality?

Vanessa: (laughing)

Th: You laugh, but often teachers don't realize that they're making assumptions about what's "normal" and "acceptable" by not questioning it.

V: How could a teacher have done that?

Th: Well, he she could have asked a student how the debates about civil unions affect the way he sees himself in terms of his sexuality. Whether it brings up questions or makes people afraid. She could ask how students identify to themselves when their feelings come out of fear or out of what their parents taught them rather than out of reason and exploration. She could ask them what made them heterosexual and put on the blackboard all the possible explanations.

V: That would have been cool.

She described the feeling of being watched and talked about and how that just made her feel self-conscious in school. But she felt she could tolerate that if she went back. What she couldn't tolerate was being asked to speak up. She was a bit afraid that her voice would crack from anger and that she wouldn't know what to say, but felt a vague responsibility to represent lesbian and gay people even though, she confessed, "I really wouldn't have the slightest idea how to."

Vanessa seemed very healthy, but I wasn't sure dropping out of school was the best decision. There were just too many activities she was engaged in that she would miss and have to set up independently. And the fact was, she wasn't going to escape homophobia in the world out there. So I asked, "Do you think you could return to school if you knew a way how to stop people from asking you about your sexuality and your sexual orientation?" She replied, "How could I do that?"

Our three sessions together focused on helping Vanessa develop a way to say no to being a spokesperson. Even using that word *spokesperson* was helpful to her as she was able to come up with a phrase, "I'm not a spokesperson for the gay community. Look it up yourself." We practiced aloud in sessions the way she might say that phrase in a class or to a jerk in the hall. "I'm not a spokesperson for Lesbians United. Go fuck yourself" was the hallway variation. Also, "I'm not a spokesperson; if you're ignorant get an education!" As she laughed and played around with these variations, she felt a little guilty saying no, and asked if maybe it was her obligation to educate. I gave her permission to do so only when she really wanted to and with people she really wanted to invest in. I confirmed that sometimes it's really painful and hard to work with people around their homophobia. There were plenty of other people who were doing that and she could concentrate on her schoolwork for now. If at some time she wanted to make a commitment to that kind of work, she could do that by first getting herself an education and some support. I think that what was most important to me was allowing her *not* to educate herself if she didn't want to but telling her there were resources out there. I wanted her to have as free an adolescence as the straight kids, and not have to make her identity a cause to adhere to if she didn't want it to be a cause.

Vanessa reentered school, simply saying to people when they asked where she was, "School sucks. I needed a break." That answer seemed to suffice. She also did say she was going to take a look at a local meeting place for gay and straight teens, maybe go to one meeting and see if it was for her. Although in general I think becoming political is a wonderful way to fight homophobia in oneself and the world out there, I wanted to let her know that she didn't have to do that. She could be herself without being political, a representative, or an educator.

COMING OUT TO A THERAPIST AND THERAPISTS COMING OUT

For teens who are relatively comfortable with a lesbian, bisexual, or gay identity, claiming it in therapy comes early, almost always in the first session. These teens are usually the ones who have found support outside of their family in community support networks or among friends. They may have boyfriends or girlfriends they want to talk about in therapy, or they may simply include their identity as a matter of fact in their description of themselves and their lives. Even though comfortable, there's often a moment after they make the statement when they search your eyes for your reaction. It's not easy coming out and even though most teens expect therapists to be accepting, they look for that simple nod of the head that says, "Okay. Go on. Thanks for telling me." I would never at the beginning of a therapeutic relationship make that small point the focus of my next question or comment unless I thought the teen wanted to talk about it. Nor would I tell a teen she was brave to tell me that so early on. There may be no bravery involved, and, as I said, teens have a right to expect that it's fine to describe themselves fully in therapy. If, though, coming out, were indeed the issue that the teen wanted to talk about, I would store away that moment of revelation because we might come back to it if only to say sometime in the future, "It seemed easy for you to tell me when we first met." The time I actually did that, the girl said to me, "Well, you looked like a liberal person and aren't all therapists accepting of sexual identity?" What trust!

Should a therapist tell a client that she too is a lesbian or he too is gay? Some therapists will self-identify or be self-identified from the beginning because they are out in the community and people may make referrals to them specifically because of sexual identity. Just as referring sources like to ask whether one would prefer a male or female therapist, some people may also ask if a teen would prefer a straight or gay therapist, man or woman. If a teen had a choice, it would be interesting to explore at some point how and why she made that choice. Did she imagine that a gay therapist might alienate her parents? Was he hoping to find the accepting mother that he doesn't have in the straight therapist?

If coming out is the issue, a client or a parent may call and ask explicitly if you are lesbian or gay. This is more unusual. It's my

experience that parents will assume that a therapist is heterosexual and will begin to talk about their gay son or daughter in a
way that they might only talk to another heterosexual parent. It
may be important to self-identify to the parent at this point if that
is one's practice. Many therapists who identify as LGB probably
wouldn't self-identify but would leave it to the parent to ask.

If a teen calls and is specifically looking for a lesbian or gay
therapist, then the teen has a right to ask. There may be some
therapists who at this point will say they are lesbian or gay. I know
of one who would give a bit of history to straight women who
came to her for help in their relationships, "I'm a lesbian now, but
I was married once to a man and am raising our children in a new
relationship." This therapist may give all this information to let
the client know that she has a range of experiences including
mothering to draw from or to let the client know that there's more
to a label than just the word. Nevertheless, that's a lot of information for a client to know right off the bat. On the phone, it may be
best to self-identify and simply say that one has experience with
straight, gay, lesbian, and bisexual clients, by way of giving information about one's practice. Then again, no therapist needs to
self-reveal over the phone. One can ask what it means to the client
and why they are asking? A teen on the phone might say, "I'm
looking for someone who won't be prejudiced against me or
shocked by anything I say," and the therapist, without self-identi-
fying, could then reply, "I have had many LGB clients in therapy
with a variety of experiences. I have a lot of respect for people and
the process they go through in understanding themselves,
deciding whether or not to come out, and their struggles living in
a homophobic society." That said, the main question is answered,
and it's the rare teen that will pursue the question over the phone.

If it happens within a session, something different may be
going on. Why might a teen ask you if you are gay or lesbian? It
may be simply a moment in which the adolescent comes out of a
self-preoccupied fog to realize there's another person in the room.

Or the therapist may have said something that seemed homophobic, the client believing in an instant that the therapist is an "other" and not present with the teen in her or his struggles. It's more likely the therapist has said something that seemed so true and real that the teen was sure that the therapist was just like the teen once and this is what gives the therapist some deeper understanding. Sometimes the question can be asked offhandedly and sometimes very directly, indicating it means a lot to a client to know. The more psychoanalytically inclined therapists will hold off and explore over time the fantasies a teen may have about the therapist. For example, the question may indicate more than a simple positive transference, that the client is hoping the therapist is just like her, or feels close to her and so they must be merged in some way. Or it may indicate a more complicated transference and attraction to the therapist. Even if one is not psychoanalytically inclined, it's a good idea to sit back and think of these possibilities before jumping in with an answer: "I'm wondering what it was that made you ask me that question today"; "I'm wondering what it might mean to you if I were gay"; "This seems important to you; let's explore why."

When a therapist reveals sexual identity to a client, it's a good idea to follow up on it, in the very least, keeping aware of how this may have changed the relationship and what the client reveals. Heterosexual therapists reveal their heterosexuality fairly regularly without giving it a second thought, buying into the idea that it is assumed, and so saying something about one's husband or wife instead of one's partner is rarely even thought of as a major revelation to a client. But it may have been. A client may have believed that her therapist was a lesbian because she worked at a feminist clinic and thus it may have been a complete surprise when the therapist inadvertently came out as a heterosexual, even to a straight client. And a gay client might believe his male therapist is also gay because he's warm and empathic, unlike the client's conservative father. The way to come to understand these assumptions is to ask or wonder aloud, sometime in the therapy, whether learning what they did has made a difference. And a therapist may be surprised that it has.

* * * *

From moment one in therapy with a gay youth, whether discussing coming out, questioning orientation, or simply living in the world, the specter of homophobia is probably in the room. In fact, if there wasn't still homophobia, there probably wouldn't be a need for therapy when a teen comes out. Realizing who you're attracted to and making that attraction a part of your identity so that your family and friends begin to know you as a relational and sexual person is a task of adolescence, similar for people of all orientations. And because of homophobia, some of the most important work will be with the families of teens who come out.

CHAPTER NINE

Working With Developmentally Disabled Teens

With Stannard Baker

Teens with developmental disabilities (DD) who come to individual or group psychotherapy are a diverse group, from those presenting with mild to moderate mental retardation to those within the Asperger's-Autism spectrum. Only a few of these teens with DD actually make it to any kind of therapy for reasons discussed below. The challenges they present in one-on-one psychotherapy may seem different at first from the challenges presented by non-DD teens, but often there are more similarities than not. With about a third of DD teens obtaining a second diagnosis of a mental disorder, the need for psychotherapy is there; however, few therapists are willing to extend themselves into this area. Those trained in talk therapies are concerned that the concrete thinking and cognitive limitations of a DD teen would prevent real progress. They may think that the level at which they will need to work is low—doing social skills training and setting up rules and regulations for behavior, something a skilled teacher could do but not usually a task in therapy—and that there wouldn't be the opportunity for symbolic work or use of metaphor. They might also think that the teen does not have the potential for deeper self-reflection and awareness. Those trained in play therapy are unaccustomed to working in this modality with teens and young adults and can feel unknowledgeable about their issues and how to address them in play. Some therapists are fearful that given the cognitive limitations, they won't be able to expect much of their clients. Some, I think, are simply uncomfortable with DD individuals. In our culture, in spite of mainstreaming in the schools and growing community integration, we have very little interaction with DD kids and adults. (Most professionals who work with DD teens, by the way, consider the teen years to continue through the 21st year.)

There are historical reasons why DD children and teens haven't been placed in psychotherapy when emotional issues have arisen. At the time of deinstitutionalization in our country, there was a strong movement to proclaim the difference between mental disorders and developmental disabilities. Not only were supporters claiming that DD was not a mental illness, but some went so far as to say that DD individuals can't have a mental illness. Today, given the number of dual diagnoses, many are in need of psychotherapy, often presenting with obsessive-compulsive symptoms. Obsessive-compulsive behavior, while anxiety provoking for non-DD individuals, can be quite comforting for the DD teen who relies on obsessive thinking to fill and structure his or her time during the day and to make the world more manageable. As for autistic and Asperger's children and teens (who, incidentally, shouldn't always be classified as DD but that's where the funding for services generally lies), intense focus that shuts out a confusing world of human social interactions provides a safe haven. Other dual diagnoses include depression, anxiety, bipolar disorder, and even schizophrenia.

So what about sex? As with non-DD teens, sexual issues emerge in therapy and sometimes are the reason for the referral; for example, they may have experienced sexual abuse or exploitation or they may be exhibiting inappropriate sexual behaviors themselves such as public masturbating. And there has been a movement over the past 20 years to ensure that we treat DD individuals according to their chronological age and not infantilize them. This means that sexually, DD teens have the same rights as non-DD teens to explore and experiment, to come into their own as fully sexual beings with preferences and attractions, and to look forward to an adult sexual life. Although DD teens have the same kind of tensions and issues as non-DD teens with their parents or guardians around independence and autonomy, formerly, DD individuals were treated as perpetual children. We can all recall the image of a 50-year-old woman in pigtails in a belted dress wearing Mary Janes and carrying a tiny little purse from an era where DD people were dressed and taken care of as if they were little boys and girls. Although some parents still want to keep their DD children young, to protect them, with help they can begin to see their children as having young adult competencies in many areas and deserving treatment as an adult.

THE THERAPEUTIC RELATIONSHIP AND SEXUAL ISSUES

Most DD teens and young adults are relationship starved. They long for a friend and the intimacy that a therapy session can provide. They've had professional helpers all their lives but often not real friends. And rarely has someone given them an hour of their time just listening to them, interested in their week. Not totally understanding the boundaries of the therapeutic relationship, they can mistake the relationship as a friendship and even a romantic opportunity. A therapist must explain what therapy is and can even refer to himself as a professional friend or professional helper rather than a peer friend. Explaining to the individual what the boundaries are is important up front, and may seem unusual to the therapist of non-DD individuals. It's not that the risk of falling in love with one's therapist is greater with the non DD (we certainly know how common that is in typical non-DD therapies); it's that it may come from a different place, a misunderstanding, as well as from that place we all know—a positive transference and a longing for that kind of attention and love in our personal lives that a therapist seems to provide. And it may be harder to undo once the idea gets into a client's head. One colleague of mine had the hardest time explaining to her client why she wasn't his girlfriend. "You stood up for me with my mother. That means you're my girlfriend," he kept insisting.

In setting up the therapeutic relationship, explaining what people generally talk about in therapy and including sexual concerns as one topic, therapy with a DD teen is not much different than therapy with a non-DD teen. Indeed, the relationship itself is the best social skills training a teen can get, with its demands for coregulation, reciprocal communication, and joint attention. We assume that high cognitive functioning people have these skills, but even with the non-DD these problems arise. If the therapist forms a relationship over time with the DD teen, it gives the teen an opportunity to have conversations or engage in joint tasks with someone that are meaningful. Far too often, DD teens have had practice talking about their day or what they're wearing; far too few have spent 50-minute conversations talking about their feelings, their desires, their plans, or engaging in some expressive activity such as sand tray therapy where the other is deeply involved in the process as a player or an observer.

With regard to sex and sexuality, it's important to be aware of some tricky issues regarding sex in terms of setting up the confidentiality parameters. Most non-DD clients come into therapy inhibited regarding talking about sex and sexual issues, afraid to share their darkest secrets or fantasies, waiting to trust the therapist before divulging their issues. Some DD teens are so used to living their lives under watch that they may tend to share too much with the people around them. Others can be withdrawn and will stick to discussions of what they did that day. And some would like to include questions about sex but are afraid it "isn't nice." The first group, the less inhibited teens, may not realize that it's socially unacceptable to describe sexual feelings to people one hardly knows. So a therapist needs to be direct at first about why it's good and helpful to talk about these feelings and fantasies in therapy if they are of concern or if the client is confused and wants more information but also that these are generally private thoughts and feelings for most people and we need to respect that.

Private feelings and thoughts? Looking around this world, one can hardly make a case that sex and sexual feelings are private. Teens see sex everywhere, and DD teens see the same images of sex and romance on TV that the rest of us see. It can be difficult to make the case that for most people, there's a difference between what they watch on TV and what they feel and do themselves. For some kids, it can be difficult to discern where and when it's appropriate to make a sexual innuendo or joke or ask a sexual question. This is also true for lots of non DD kids and teens, those who are impulsive or who have been diagnosed with attention-deficit disorder. But in order to talk about sex in therapy, it's a good idea to place a circle around it, a boundary that explains the more complicated idea that one's own sexual feelings and thoughts are private and that therapy is a place where private thoughts and feelings can be talked about, especially if kids have some worries or thoughts they keep thinking about over and over. As with trauma issues, it's also a good idea for a therapist to understand the window of opportunity afforded in each session. The window is the open space, sometimes short, to talk about sexual issues. DD teens benefit from a time of grounding at the end of each session to reenter the real world in a self-regulated state.

With that caveat, service agencies generally support the value of presumed competence in many areas, including the sexual. This doesn't mean talking above someone's head, as one wouldn't with a non-DD teen, but that as therapists we need to assume that DD individuals are competent in one or several areas rather than disabled in all areas of their lives, and that they may be quite competent to form sexual relationships with others. A second core value at the Howard Community Services in Burlington and in other DD service agencies in Vermont is to give DD individuals "dignity of risk"; people should be allowed to take reasonable risks in life. Other important core values are self-determination, community inclusion, and the right of everyone to articulate their hopes, dream, and goals. This should happen in a climate of safety, choice, and empowerment.

RISKS OF SEX FOR DD TEENS

What is reasonable risk for non-DD kids, let alone DD kids? In writing this book, I tried to no avail to find out what is the actual risk of a heterosexual female contracting HIV/AIDS from a random one-night stand with a non-drug-addicted heterosexual male. The answer from every HIV/AIDS expert was, "We don't know that, but a teenage girl should be told to always use a condom." And yet, there isn't a sexually active heterosexual female I know who hasn't taken that risk at least once. Is this a reasonable risk? How do we balance the need for safety with the need for independence for DD teens—or for all teens, for that matter?

A major risk for DD teens is exploitation. Estimates show the risk of abuse and exploitation is higher for DD children and teens. For example, non-DD teens and adults can use these kids sexually while the kids are unaware, experiencing themselves as consenting and part of something. This is a tricky issue because we don't actually believe that DD teenagers can give consent. But of course they can. They simply can't always recognize deception and exploitation, nor lack of mutuality. Sometimes when they do, they choose the pseudofriendship over none at all. Even when DD teens and adults have received good education about protection and identifying unwanted sexual contact, it is still difficult for them to see themselves as responsible for their sexual choices (Garwood & McCabe, 2000). This is a problem for non-DD kids too, one that we work on in therapy, helping them to consider whether they are making a choice to let others exploit them and treat them badly or whether they just don't see what is happening to them as exploitation. Because DD teens are often starved for intimacy, they will accept negative attention from peers rather than no attention at all. They feel connected in some way, even if they are being teased. The line between giving one's lunch money to bullies and giving one's body sexually to an aggressive peer is very thin. Role-playing various social and dating interactions with a DD teen in therapy is a good way to help build the ability to discriminate between mutual and exploitative interactions. Indeed, the idea that one is responsible for one's sexual choices is a concept that lots of teenage girls and boys are still learning. If a non-DD teenage girl has sex with a bullying teenage boy because she feels awkward saying no, it's a problem. But if the same thing happens with a DD teen, it's a legal problem.

Marie would hang out at the park near her home where other teens would be smoking weed and sneaking beers. There seemed to be a quasi acceptance of her among the non-DD teens there. As she saw other girls and boys with their arms around each other, she might have wanted that same intimacy. In her mind, this might have been the crisis-laden "intimacy" that she saw on soap operas and reality shows. It's also possible that these scenes were arousing to her and that it wasn't simply intimacy that she longed for. We as therapists need to be careful about making assumptions based on gender stereotypes that girls want intimacy and boys want sex. In Marie's case, some of the boys saw whatever need she was expressing and convinced her to let them touch her breasts. They then taught her how to give them blow jobs in the woods behind the park. To them, Marie seemed happy to comply, happy for the attention, happy to please, perhaps even happy for the sex.

The girls in the crowd, it came out afterward, thought it was fine because Marie was giving consent. The boys were exploiting her but they were doing so in a friendly way that must have been confusing to her.

It all came out when Marie reported to her therapist that she had "one-night boyfriends." The therapist pursued this odd phrase and figured it out. While Marie was happy to have a boyfriend even for a night (usually a couple of hours at the park), this was exploitation, and it was illegal. If not hurtful ostensibly, it taught Marie that her worth to these guys was in her ability to please them sexually. Perhaps she was shielded because of her cognitive impairments from the fact that they weren't really interested in being her boyfriend or knowing more about her life. Whereas a non-DD girl might understand the lack of mutuality, Marie did not understand that this wasn't what girlfriends and boyfriends do, nor the way to get a boyfriend. Or maybe she did. For non-DD girls as well as the more vulnerable DD teens, it's hard to know if the issue is better negative attention than no attention at all or truly wanting to do what they are doing even if the attention is not real. With Marie, however, it became clear that it was more about the attention than the sex when she said that what hurt her was being ignored the next day by her "boyfriend."

Working with Marie then focused on her hopes, many of which were very simple stereotyped girlfriend–boyfriend activities—to have a boyfriend, to sit with him on the swings at the park and hold hands, to have him go on walks with her, to watch TV together, to kiss and hug, to make her feel like the best girl in the world, to go the movies. Then together she and her therapist talked about what was different about this situation in the park and how to recognize when someone was interested in something more mutual. I'd like to argue that this is more than social skills training, for when these conversations happen in therapy, they don't seem like social skills training to the teen; a real conversation is happening in a real relationship. These conversations are about honoring one's hopes and wishes, understanding the feelings a client hopes to have in relationship, understanding why clients are likely to put themselves in situations that are risky, coming to understand self-worth, imagining possible selves, and about finding the presence in oneself to be able to hold out for what one wants. Good therapy builds a sense of social competence and the skills inherent in that competence.

Holding out for what one wants may be more conflictual than it seems. It is even harder for DD teens than other teens to learn to use delayed gratification. Most people are ambivalent about what they want. And when Marie knew at some level that she was being exploited, would she be able to inhibit her desire in the moment to be a part of things, to be wanted by a guy? That was also an important goal.

PARENTS AND DD TEENS

It's really great to involve parents at times in therapy with their DD kids. All children and teens want approval from their parents for their adult selves, to have their parents recognize and admire the way they're growing up. And too often, they are fearful that some of the things they do that feel grown-up are the very things their parents will be angry about.

Pendler and Hinsburger (1991) wrote that we shouldn't assume that parents are against sexuality in their kids, arguing with a number of previous writings. They cited research that shows that some group home staff can be more punitive and restrictive than parents. But it seems clear why that might be. Group home staff have some legal responsibilities, including reporting to parents and guardians. Also, they can be less well trained on the subject of developmental disabilities than parents of kids who've grown up with disabilities. Given the low pay of the job in most parts of the country and the occasional hardening of the senses that comes from working in the same position forever, they can be more interested in management than personal growth issues for their clients.

There are also many committed workers who are frustrated with parents who want to baby their kids and are afraid to allow them their own sexuality and choices. For parents of DD teens, there is often no rite of passage that helps them begin to let go. These parents need their own lives and their kids need independence at some point. But this is difficult to achieve, and they show deep ambivalence about their child growing up. And they worry about the risks of disease, and for girls, pregnancy, exploitation, and abuse.

When parents can come to see their children as sexual, then their vision of what kind of sex and sexuality is right for their kids is much more traditional than it might be for a non-DD child. Issues like promiscuity, exploration of oral sex, illicit affairs with inappropriate individuals, and sexual orientation become more difficult for parents if encountered with their DD teen. They may see their kids as following someone else's lead, vulnerable, and unable to give real consent, rather than having real interests.

Thus, some of the work a therapist might do is with parents. Can a therapist help parents to imagine a sexual life for their child in which their child can both explore and be protected? Do they believe that their child can retain the knowledge he needs to protect himself? And who will give their child that knowledge? There's often the fear that if you teach DD kids about sex, they will act impulsively and go out and do it. But all the research on sex education in non-DD kids shows that it creates more self-reflection and less action. There is also some research and writing on sex education groups with DD teens and young adults, none of which indicates acting-out behaviors after sessions or group. Importantly, therapists of DD clients know to structure sessions with a beginning, middle, and end to help the child leave in a reg-

268

ulated and calm way, not overstimulated by the material presented.

THERAPY AND SEX EDUCATION

Parents are the best educators about sex in many ways because they are free to convey their values as well as the information. But sometimes kids don't want to learn about sex from their parents. And sex education groups have been used with success among DD teens. Therapists will provide sex education in therapy as it is relevant to the issues at hand, but they need to be prepared.

In providing sex education, whether in group or one-on-one with an individual client, it's important not to start at too high a level. This may be true for non-DD teens as well. We might assume that because they're having intercourse or living in this hypersexualized world that they know some of the basics about reproduction and sexual functioning. And we would be wrong. Many have been excluded from even the simple sex education available in the schools they've attended, for various reasons, among them the fear that a DD teen will act out or is too immature to understand. With DD teens, it's good to have some prepackaged drawings of body parts and people simply to establish a common language about sex. These can be ordered from companies that provide educational materials for DD youth. And in perusing such pictures, a therapist can address the taboo that some have been taught that it's "not nice" to talk about sex. "We talk about sex in this room because it's therapy, and in therapy you learn about yourself in all kinds of ways. You also can ask questions about private things in therapy and talk about your feelings about private things like sex." The therapist will want to remind DD teens what kind of conversations about sex and sexual issues will get them in trouble in settings other than the therapy room.

But talk is not the only modality. Therapists need to be able to work in a number of symbolic and expressive modalities for several reasons. There may be verbal disabilities and problems with speech. Some sexual issues result from early trauma—trauma that may have been experienced on a nonverbal level. Expressive modalities are often the therapy of choice for these issues. When a child or teen can't seem to speak in abstractions, they often still can understand more abstract concepts when presented symbolically, and these modalities free a child or teen to explore issues that may be too difficult to explore in conversation. For example, many DD teens use drawing as a way of externalizing their history, thoughts, and feelings. A pattern of drawings literally helps paint a complex picture for the therapist of what is happening inside the teen's mind with minimal or no words being spoken. The trick is to not infantilize the adult through play, but to offer modes of play as a mutual resource to the therapy. Puppets, drawing, a sand tray with miniatures, and even a dollhouse can open up possibilities for understanding and expression. Play in these areas is not merely helpful because teens can communicate better by displacing what happened or what they want onto dolls. Through the interactions and the feelings that arise and are placed onto the dolls, they can express worries, fears, and desires in ways not possible through talk.

Working in an expressive modality is less threatening than face-to-face talking for many DD teens. The expressive therapy modalities include art, play, music, movement, and drama. They are flexible, safe, engaging, and reciprocal. An internal, nonverbal image can be expressed in any or several of these modalities. Staying in the metaphor without direct verbal interpretation lets teens explore issues more completely and reach a more helpful resolution. When teens are stuck around sexual issues in their thought or feeling process, expressive work literally moves them out of their stuck place. Physical or expressive movement equals emotional and cognitive movement.

While it may seem odd to introduce these kinds of activities in therapy with a non-DD teen, working in an expressive modality can frequently feel less threatening than face-to-face talking for many DD teens. When a sexual issue comes up, a therapist can try to go over what the client knows by talking, bringing over some dolls, or using pictures. (Therapists can also refer to Planned Parenthood, which often has specialists in educating DD teens.) I've used a sketch pad and markers so that while talking we can also laugh at my drawings. Also, my clients can then take the marker and show me things of interest and concern on my makeshift human body. But there needs to be a shift from education to feelings, and after establishing some basic knowledge, it's important to ask a client about her or his hopes, dreams, and desires as well as worries and fears. When this happened in relation to talking about a teen's abuse, the simple drawing of a picture and labeling parts was transformed into attacking the page with markers to show anger.

Within periods of talk and play regarding sex, therapists need to keep an open mind with regard to what sex is for their clients. I would never jump right into the drawing of private parts on a sketch pad nor even to educating the teen with regard to what these parts of the body are called. I would begin with hopes and wishes. A few may say they want to have intercourse with someone. Many, though, will say they want a boyfriend, a girl-friend. When pressed further to describe what they picture they might do with a girlfriend or boyfriend, it may be something as simple as holding hands and kissing. Some also want marriage and children, markers of normality to them.

I had a client, LaToya, who thought of sex with a boyfriend as holding hands, hugging, and kissing. Doing this gave her nice feelings. Intercourse or anything to do with her vaginal area did not seem nice to her because she had been raped and sexually abused by her grandfather. Was it my duty to tell her that other sex acts could be nice too? I thought so. It was important for her to understand that this grandfather robbed her of some feelings and the opportunity to discover more pleasant adult sexual feelings. Why?

271

Because she needed to make a choice about these adult acts that came from knowledge, not from fear. We processed her hateful feelings toward her grandfather, as well as the fear she felt at the time. We even used markers to slash at the makeshift drawing I drew of him. And she drew bars across him to show me he was in jail or should have been put in jail. She also drew tears on the face of the girl I drew. We had a limited way of talking about this: "He made you sad"; "He hurt you"; "You wanted to say no"; "You wanted a boyfriend to share things with you"; "You didn't want a man to stick his penis in you then"; "It hurt"; "You were quiet because you were afraid"; "You were frightened." And in this way we created a narrative of her abuse that was based on her feelings and perspectives.

Then I wondered whether I should tell her that adults have sex and it is pleasurable, to give her some more positive idea of sex and sexuality. Because her caseworker thought she might have some sexual preference toward other girls, I had to be careful about how I worded it.

Therapist: Often when people are grown up and married or when they have someone they love and want to be close to, they have sex and it feels nice.

LaToya: No.

Th: No, they don't? Or no, it doesn't feel nice?

LT: Doesn't feel nice.

Th: What do you think adult couples do?

LT: Hug and kiss.

Th: They do that too, but sometimes they want to do more and they're not scared or unhappy. They like it because it feels good and they like the person. They choose to do it.

LT: Do Melissa and Neil have sex? [*This was the couple she had been living with in foster care for the past six months.*]

Th: I think they might. [*I forgot to warn her that this was private between Neil and Melissa. Or perhaps I just wanted to normalize it for her.*]

She went home that day and became angry at Melissa. Melissa called me and said that LaToya came up to her and yelled, "You have sex with Neil," in an accusing way. Melissa didn't know what to say, given how angry LaToya was, and she wasn't sure what the anger was about. I encouraged Melissa to talk to LaToya about the reasons grown-ups have sex, about reproduction as well as love and pleasure. But I also cautioned her to ask LaToya first if she was ready to talk about it. It seemed that she was quite overstimulated by our talk.

Although LaToya insisted that she wanted a boyfriend to hug and kiss, it seemed as if she had some sort of sexual attraction to Melissa, whom she occasionally would hug too closely. Melissa had already had to create some boundaries around hugging to prevent too close contact for her comfort. So back in therapy, LaToya and I talked about her anger at Melissa. I asked if it was upsetting because she thought that sex was bad and hurtful. She said yes. I said that it must be confusing if Melissa would do that on purpose. "Maybe she likes it," I offered. LaToya looked angry at that and I said, "Maybe you don't want her to be that close to Neil." She looked up quickly and deeply into my eyes, as if I had hit on something. I went on, "She is still your foster mother and still cares about you so much, but this is something private she has with Neil."

Was LaToya sexually attracted to Melissa, or was this simply jealousy about her foster mother giving attention to someone LaToya considered a rival? I couldn't tell, and maybe there wasn't such a difference. DD teens often have difficulties when caregivers split attention, and it's not uncommon for them to sexualize intimate relationships with caregivers. Moreover, LaToya had grown up in a home with few boundaries. She was exploited and perhaps taught to sexualize others too easily. Her dream relationship was based on TV romances, a boyfriend to hug and kiss. But her inner life may have pushed her toward a very powerful crush on

Melissa, whom she had known less than a year and who was caring and good to her. She may have had very strong feelings toward Melissa, even sexual arousal, but it's unclear whether these feelings translated into anything adults would consider sexual, given that LaToya's idea of sexual intercourse was one of harm. How confusing it must have been to learn that Melissa had sex with someone else right after learning that sex can mean intimacy, love.

The therapy with LaToya continued over many months, differentiating between the various kinds of love and caring feelings, various forms of relationships, and various types of sexual relationships a person can have. Then something unexpected arose: LaToya announced she had a boyfriend. For weeks she talked about Jason after she met him at a dance. They danced several dances and talked. She and I talked about when she might see him again and how she might arrange to meet him somewhere to walk, talk, or do some other activity together.

But I soon found out that the person she considered her boyfriend was a staff member who had danced with her at a party. Given the confidentiality and privacy of our sessions, I had no way initially of knowing whether this boyfriend was appropriate or not for her. From what she told me, he seemed appropriate. He was another teen at the dance. But wait. Did I ask if he was a teen? Did I ask if he was DD like LaToya? No and no. When her service provider, who brought her to therapy, told me who Jason was, I felt incredulous and guilty. Here I was, leading her on, as if this could be a real relationship for her. Staff and clients are not allowed to date for obvious reasons, but should I drop our discussions? Should I be the one to tell her? The service provider reassured me that they had told her many times that Jason was not an appropriate boyfriend for her.

I decided to treat this like any schoolgirl crush. If others were telling her no, and she was still enjoying talking to me about this potential boyfriend, then why not continue? I decided to let *her* tell me that things didn't work out. And in the meantime, we continued "practicing," in my eyes, what she might do if she did have a crush on someone more appropriate, fantasizing of a relationship to come, the planning of how she might meet him. Rather than raising unrealistic expectations, I thought of when I was young, in middle school or earlier, and my friends and I talked endlessly about our "relationships" with boys we had crushes on, boys who barely knew we existed, especially when these boys were George Harrison and Paul McCartney. In the grand scheme of things, this is the way we learn, by playing around with ideas before acting on them.

She eventually stopped talking about Jason. After a few weeks, I brought him up, and she said she wasn't interested in him anymore. Why? She didn't tell me he was staff. She simply said, "I never see him." That was a good sign. She wanted a real boyfriend, in the flesh, but for now knew some things about how she might feel, what she might want, and how to respond when a real one came along.

KIDS WHO DO DANGEROUS THINGS

Graham was the 17-year-old son of very conservative Christian parents who found out from his developmental home provider that Graham had been seeking out male-to-male contact. Graham had discovered, nobody knew quite how, that the space behind the bandstand in the park, bounded by both the back of the bandstand and the beginning of some woods, was a meeting place for a small group of men to have casual sex with other men. This was a place that his caseworker, David, a gay male therapist, knew about but had never visited. He had heard that straight and married men as well as closeted men frequented such spots, and he seemed appalled by it all. In a long-term relationship himself, he disliked the idea that Graham, if he had same-sex attractions, had had his first experience in a place like this, and wished there were healthier places for Graham to meet other DD guys or gay males who would be his friend first and with whom he might establish a relationship.

At the center that ran the set of group homes where Graham lived, in spite of David's efforts to educate them, the administrators and other counselors were adamant that Graham was to have no gay sex anytime, anywhere, let alone in that more dangerous venue behind the bandstand. They asked the group home to watch him 24–7. But there also was an "alone-time agreement" that left Graham responsible for what he did and where he went at certain times.

It was not difficult for Graham to find sex behind the bandstand once he put himself in that situation. From what David gathered, Graham would simply go behind the bandstand and when he saw a man alone there, he would expose himself and hope that this would start the action. David told him that he needed to stop going there and exposing himself. Graham said he understood the risks, and he said he would stop, but then he continued.

Although Graham looked 17, or even younger, he did not appear to be developmentally disabled, and so his sexual partners may not have known that about him. These older men (most only a few years older) should not have been taking advantage of a teenager, DD or not, but probably saw him as a questioning youth, looking for a thrill or a new experience. In a different world, his caseworker could have offered Graham events and groups where he might meet kids his own age and where the contact between them, if the contact happened to involve sex, would at least be mutual, the power differential less problematic. There were groups in the area for questioning teens that held support sessions and scheduled activities like bowling and pizza—but they didn't seem right for a DD teen.

It was after a weekend home when his parents, particularly his father, absolutely forbid him from going behind the bandstand, that Graham began to change the way he described his trips. We guessed that his parents had told him that what he had done was sinful, but we hoped that they also might have described it as dangerous for other reasons. Perhaps they told him that he was being exploited. We don't know exactly what went on that weekend, but when he returned to the developmental home, he started describing what happened differently. He was unable to keep private what he did when his home provider asked him. But he fudged it by saying he was lured by older men: "He made me do it" was the refrain.

In therapy, this was not a difficult issue to discuss. It was one of agency and independence from his parents. Even though he was saying that men made him do things, it was clear that what was occurring followed the same pattern as before. After all, why was he going to the bandstand? This new way of presenting it arose so that he wouldn't get in trouble with his parents. When asked if he wanted to go behind the bandstand, he would honestly say yes. David asked, "But how does it feel when it happens and afterward?" Graham paused and said, "It feels good. And then I feel funny." After some exploration, it seemed that what he might be describing was the positive sexual feeling followed by a feeling of shame or having done something wrong.

Believing that Graham had a right to pursue and explore his own sexuality, his caseworker began looking into the possibility of starting a sex and sexuality group for DD teens and young adults, a rare group offering anywhere. What questioning youths need is to know that others like them are out there. This therapist also thought it was important to talk about norms for kids his age who are gay.

Therpist: What do you think boys your age who want sex with men do?
Graham: Go to the bandstand.

That was all Graham could think of. His therapist then offered some alternatives.

Th: Some masturbate, and they use pictures of men that they like, often pictures from magazines and the Internet, and masturbate while looking at them.

They also discussed Internet safety and made some clear agreed-upon rules that Graham would follow in his Internet use.

Th: And they look for kids their age who might be interested in starting something, first as friends and then maybe as boyfriends. Most kids are waiting to find someone they like to have sex with, whether it's a boy or a girl.

Graham replied that masturbation didn't feel good. At first his therapist wondered if Graham was hurting himself while masturbating or simply whether he preferred other people in the flesh. It is not uncommon for DD teens to use strange objects for masturbation or not to know how to bring themselves to orgasm. In their conversation, it became clear that Graham didn't seem to know how to masturbate himself to orgasm. His therapist explained how a person could do that, and also explained quite simply that some people did some things that hurt their penises and that Graham should make sure that he was not being too rough. He suggested that maybe he needed to press hard enough to make himself have an orgasm or use lotion. Graham seemed eager to try, so eager that his therapist was certain he was going to leave the session and go straight to the bathroom of his developmental home.

There was another issue to address, and that was Graham's independence from his parents. Through many sessions, the two struggled with the fact that his parents did not like that he wanted to have sex with men or that he might even have a boyfriend someday. As with any teen, the two of them worked on issues of autonomy. Could he keep secrets from his parents? If he had concerns, could he bring them to his therapist, who could keep a secret? How could he cope with feeling bad, knowing he was doing something his parents didn't like him to do?

The therapist told the parents at parent meetings that he was helping Graham to make sensible choices and that they worked on his not being exploited and not putting himself in physical danger, but that it wasn't his inclination to try to undo Graham's leanings toward homosexuality. As with all parents whose children come out in the teen years, the parents struggled with losing their control. They liked the developmental home and provider in other ways and because there were so few other alternatives, they kept Graham there. The therapist then worked with the parents on and off, but rather than focusing on Graham's sexuality, they talked about how to let go and accept that Graham might have a separate adult life in a few years, to which they might not be privy.

Neither sexuality nor letting go are easy issues for parents and adolescents. As with all therapy with adolescents, issues of autonomy, values, and difference are at the forefront during these years. Both the parents and the adolescent need support through these times.

SEX AND THE BEAUTIFUL BOY

George was a gorgeous adolescent boy, one to whom girls, women, and guys too were drawn. Tall and structured, he enjoyed compulsively working out and lifting weights, which his father encouraged, in their basement. He had the look of a young rock star, his Greek features shining through his dark hair and eyes. Workers at his group home noticed that girls swooned and boys took notice when he walked by.

His beauty also brought him more attention and help than other DD kids, although his placid, laid-back personality might have helped too. He had more service providers and a larger support system than most kids, DD or not. First, he had his father, who lived near the group home and encouraged George to stop by anytime. Then he had the Greek Orthodox Church members who got to know him while he was growing up because his father was active in the church. He would run into these people downtown when he was hanging out and they would often stop to check in with him on how he was doing. The workers in the home all liked him. The service providers he had over the years kept in touch. And new people who met him felt that they were willing to go the extra mile to provide services, rides to places, lunch money, and so on.

George could pass as non-DD. Although he wasn't able to drive, he was able to get a high school diploma and was working on it. Because he could pass, and because he was rather high functioning, he was embarrassed and ashamed about his disability. He knew that the friends he hung out with on the benches by the river weren't truly friends, but they were cool kids and seemed to like him well enough. In talking with his therapist, he would say, "I shouldn't go to the river, but I can't stop myself. I want to be by my friends." But going down to the river meant that these friends would use his money to buy drugs, and share the drugs with him, and that he could have sex with some of the girls who would come by night.

It was unclear whether these river kids were exploiting George. They could have enjoyed his company. And it could have been the case that none of them had real and trusting relationships with one another. It may have been the case that whoever among them had money just threw it into the communal pot (so to speak) for drugs. But of course they must have come to know over time that George had some cognitive issues—as well as some available money.

With regard to sex, like a ping-pong ball, George bounced from one girl to another girl, having sex with whoever was interested that night. He in fact had had more sex than most teen boys, probably because of the crowd he hung around with as well as his good looks. Given the gruff silence of most teen boys, it was the rare girl who could detect his cognitive disability if George kept his mouth shut.

And George was a bit more experienced than most boys. At the age of 16 he had been taken by his father to a prostitute in New York City, whom his father found through some of his connections there. This woman was asked to teach George about having sex as well as how to please a woman. All this George related to his therapist, which perhaps explained to him why George seemed to be confident in his ability to have sex with a number of different girls.

But when George's therapist began to talk about relationships rather than sex, George began to change. It is common for educators to describe sexual relationships as a pyramid, with sexual intercourse at the apex and commonly accepted relationship skills at the base. Using this information, George's therapist drew a pyramid and put intercourse at the top. On the broad base were a number of things that had to do with relationships: talking about your dreams, listening, sharing things you like, holding hands, and feeling close. It wasn't that George's therapist was against meaningless sex; it was that she wanted George also to know that there was potential for something else, and not just something else with girls, but with his male friends who were pretty much only drug buddies. Her point was that sexual intercourse is only a small part of intimate human relationships, with so much else available as foundation experiences. "What do you want in a relationship?" she would ask. "Where do you find the right person? How do you know if someone is using you or wants to really get to know you?"

Their work progressed to the extent that George began to see his one-night stands as potential relationships. And he became sad when they were only one-night stands. He came up with the goal of having a girlfriend but specifically said that he didn't want her to be DD; he wanted her to be "normal."

One night George hooked up with a girl he really liked a lot. They were at the river and spent the night walking around the town after they hooked up, holding hands and talking. As the weed they smoked wore off and the two became sleepy, a change happened. The girl seemed to realize that George was disabled. Was it his indication that he lived in a group home they passed? Was it something he said? George described feeling her extract herself from the conversation, from him. In his depiction of what happened, the therapist became distinctly aware that this girl may have realized she had just slept with a DD youth. Was she horrified? Did she see herself as an exploiter? She had said to him that the two of them weren't the same "kind of people" and so shouldn't see each other again.

George was devastated. Because he was so upset, his therapist made the point that when a person really wants a relationship, easy sex is more difficult to manage. It brings up feelings of desire for more than just sex. And that makes rejection all the harder. Their work continued, with George desperate for skills to make relationships last longer. Fun, help, gifts, and even sex had come easy because of his looks and his simple charm. Now he had to work to get what he really wanted.

Was this therapist wrong to introduce desires George may not have been fully aware of? She was the one who brought up the idea that maybe he wanted something more than a one-night stand. Her feeling was that this is what most people want, and that a real relationships would ultimately be more fulfilling and would help him to attain adult autonomy from a loving but confused father.

* * * *

If sex is a part of being human, a pleasure that can be enjoyed alone but that adds to the intimacy in relationships, then it's our responsibility to help DD teens to gain competency in this area, to feel fine about pursuing pleasure, and to form relationships that can become sexual. The issues regarding pleasure, guilt, relationship, sexuality, choice, and autonomy regarding sex are similar for DD and non-DD kids. But with DD teens, there is much more potential for exploitation, and developmentally they may take things slower.

If a therapist sees a DD teen one-on-one, it's probably for a host of issues and not a simple sexual problem. But sexual issues will arise and it's good to be prepared. Starting simple and working with clients on their desires as well as their feelings conveys to them that we as therapists aren't about social skills training. Real conversations with a real therapist about skills that are more than skills when enacted in the real world with real people are what it's all about. Many of these kids haven't had a lot of long conversations that focus on their insides, their wishes and dreams. And it's important to go there.

CHAPTER 10

Sexual and Moral Feelings in the Therapy Hour

You don't necessarily need psychoanalytic training to recognize when you're getting too involved with a patient, but it helps. When talking about sex and sexual activity, the chance that transference and countertransference reactions will occur is great, and many therapists ought to seek supervision early when they suspect there may be counter-transference issues. Transference is healthy. Patients do respond to therapists in ways that replicate their deepest longings for love and intimacy. But when therapists respond back, forgetting about boundaries, the patient's best interests, and the meaning and origin of the patient's longings, therapists are in the troubling waters of countertransference. Pope, Tabachnick, and Keith-Spiegel (1987) found that around 85% of therapists have had sexual feelings towards clients, but far fewer have talked about it in supervision (Ladany, O'Brien, Hill, Melincoff, Knox, & Peterson, 1997).

Most therapists aren't in the practice of reflecting on their own sexual lives and feelings, and this lack of awareness may make us overly interested in our patients' sexual lives, reliving our own less exciting adolescence vicariously through teens, or alternatively shying away from arousing or embarrassing material. As with any difficult and emotional memories, when teens talk about sex, we therapists need to make sure that our minds do not wander, that we don't shut down, or that we don't become lost in memories of our own experiences. We need to be aware of our sexual histories and fantasy life, so that we can separate them from our interest in the sex lives of teens.

Therapists aren't immune from cultural influences. If we watch TV, read the papers or magazines, and go to the movies, we are titillated by nonstop stories of teen sex, some in the guise of journalism. If we only read and watch that kind of fare, we begin to lose track of what real teens are like, and the knowledge that real sex comes with ambivalences, anxieties, and insecurities as well as the potential for pleasure.

Remember, too, that many psychotherapists were sexually abused as children, and that this too can be a source of feelings of overstimulation or fear and avoidance. One colleague of mine expressed the envy he felt when he talked to youths about their new sexual experiences. His clients had a chance to do it right. He was sexually abused as a teen by a priest and didn't have that chance.

Even when a person was not abused as a child, it's important for therapists not to use our own childhood or adolescence as a basis for what's normal. Sexual play and games may seem very odd to a therapist who grew up with none of that. For one who did play these games, the stories her client tells may not sound so different.

TRANSFERENCE AND
COUNTERTRANSFERENCE REACTIONS

Transference, originally a term from psychoanalysis but now used by all kinds of practitioners, refers to the strong feelings a patient develops toward the therapist that may reflect unconscious feelings toward an early parent. In a positive transference, those feelings can involve a powerful love, sexual interest, and even lust; in a negative transference, rage or sadness at the therapist's inadequacies or mistakes, both imagined and real, can result. Transference has been seen as a natural part of the intense nature of therapy. Countertransference occurs when a therapist responds to that transference, acting or feeling like the parent, the lover, or the beloved or hateful object. Countertransference feelings may well up in therapy sessions, and we have a responsibility to reflect on these and cope with them in supervision outside of therapy so we don't act on those feelings, doing or saying things that might not be so helpful to our clients.

Usually countertransference is described as a reaction to the patient's transference, but sometimes it occurs on its own. Take, for example, the therapist who gets overinvolved in a teen's sex stories. If a teen senses the increased interest of a therapist, he or she may avoid such subjects or act out in a session, spinning tales to delight and shock. Let's say a therapist is drawn in and makes a more personal statement like, "I remember when I was that age and obsessed with girls." The therapist might ask himself why he was compelled at that moment to respond with a statement that described himself as being like his patient. Was the teen placing him in that position, the position of buddy or friend, in the way he was telling his story to his therapist? Was he afraid of judgment by the therapist and trying to ensure the therapist was a buddy who wouldn't make him look too hard at his actions? Was he simply seeking some reaction that confirmed his normality? Or maybe he was trying to neutralize his sexual feelings toward the therapist by making his therapist just a buddy. Some clients may describe their sexual experiences in such a way that therapist and client together can share a sexual experience symbolized through talking.

More disturbed teens might take this transference a bit further. My colleague Jules was treating a teenage girl who had had a psychotic break in which she was talking about having sex with

Jesus. This break came after having a two-year relationship in high school with her photography teacher. The relationship she began to develop with Jules had aspects of both kinds of relationship, a relationship with a teacher and a confessional relationship with God, and so it was quite natural that it should develop into some kind of transference. In the first year of therapy, she began to feel that she had a loudspeaker in her head giving her commands from her therapist. These commands were to have sex with many different boys in her school. Before she had had the affair with her teacher and her subsequent breakdown, she was quite active sexually with kids her own age, so sexual activity was not new. She also felt that she had initiated sex with this teacher; she stated to Jules that she was attracted to him and was "up for it."

What Jules remembered about this case was the difficulty they both had in the sessions during her telling of the events because as they emerged they were eroticized. She seemed to be retelling the events, of her exploitation by this teacher, in a very erotic and sexual way. When Jules realized that this was dangerous for her, a reenactment of sorts, he became quiet and neutral. This was difficult and he had to work at it through supervision outside of sessions and by actively thinking about his responses within the sessions. He also felt that he couldn't confront her with her own excitement in telling him these stories and wanting to arouse him. Instead of confronting her with the stimulating way she told her stories, he spoke with her of the ambivalence that was barely present in her speech, asking her about moments of fear or sadness, complicating the emotions that she presented. Surely these were complex emotions at the time or they would not have led to a breakdown. And as he kept in his mind that this girl was inviting him to exploit her rather than help her, he became focused on how to help and what she really needed from him.

Male therapists have confessed to me that sometimes it's difficult to keep these thoughts in mind with female teenage clients. One friend, who predominantly sees male adolescents, admitted,

"I'd probably be pretty aroused if I listened to teen girls' escapades." I didn't actually think this would be so. In the abstract, he thought he might be, but I believe that in a session this therapist would be able to focus on what his client needed from him rather than his own fantasies. In fact, Scott Okamoto's (2002) research with male therapists of young female clients showed them to feel more fatherly and frustrated with their clients' suspicions of them as potential partners and potentially abusive males rather than being turned on.

For male staff in residential homes and treatment centers, with less training and perhaps less time to reflect, girls' sexualizing the relationship can become very difficult. Okamoto wrote of girls who will purposely get a male staff member to restrain them or who will wear halters or tank tops and draw attention to their breasts by asking the staff to look at a pager or a button or some other thing attached to the strap. In some homes, staff members have training that teaches them to confront girls directly when this happens, in a way that's not meant to shame them but to invite later discussion about sex, sexuality, and boundaries. I've heard of this being done and although I like the motivation behind the intervention, I don't like the way it usually pans out. These kinds of direct comments are made in one home in which I have supervised students. Staffers respond to kids by saying things like, "That's sexualizing!" or "That's inappropriate!" But then they walk away, ignoring it. A brief statement like that can be shaming and doesn't make clear that it's not the sex that's wrong, it's wrong because of the boundary violation and because it can be disrespectful, treating someone as a sexual object rather than a person.

Okamoto wrote about how in some residential centers, teens can try to get staff to restrain them just for the "intimacy" or the sexual contact. Restraints are always tricky, even with the best of training. Instead, a staff member can say, "Marcy, you're escalating things in a way that makes me think you're looking to have me restrain you. I'm not going to do that and am going to get a female staff member to do that if this continues. But if sometime you want to talk about sexual or angry or out-of-control feelings in a serious way, maybe I can do that with you." Also a staff member can say, "Una, I'm a staff member and when you show me that button, you're also showing me your chest. Can we talk about how that's flirting with me and not appropriate because I'm staff? I want to be someone you turn to for real help, not just to give you sexual attention. It feels demeaning to me to be treated that way." The point would be to work on a relationship in which staff can talk to girls about their tendency to seek self-esteem through sexualizing themselves and through attention from men. Okimoto suggested that at the beginning of the therapeutic relationship, the male therapist needs to set up and be consistent about professional boundaries, monitoring his physical differences and using language carefully. If he can focus on establishing rapport rather than confronting clients on sexual issues, later on in the treatment they will be less likely to misinterpret or misuse efforts to help them understand their sexuality and sexual behavior.

Do women therapists and staff also get aroused? Of course. When that happened to me, I instantly began to question myself and what was going on in the session. It frightened me and made me doubt myself. I remember that I became uncomfortable and less responsive, turning inward to ask what I was doing wrong? My reaction came out of a fear of the sexual. But the sexual is going to be a part of many human encounters, and instead of asking what I was doing wrong, I might instead have asked what was happening in the session that day that made those feelings. What was my client talking about and in what way?

A very fine therapist I know quit doing therapy because her own self-doubts about boundaries led her to feel very uncomfortable with kids and teens in session. She remembers a child of 8 or 9 tying her up around a pole in her office and that she felt very aroused by this act but frozen in what she should do about it. If she stopped the play, he would certainly feel that something was wrong about the fantasies that he was enacting. If she recognized these sexual feelings as something that he evoked as part of his fantasy, how could she talk about that with an 8-year-old boy? Instead she felt that something was wrong with her for becoming aroused by being tied up, for being aroused by an 8-year-old boy, and for not being able to focus outward instead of on herself and her own feelings within that session.

Pope, Sonne, and Holroyd (1993) formulated guidelines for psychotherapists to help them not act out in situations in which they have become aroused. I name a few here that are particularly relevant for work with children and teens. When a therapist is feeling sexual feelings, these can be powerful and confusing—instead of responding in the moment, it might be better to wait for clarification of these feelings. Clarification might mean understanding what was happening in the session at that moment or what is going on in the therapist's life in the present that would invite such feelings. Before speaking or acting, it's also important to check in with oneself by asking what is in the best interest of the client at that moment. If it's unclear, then therapists should wait until they can better adopt the client's view and play out in their mind how it might feel to the patient to have a therapist respond in such a way. Another consideration would be for therapists to ask themselves how competent they are to carry out the conversation or intervention. For example, if a psychotherapist is deciding to bring in pornographic materials to help a client with an addiction, has the therapist looked up the guidelines for use of such material? Would there be some need for supervision or training in this particular use? A question Pope and colleagues ask of therapists is to consider whether what they are about to say or do is unusual or uncharacteristic. It is uncharacteristic of a therapist to tell a client that he has had a sexy dream about her. It is uncharacteristic to call up Internet porn sites on the Web with a client. It is uncharacteristic to ask a patient to cover up her breasts or dress more respectably when coming into the office. All of these might be done with care and consideration, but it is not likely.

Finally, Pope and colleagues ask therapists who are considering a conversation or act that might cross boundaries to consider whether they feel they must keep it secret or can discuss it with a colleague. I once almost crossed a boundary, although not a sexual one, but was talked out of it by colleagues. A psychotherapist friend of mine received a referral she did not take. When discussing it with me over the phone, we realized that this client was a former patient of mine, one I had discussed in supervision with this friend years ago. I immediately wanted to call this client and offer some help to her. I now lived in a different state but had often thought of her and wondered how she was doing. My feelings of missing her and my desire to be there for her (perhaps even my guilt for having left her by moving away) were so strong that I thought it would be okay to call her and try to offer some support and help over the phone. I knew this would be unusual and asked my friend if she thought I could do such a thing. She said no, kindly but firmly. And I let it go. But I remember distinctly the desire and the continuing mental justifications for making this call that my friend thought would be wrong. It was only a niggling rational feeling that she must be right as well as the knowledge that this would be very uncharacteristic of a therapist that prevented me from calling this client. How many people do we know who, out of the blue, got a call from a former therapist asking, "Hey, how're you doing? I've been thinking about you!"

Amid these powerful desires, it may be hard to call a colleague or seek supervision. Therapists most likely will be ashamed of such feelings or fantasies and afraid of being judged by the supervisor, who often seems so much more experienced and immune to these kinds of responses. A therapist who can't discuss these feelings with a supervisor ought to seek out psychotherapy. In the very least, knowing that it might be important to get supervision before acting is key. Instead of seeking supervision, however, many therapists blames their own feelings on the client. "She keeps showing me a bit of leg," said one guy to me when we were in training, and I wondered why he didn't say, "I kept finding myself staring at her legs or attracted to her legs." Patient-blaming talk, which is common among therapists, is a defense against the shame of having sexual attractions in psychotherapy.

It also may be common for therapists to project their own worries about sexual feelings onto other therapists rather than recognizing them in themselves. Therapists delight in stories of other therapists' downfall through sexual acting out. It helps them to feel more moral and to reassure themselves that they would never do such a thing. I was once the object of an attack by another therapist. When I was an intern at Massachusetts General Hospital, the emergency room called me in the middle of the night to say that they were thinking of hospitalizing a patient of mine, Rebecca, who was suicidal. I got on the phone with her and she was a mess. My heart went out to her and I told the ER psychiatrist that I would come down to the hospital to see if I could calm her. I arrived at three in the morning and found Rebecca to be hysterical. I sat next to her in the room, and I put my arm firmly around her, sometimes moving my hand up and down her upper arm for reassurance. This was something my own therapist had done for me when I was crying uncontrollably in her office. My feeling at the time was to provide support through her attachment to me as a mother figure. In a very short while, she calmed down and said she no longer wanted to kill herself. We made an appointment for the next day, and the ER psychiatrist decided to keep her that night in a bed in the ER for observation. I went home.

The next day I discovered that I was the main topic at morning rounds. The psychiatry intern awoke that night and wondered if I was having a sexual relationship with my client and questioned her about it after I left. The psychiatry, ER residents, and interns had discussed what was wrong with touching clients and when I came in to work later that day, the chief of psychiatry brought me in to find out more. I felt scolded and accused. I felt particularly bad when the chief psychiatry resident, whom I had been working with and who provided medication consults to this young woman, condemned me. When I saw my client, she was confused and horrified by their questioning. She thought that she had gotten me in trouble and felt terribly guilty. "See?" she said. "I'm no good. I got you in trouble." I reassured her that I could handle this and that it was somewhat unusual for people in our profession to hug clients—the young psychiatrists-in-training had never seen that before in the ER. We processed what it meant for me to hug her and she said that it felt reassuring. What saved me from the humiliation of this incident was that three female psychiatrists secretly came to my aid, confessing to me that they too at times hugged their clients. They went to the chief of psychiatry and told him the same.

The end of this story was that years later, I learned that this chief psychiatry resident had been accused of having a sexual relationship with one of his patients. They recently settled out of court for $750,000. And I wondered whether his condemnation years ago was a projection of the shame he felt for his own longings, longings that might have been aroused by our beautiful young patient.

Should a therapist avoid hugging a patient? Probably, when working with teens. One of my fellow interns at Massachusetts General was found to be taking a 13-year-old boy onto her lap for some reparenting experiences! Although this boy was a young 13-year-old and likely to experience this as nurturing as well as sexual, the rest of us couldn't help but see this as far too stimulating for him sexually. Same-sex hugging is less likely to raise questions from the client or from colleagues. But before a therapist touches a patient or client who may be crying very hard, the therapist ought to ask, "Would it be helpful if I put my arm around you or touched your arm right now?" At the end of a session, sometimes a teen will just spontaneously want to hug you. If this is a patient whom I've seen for quite some time or after a particularly moving or meaningful session, I accept the hug. I know that these sorts of contacts need to be discussed afterward, but having had a therapist who hugged me at the end of every session, I also know that this can simply be a part of the therapeutic process.

MORAL ISSUES AND FEELINGS

We live in a time when the use of the term *moral values* seems to refer to the values of one group. The co-optation of the phrase *moral values*, however, does not mean that this group has the last say on what it means to be a moral human being. Throughout my 25 years as a therapist and as a member of the Association for Moral Education, I've thought quite a bit about the development of morality in children and teens and the moral messages that therapists can and often do provide. As a rule, therapists take what their clients bring them and don't judge in order to more and closely examine feelings, thoughts, and behaviors. But refraining from judgment isn't always a good thing, and temporarily refraining from making any judgments does not mean giving up one's personal moral views.

There are some moral views that would preclude doing therapy unless the therapists advertise that they do a particular kind of therapy from a particular worldview. For example, if a therapist has strong feelings that male-to-male or female-to-female sex is morally wrong and a teen brings up sexual feelings toward someone of the same sex, this therapist should refer the teen elsewhere, trusting that a colleague with a specialty in this area can provide better counseling. If a therapist has strong feelings that premarital sex is morally wrong, she must decide whether those feelings are interfering with her ability to listen to the struggles of an adolescent and then refer out if they are. Perhaps these therapists can keep these moral views to themselves and focus on the idea of psychological and physical health. But I doubt it. It would be wrong to set up a therapy relationship in a way that invited openness and exploration and then to switch strategies when the adolescent got personal, setting a goal of abstinence and teaching the teen ways to be strong in the face of temptation.

Those who promote moral education hope that children and teens will come to know the good and to know what's fair and just, through reflecting on the world around them, through reasoning and discussion, through putting themselves in the shoes of others, and through empathy. But moral education above all helps children to have and express morals via a process that engages them in the world. The expectation is that they won't simply take in and regurgitate the morals of parents, schools, and religious institutions, but that they will internalize these values so they feel like their own. And if this happens, just acts will be motivated by a love of justice and not a fear of disapproval, and service will be motivated by caring and not by trying to please some elder or peer group.

The two moral values that a therapist is confronted with when dealing with kids and teens around issues of sex and sexuality concern harm and unfairness; that is, it's wrong to harm others (and the self perhaps) and it's wrong to treat others unfairly, like objects, as means to personal ends. But the way these issues come up in therapeutic conversations is different than the way they are talked about from behind the pulpit. As therapists, we encourage kids to know their own feelings and guess at the feelings of others in reaction to their behaviors. And we help kids to be aware of differences in power, status, knowledge, age—in short, to understand the other from the other's perspective.

While we may be horrified by the way a client treats his girlfriend, we know that it might not be helpful in the moment to express that horror. Instead, we tend to ask about his feelings leading up to his acts, his feelings about his acts, his thoughts, his justifications. Then we ask him to reflect on how his girlfriend reacts and how that makes him feel. We might express sympathy for the girlfriend in that moment, but also empathy for our client's wounded pride or feelings of humiliation that might have led to that act. We might point out the consequences of such behavior in terms of his relationship or even, when it applies, legally. We might ask him to look at his feelings of vulnerability in other situations and how he handles them. We might ask if he wants to be acting in this way or whether he could imagine himself doing something else. In the end, we psychotherapists seem to trust that by reflecting on his own feelings more deeply, he may make different choices later and may be able to see other people as people with feelings and motivations that deserve respect.

In the end, sex and sexual development are about relating to another person. And the goal of each individual in developing sexually is to have sex in relation to another person, and have it work, and be nice, and even be great someday (or on some days). And if we remember that when working with kids and teens, we can focus on their growing ability to see outside themselves. Knowing oneself is not simply an exercise in knowing oneself, but in understanding oneself so as to relate better to others and the world in which we live.

As in therapy for all sorts of issues, we do give moral messages when talking about sex: Be good to yourself, be good to other people, be fair in the way you act, think of others, practice self-worth. How do we convey these values? By asking children and teens to reflect on their feelings, to come up with plans to wait or move forward in ways that will be safe and healthy for themselves and other people, to become aware of others' reactions to their words and behaviors, to understand what their fantasies mean about their views of themselves and the people around them. Do we advocate self-restraint in a world gone sexually mad? I suppose we do. But asking people to reflect before acting is always a message about self-restraint, or rather, a message about where and when to self-restrain, as well as when it is safe to let go.

References and Resources

GENERAL SEX EDUCATION LITERATURE FOR USE WITH TEENS

Bell, R. (1998). *Changing bodies, changing lives.* New York: Random House.

The Boston Women's Health Book Collective. (2005). *Our bodies, ourselves.* New York: Simon and Schuster.

Mosher, W. D., Chandra, A., & Jones, J. (2005). Sexual behavior and selected health measures: Men and women 15–44 years Age, United States, 2002. *Advance Data form Vital Statistics, 362.* Washington, DC: Centers for Disease Control.

INTRODUCTION

Works Cited

Crosby, R. A., & Yarber, W. L. (2001). Perceived versus actual knowledge about correct condom use among U.S. adolescents: Results from a national study. *Journal of Adolescent Heath, 28,* 415–420.

Jayson, S. (2005, October 19) Teens define sex in new ways. *USA Today.* Available at http://www.usatoday.com/news/health/2005-10-18-teens-sex_x.htm

Hockenberry-Eaton, M., Richman, M. J., Dilorio, C., Rivero, T., & Maibach, E. (1996). Mother and adolescent knowledge of sexual development: The effects of gender, age, and sexual experience. *Adolesence, 31,* 35–47.

Lamb, S. (2002). *The secret lives of girls: What good girls really do—Sex, aggression, and their guilt.* New York: Free Press.

Levy, A. (2005). *Female chauvinist pigs: Women and the rise of raunch culture.* New York: Free Press.

Additional Resources

Ellis, B. J., Bates, J. E., & Dodge, K. A. (2003). Does father absence place girls at special risk for early sexual activity and teenage pregnancy? *Child Development, 74,* 801–821.

Jaccard, J., & Dittus, P. (1991). *Parent-teen communication: Toward the prevention of unintended pregnancies.* New York: Springer-Verlag.

Leitenberg, H., Detzer, M. J., & Srebnik, D. (1993). Gender differences in masturbation and the relation of masturbation experience in preadolescence and/or early adolescence to sexual behavior and sexual adjustment in young adulthood. *Archives of Sexual Behavior, 22*(2), 87–98.

Miller, B. C., Benson, B., & Galbraith, K. A. (2001). Family relationships and adolescent pregnancy risk: A research synthesis. *Developmental Review, 21*(1), 1–38.

Kirby, D. (2001*). Emerging answers: Research findings on programs to reduce teen pregnancy.* Washington, DC: National Campaign to Prevent Teen Pregnancy.

Saewyc, E. M., Bearinger, L. H., Heinz, P. A., Blum, R. W., & Resnick, M. (1998). Gender differences in health risk behaviors among bisexual and homosexual adolescents. *Journal of Adolescent Health, 23*(2), 181–88.

Smith, M. A., Rosenthal, D. A., & Reichler, H. (2005). High schoolers' masturbatory practices. In M. Kimmel & R. Plante (Eds.), *Sexual identities* (pp. 99–105). New York: Oxford University Press.

Snow, L. F., & Johnson, S. (1978). Myths about menstruation: Victims of our own folklore. *International Journal of Women's Studies, 1,* 64–72.

Thornton, A. (1990).The courtship process and adolescent sexuality. *Journal of Family Issues, 11,* 239–273.

Whitbeck, L. B., Yoder, K. A., & Hoyt, D. R. (1999). Early adolescent sexual activity: A developmental study. *Journal of Marriage and the Family, 61,* 934–946.

CHAPTER 1

Works Cited

Kirby, D. (1997). *No easy answers: Research findings on programs to reduce teen pregnancy.* Washington, DC: National Campaign to Prevent Teen Pregnancy.

Lamb, S. (2002). *The secret lives of girls: What good girls really do— Sex, aggression, and their guilt.* New York: Free Press.

CHAPTER 2

Works Cited

Cavanaugh Johnson, T. (2004a). *Helping children with sexual behavior problems: A guidebook for professionals and caregivers.* 2nd edition. South Pasadena, CA: Author.

Cavanaugh Johnson, T. (2004b). *Understanding children's sexual behaviors: What's natural and healthy.* San Diego, CA: Family Violence and Sexual Assault Institute.

Girl Scouts of America (2000). *Executive Summary: Girls speak out: Teens before their time.* New York: Author.

Meichenbaum, D., & Deffenbacher, J. L. (1988). Stress inoculation training. *Counseling Psychologist, 16,* 69–90.

Lamb, S. (2002). *The secret lives of girls: What good girls really do— Sex, aggression, and their guilt.* New York: Free Press.

O'Donnell, L., Stueve, A., & Wilson-Simmons, R. (2006). Heterosexual risk behavior among urban young adolescents. *Journal of Early Adolescence, 26,* 87–109.

Additional Resources

Winnicott, D. W. (1971). *Playing and reality.* Oxford, UK: Penguin.

CHAPTER 3

Works Cited

Foa, E. B., Hembree, E. A., Cahill, S. P., Rauch, S. A., Riggs, D. S., & Feeny, N. C. (2005). Randomized trial of prolonged exposure for PTSD with and without cognitive restructuring: Outcome at academic and community clinics. *Journal of Consulting and Clinical Psychology, 73,* 953–964.

Additional Resources

Gil, E. (1991). *Healing power of play: Working with abused children.* New York: Guilford Press.

Gil, E., & Johnson, T. C. (1993). *Sexualized children: Assessment and treatment of sexualized children and children who molest.* Rockville, MD: Launch Press.

CHAPTER 4

Works Cited

Aylwin, A. S., Studer, L. H., & Reddon, J. R. (2003). Abuse prevalence and victim gender among adult and adolescent child molesters. *International Journal of Law & Psychiatry, 26*(2), 179–190.

Stirpe, T. S., & Stermac, L. E. (2003). An exploration of childhood victimization and family-of-origin characteristics of sexual offenders against children. *International Journal of Offender Therapy and Comparative Criminology, 47,* 542–555.

Widom, C. S., & Ames, M. A. (1994). *Criminal consequences of childhood sexual victimization. Child Abuse and Neglect, 18*(4), 303–318.

Worling, J. R. (1995). Sexual abuse histories of adolescent male sex offenders: Differences on the basis of the age and gender of their victims. *Journal of Abnormal Psychology, 104*(4), 610–613.

Additional Resources

Bagley, C. (1997). *Children, sex, and social policy: Humanistic solutions to the problem of child sexual abuse.* Brookfield, VT: Avebury Press.

Cavanaugh Johnson, T. (2004). *Helping children with sexual behavior problems: A guidebook for professionals and caregivers,* 2nd ed. South Pasadena, CA: Author.

Finkelhor, D. (1979). What's wrong with sex between adults and children? *American Journal of Orthopsychiatry, 49,* 692–697.

Fitzpatrick, C., Deehan, A., & Jennings, S. (1995). Children's sexual behaviour and knowledge: A community study. *Irish Journal of Psychological Medicine, 12,* 87–91.

Freud, S. (1961). Three essays on the theory of sexuality. In J. Strachey (Ed. & Trans.), *The standard edition of the complete psychological works of Sigmund Freud* (vol. 7, pp. 123–245). London: Hogarth Press. (Original work published 1924)

Friedrich, W. N., Grambsch, P., Damon, L., Hewitt, S. K., et al. (1992). Child Sexual Behavior Inventory: Normative and clinical comparisons. *Psychological Assessment, 4,* 303–311.

Haugaard, J. J. (1996). Sexual behaviors between children: Professionals' opinions and undergraduates' recollections. *Families in Society: The Journal of Contemporary Human Services, 77,* 81–89.

Lamb, S. (2002). *The secret lives of girls: What good girls really do— Sex, aggression, and their guilt.* New York: Free Press.

Leitenberg, H., Detzer, M. J., & Srebnik, D. (1993). Gender differences in masturbation and the relation of masturbation experience in preadolescence and/or early adolescence to sexual behavior and sexual adjustment in young adulthood. *Archives of Sexual Behavior, 22*(2), 87–98.

Leitenberg, H., Greenwald, E., & Tarran, M. J. (1989). The relation between sexual activity among children during preadolescence and/or early adolescence and sexual behavior and sexual adjustment in young adulthood. *Archives of Sexual Behavior, 18,* 299–313.

Ryan, G. (1999). Childhood sexuality: A decade of study. Part I— Research and curriculum development. *Child Abuse and Neglect, 24,* 33–48.

Wyatt, G., Newcomb, M. D., & Riederle, M. H. (1993). *Sexual abuse and consensual sex: Women's developmental patterns and outcomes*. Thousand Oaks, CA: Sage.

CHAPTER 5

Works Cited

Cassell, C. (1984). *Swept away: Why women fear their own sexuality*. New York: Simon and Schuster.

Collins, R. L., Elliott, M. N. Berry, S. H., Kanouse, D. E., Kunkel D., Hunter, S. B., & Miu, A. (2004). Watching sex on television predicts adolescent initiation of sexual behavior. *Pediatrics*, *114*(3), 280–289.

Collins, R. L., Elliott, M. N., Berry, S. H., Kanouse, D. E., & Hunter, S. B. (2003). Entertainment television as a healthy sex educator: The impact of condom-efficacy information in an episode of *Friends*. *Pediatrics*, *112*(5), 1115–1121.

Conan, N. (2004, June 10). Friends with benefits. *Talk of the Nation*. Available at http://www.npr.org/templates/story/story.php?storyId=1952884

Denizet-Lewis, B. (2004, May 30). Friends, friends with benefits, and the benefits of the local mall. *New York Times Magazine*, 30–55.

Fredrickson, B. L., & Roberts, T. (1997). Objectification theory: Toward understanding women's lived experiences and mental health risks. *Psychology of Women Quarterly, 21,* 173–206.

Henshaw, S. K., & Kost, K. (1992). Parental involvement in minor's abortion decisions. *Family Planning Perspectives*, *24*(5), 196–207, 213.

Additional Resources

Lamb, S., & Brown, L. M. (2006). *Packaging girlhood: Rescuing our daughters from marketers' schemes.* New York: St. Martin's Press.

Tolman, D. (2003). *Dilemmas of desire.* Cambridge, MA: Harvard University Press.

CHAPTER 6

Works Cited

Brooks, G. R., & Gilbert, L. A. (1995). Men in families: Old constraints, new possibilities. In R. F. Levant & W. S. Pollack (Eds.), *A new psychology of men* (pp. 252–279). New York: Basic.

Carnes, P. (2001). Cybersex, courtship, and escalating arousal: Factors in addictive sexual desire. *Sexual Addiction and Compulsivity, 8,* 45–78.

Horne, A. M., & Kiselica, M. S. (Eds.) (1999). *Handbook of counseling boys and adolescent males: A practitioner's guide.* Thousand Oaks, CA: Sage.

Joliff, D., Newbauer, J., & Blanks, B. (1999). Treating adolescent sex offenders. In A. M. Horne & M. S. Kiselica (Eds.), *Handbook of counseling boys and adolescent males: A practitioner's guide* (pp. 217–236). Thousand Oaks, CA: Sage.

Kimmel, M. S. (2005) *The gender of desire: Essays on male sexuality.* Albany: State University of New York Press.

Kindlon, D., & Thompson, M. (2000). *Raising Cain: Protecting the emotional life of boys.* New York: Ballantine.

Kiselica, M. S. (2003). Transforming psychotherapy in order to succeed with adolescent boys: Male-friendly practices. *Journal of Clinical Psychology, 59,* 1225–1236.

National Association for the Development of Work with Sex Offenders, Ethics Committee (2000). Working with adults and adolescents who exhibit sexually abusive behavior: The use of sexually salient and pornographic materials. *Journal of Sexual Aggression, 6,* 102–110.

Peele, S., & DeGrandpre, R. (1995, July/August). My genes made me do it. *Psychology Today,* 50–53, 62–68.

Pleck, J. H. (1981). *The myth of masculinity.* Cambridge, MA: MIT Press.

Pleck, J. H., Sonenstein, F. L., & Ku, L. C. (2004). Adolescent boys' sexual behavior. In N. Way & J. Chu (Eds.), *Adolescent boys: Exploring diverse cultures of boyhood* (pp. 256–270). New York: NYU Press.

Pollack, W. (1998). *Real boys.* New York: Simon and Schuster.

Ponton, L. (2000). *The sex lives of teenagers.* New York: Plume.

Price, D. (2003). A developmental perspective of treatment for sexually vulnerable youth. *Sexual Addiction & Compulsivity, 10,* 225–245.

Schneider, J. P. (2000). A qualitative study of cybersex participants: Gender differences, recovery issues, and implications for therapists. *Sexual Addiction and Compulsivity, 7,* 249–278.

Tolman, D. L., Spencer, R., Harmon, T., Rosen-Reynoso, M., & Striepe, M. (2004). Getting close, staying cool: Early adolescent boys' experiences with romantic relationship. In N. Way & J. Chu (Eds.), *Adolescent boys: Exploring diverse cultures of boyhood* (pp. 235–255). New York: NYU Press.

Additional Resources

Diamond, L. (2003). Love matters: Romantic relationships among sexual minority adolescents. In P. Florsheim (Ed.), *Adolescent romantic relations and sexual behavior: Theory, research, and practical implications* (pp. 97–105). Mahwah, NJ: Lawrence Erlbaum.

Griffin-Carlson, M. S., & Schwanenflugel, P. J. (1998). Adolescent abortion and parental notification: Evidence for the importance of family functioning on the perceived quality of parental involvement in U.S. families. *Journal of Child Psychology and Psychiatry, 39,* 543–553.

Henshaw, S. K., & Kost, K. (1992). Parental involvement in minors' abortion decisions. *Family Planning Perspectives, 24,* 196–207, 213.

Kiselica, M. S. (1995*). Multicultural counseling with teenage fathers: A practical guide.* Thousand Oaks, CA: Sage.

Korobov, N., & Bamberg, M. (2004). Positioning a "mature" self in interactive practices: How adolescent males negotiate "physical attraction" in group talk. *British Journal of Developmental Psychology, 22,* 471–492.

Levant, R. F., & Pollack, W. S. (Eds.) (1995). *A new psychology of men.* New York: Basic.

Longo, R. E. (2004). Using experiential exercises in treating adolescents with sexual behavior problems. *Sexual Addiction and Compulsivity, 11,* 249–263.

Richmond, K., & Levant, R. (2003). Clinical application of the gender role strain paradigm: Group treatment for adolescent boys. *Journal of Clinical Psychology, 59,* 1237–1245.

CHAPTER 7

Works Cited

Goodrich, T. J. (Ed.). (1991). *Women and power: Perspectives for family therapy.* New York: Norton.

Hare-Mustin, R. (1978). A feminist approach to family therapy. *Family Process, 17,* 81–194.

Holland, J., Mauthner, M., & Sharpe, S. (1996). *Family matters: Communicating health messages in the family.* London: Social Science Research Unit, Institute of Education.

Lamb, S. (2003, May/June). Not with my daughter. *Psychotherapy Networker,* 44–49.

Levine, J. (2002). *Harmful to minors.* Minneapolis: University of Minnesota Press.

Minuchin, S., & Fishman, H. C. (1981). *Family therapy techniques.* Cambridge, MA: Harvard University Press.

Pollack, W. (1998). *Real boys.* New York: Simon and Schuster.

Rosenthal, D. A., & Feldman, S. S. (1999). The importance of importance: Adolescent perceptions of parental communication about sexuality. *Journal of Adolescence, 22,* 835–851.

CHAPTER 8

Additional Resources

Bohan, J. (1996). *Psychology and sexual orientation: Coming to terms.* New York: Routledge.

Bohan, J., & Russell, G. (1999). *Conversations about psychology and sexual orientation.* New York: NYU Press.

DeAngelis, T. (2002). New data on lesbian gay and bisexual mental health: New findings overturn previous beliefs. *APA Monitor, 33,* 46–47.

Diamond, L. M. (2005). A new view of lesbian subtypes: Stable vs. fluid identity trajectories over an 8-year period. *Psychology of Women Quarterly, 29,* 119–128.

PFLAG, Parents and Friends of Lesbians and Gays. Availavble at http://www.pflag.org

Russell, G. M., Bohan, J. S., & Lilly, D. M. (2000). Queer youth: Old stories, new stories. In S. Jones (Ed.) *A sea of stories: The shaping power of narrative in gay and lesbian cultures* (pp. 69–92). Bringhamton, NY: Haworth.

CHAPTER 9

Works Cited

Garwood, M., & McCabe, M. P. (2000). Impact of sex education programs on sexual knowledge and feelings of men with a mild intellectual disability. *Education and Training in Mental Retardation and Developmental Disabilities, 35,* 269–283.

Pendler, B., & Hinsburger, D. (1991). Sexuality: Dealing with parents. *Sexuality and Disability, 9,* 123–130.

Additional Resources

Katz, G. (1998). Sexuality groups for adolescents with developmental disabilities. *Journal of Developmental Disabilities, 6,* 73–88.

Koller, R. (2000). Sexuality and adolescents with autism. *Sexuality and Disability, 18,* 125–135.

CHAPTER 10

Works Cited

Ladany, N., O'Brien, K., Hill, C. E., Melincoff, D. S., Knox, S., & Petersen, D. (1997). Sexual attraction toward clients, use of supervision, and prior training: A qualitative study of psychology predoctoral interns. *Journal of Counseling Psychology, 44,* 413–424.

Okamoto, S. K. (2002). The challenge of male practitioners working with female youth clients. *Child and Youth Care Forum, 31,* 257–268.

Pope, K. S., Tabachnick, B. G., & Keith-Spiegel, P. (1987). Ethics of practice: The beliefs and behaviors of psychologists as therapists. *American Psychologist, 42,* 993–1006.

Pope, K., Sonne, J. L., & Holroyd, J. (1993). *Sexual feelings in psychotherapy, explorations for therapists and therapists-in-training.* Washington, DC: American Psychological Association Press.

Additional Resources

Association for Moral Education. Available at www.amenetwork. org

Ladany, N., Friedlander, M. L., & Nelson, M. L. (2005). *Critical events in psychotherapy supervision.* Washington, DC: American Psychological Association Press.

Index

abortion
    parents' knowledge of, 135
abuse, sexual
    "distinguishing play from abuse" case
        example, 107–110
    normative behavior and, 7–8 sexual
        play vs., 72–73, 98 boundary
        violation, 72, 98
    coercion, 72, 97
    harmful to child, 72, 97
    persistent, compulsive, obsessive,
        72, 97
abused children, 79–96
    addressing abuse directly, 79–80
    boundary violation case example,
        82–86
    chronically out of control child
        example, 89–90
    indirect processing of play, 88
    normative sexual development and,
        81–82
    play as reenactment, 80–81, 86–87
    recapturing personhood, 87–88
    role of play in therapy, 80–82
    sex education, 38–39, 90–96
    signs of overstimulated play,
        86–87
academic achievement
    early sex and, 12
acting-out behavior, 97–120
    "Am I a sex offender" case example,
        102–107
    children's age differences and,
        110–114

"complicit younger child and
    immature older child" case
    example, 110–114
"distinguishing play from abuse" case
    example, 107–110
emotional characteristics of, 98–99
overwhelming thoughts and feelings,
    99–100
from problematic behaviors to sex
    offenders, 114–118
teenage boys, 189–192
trying to gain control via, 99
using sex offender term for children,
    118–119
from victim to offender, 100–102
affect
    modulation of, 21–22
aggression
    boys and integrating into caring
        relationships, 159, 161, 162,
        181–183
    fantasies of, and teenage boys, 162
alcohol use
    early sex and, 12
Ames, M. A., 101
anxiety
    pregnancy or HIV scares, 130–136
    teenage boys and sex, 164–166
AOL's Instant Message, 178
Asperger's Disorder children with, 260
attachment
    attachment difficulties, 217
    bedtime scenes, 74
autistic children, 260

313